ISBN: 9781314062670

Published by:
HardPress Publishing
8345 NW 66TH ST #2561
MIAMI FL 33166-2626

Email: info@hardpress.net
Web: http://www.hardpress.net

THE MARRIED LIFE OF
QUEEN VICTORIA

Queen Victoria

BY

CLARE JERROLD

Author of " The Early Court of Queen Victoria."

" Alexandrina Victoria Fidei,
Hm—hm—how runs the jargon? being on the throne."—
Calverley.

LONDON

1913

TO
A. M. BROADLEY
MOST GENEROUS OF BIBLIOPHILES
IN GRATITUDE

PREFACE

THE married life of an individual predicates a second individual, and this volume is as much a consideration of the character of the Prince Consort as of that of Queen Victoria. Though in his youth he professed liberal tendencies, the Prince was a strong upholder of Monarchy, and resisted with all his strength anything that he considered an encroachment on the powers of the Crown. He went further, for his life in England was, on one side of it, a long attempt to put back the hands of the clock and reinstate authority which had already been delegated to Parliament.

Had the Prince lived long, the history of England would have been very different from what it is, for either our Parliament would have succumbed to his ideals, and England would have become reactionary, or the struggle between the people and the Crown would have ended in the abolition of the Monarchy; and it is not difficult to believe which part the English people would have chosen in the critical time of thirty and forty years ago.

Furthermore, had the Prince lived there would have been no "great" Queen Victoria, for by 1860 the

Queen had so entirely transferred all work to her husband that, excepting as an appearance and a signature, the Queen-Regnant may almost be said not to have existed—a state of things which would eventually have had to be acknowledged; it would have been upon that point that an English revolution would have occurred. However, the Prince was not physically strong enough to bear the burden.

That I have written more fully about the first ten years of the "married life" than about the second is due to the fact that the Royal pair were more interesting to the public then than later; they were more studied, more thought about, and more written about. Later, when they had become a habit, it needed special events to raise marked comment.

It is a curious fact that of Prince Albert only two "Lives" have been written : the five-volume work by Sir Theodore Martin, and "The Early Years of the Prince Consort," by the Hon. C. Grey—both written by command of Queen Victoria, to both of which she supplied all personal matter, and both of which were therefore essentially her books. Among recently published volumes I have found Mr. Edmund B. d'Auvergne's work on "The Coburgs" helpful.

To my friend, Mr. A. M. Broadley, I must acknowledge my great gratitude for allowing me to make use of his fine library, and of selecting from his valuable collection of prints the illustrations to this volume.

C. J.

HAMPTON-ON-THAMES,
   January, 1913.

CONTENTS

x

CONTENTS

LIST OF ILLUSTRATIONS

N.B.—*The illustrations marked with an asterisk* (*) *are reproduced from
prints in the collection of Mr. A. M. Broadley.*

THE MARRIED LIFE OF QUEEN VICTORIA

CHAPTER I

THE QUEEN'S BRIDEGROOM

WHEN Queen Victoria and Prince Albert married in 1840 the formula "they lived happily ever afterwards" might have been uttered about them, for "ever afterwards" implies but "while life lasts." In spite of her autocratic bearing, she was by nature both simple and plastic, and while she would certainly have resented any attempt to force her choice, she yet yielded unconsciously to steady half-hidden pressure. It was no secret that her impressionable youth had responded to the admiration which had been offered by Lord Elphinstone; and Lord Alfred Paget—who was reported to be so much in love with her that he not only wore the portrait of her round his neck, but tied another round the neck of his dog—was always a person to be considered in her Majesty's mind. But as it was impossible for her to marry either of these, and as all other princely suitors had been dismissed by her mother and uncle Leopold, and as matters had been so worked that all Europe regarded Albert as the man of her choice, there was nothing for Queen Victoria to do but definitely to declare her mind.   In the summer of 1839 she did this by refusing a second time to consider for some years to come a marriage with her cousin, upon which Leopold made plans which would ensure a visit from the Prince to England in October, when the young Queen would have few Parliamentary, State, or social distractions.   It was the last resource, for if the hesitating girl failed to be won by Albert's personal appearance and address, she would not be won at all.   Three and a half years had passed since the cousins had met, and those years had made a great difference in the Prince; from being a short, fat boy he had grown into a fairly tall man, superfluous tissue had disappeared, and his delicate profile had gained from the change.   So he came and saw—or was seen—and conquered, and for nearly twenty-two years after was one of the hardest-worked men in England.

Much has been said about the marrying Coburgs, those young men and women who at that period were being dispersed over Europe, as Kings, Consorts or rulers of small countries.   It was a subject which was returned to every time the Prince had the misfortune to get talked about in England; I say misfortune, for the people scarcely ever talked of him excepting to grumble; when they pretended to praise an antidote

was always administered, as in the following paragraph from a provincial paper: "Prince Albert is a
prince respected and to be respected for all his conduct since he came among us. But, besides and
beyond him, we see Coburgs in France! Coburgs in
Belgium! Coburgs in Portugal! and we verily believe
that if the billionaires among the children of Israel
should buy Jerusalem and all the land about Jordan,
we should doubtless see all the machinery of diplomacy instantly at work with a Coburg King of the
Jews."

But though there may be a certain dignity in sitting
on the apex of any social structure, it is scarcely a
comfortable position; Ferdinand of Portugal was in
trouble with the country of his adoption for a quarter
of a century, mostly through his determination to be
the Commander-in-Chief of its army; King Leopold
of the Belgians spent as much time as possible out
of his kingdom, causing his niece anxiously and often
to remonstrate with him; and Prince Albert took his
position with such immense seriousness that, while
still a young man, he had worn out his very desire to
live.

It is curious that we know so much and yet so little
of the twenty-two years of married life which Albert
and Victoria spent together. There are numberless
letters on public affairs, numberless accounts of
journeys to north or south, anecdotes galore about
cottagers at Balmoral or Osborne—the Windsor
cottagers were not popular—many complaints of the
uncourtly ways of Lord Palmerston, "who has em-

B 2

bittered all our life," and a whole album of opinions upon the moral perfection of Prince Albert.   But with all this we know very little of the Palace domesticity excepting the Queen's saying : " I will venture to say that not only no *Royal ménage* is to be found equal to ours, but *no other ménage* is to be compared to ours"; and we are never given a real conception of Albert's character, for his character has been buried deeply under words, words, and yet more words.   The frantic endeavour to canonise him led to a deliberate suppression of any knowledge about one side of his personality, and of the other what was told of him was so overlaid with sentiment that it is difficult to know what is and what is not real.   It is true that there are still rare books and pamphlets extant, the production of which caused much annoyance in the Royal bosoms, so much annoyance that great efforts were made to suppress or buy them up; but these dealt only with isolated incidents affecting subjects, in which some injustice was felt to have been inflicted; they had nothing to do with the life in the Palace. If Prince Albert was the extraordinarily brilliant man, mentally, that so many have agreed in thinking him, why is it that of him only one Life has been written and one partial Life extending merely to his marriage, both of which books were inspired by Queen Victoria and annotated by her?   The reason probably is that no one would have dared to write of the Prince as a real man in the Queen's lifetime, for she would certainly have set her face against such a publication. And she lived so many years beyond him, and held him up so long to her subjects as such a wonderful pattern of infallibility, that public sentiment was divided between happy forgetfulness of the dead man's existence and a peevish distaste for the person they were asked to regard as the Prince Consort. It might perhaps be said that for all ordinary purposes to-day there either is no Prince Albert at all or there are two Prince Alberts.

On the one hand we have a Prince who never did wrong, a wise, kind, loving boy and man, assiduous at work, devoted domestically, pious in aspiration, and pure in every way. Indeed, such emphasis is laid upon his purity of habit, of thought, and of will, that those who read might excusably weary of the refrain were it not that purity of any sort must have shone like a beacon light—variously appreciated—in a period immediately succeeding that of the Hanoverian Kings.

In this description there is an ideal, an impossible perfection, but there is no man; being human, we do not believe in human perfection; it is a reproach to us personally and collectively; we feel abashed, for we know our own faults and weaknesses; and then we save our self-respect by asserting—and with reason— that we have been deceived. In place of a human being we are shown a light, and told that we must call it Albert the Good, and, indeed, that we should not be far wrong if we regarded it also as a saint. Well, that is the way that saints are made. If we knew the real life of Edward the Confessor it is fairly certain that our regard for him as a saint would be evaporated by our laughter at the idea.

The other side of the picture is the exact reverse. It was drawn during the Prince's life by those people who perhaps were not pure in heart—by those who considered it an affront that any young man from another country—an inferior country filled with " beggarly princes," for Germany was but a confederation then—should dare to prove definitely to English nobles of high degree that it was easily possible to live without debasement, to drink without getting drunk, to use money without squandering it, to have intellectual rather than fleshly tastes.   Poor Prince Albert!   This second picture shows him possessed of every little, insignificant fault, apart from personal impurity and excess.   He was mean, he was an Anglo-phobe—only the word itself had not been invented then—he was a traitor, playing into the hands of Russia and Germany; he influenced the Queen to her people's detriment; he was worthy of no better fate than the Tower and the axe.   More than once a howl of execration over him rolled from one end of England to the other, and the echoes of it still linger, though it was first heard more than sixty years ago.

But this impression is no more true than the other. The Prince Consort was not guilty of the offences laid to his charge any more than he was guilty of possessing all the saintly virtues.   Somewhere between these two extremes was the man himself; but he has been lost, smothered under Queenly sentiment, shut off by Princely reserve.   The curious thing is that Albert himself was partly responsible for destroying his own personality—he voluntarily turned to the public a blank surface. He said, literally : " My life is my own, and it is a private thing ; you, you curious public, have no right to know anything about me or about my home. I have a right to know all about you, but you are overstepping propriety when you desire to know anything about me. In *my* country, through the police and by other means, we at Court know everything about everybody. Here you have the impertinence to reverse that custom; I can get to know nothing of you, but you tempt the servants in my house to become reporters that you may see in print all the things I do."

The Prince went further : he made the members of his household promise most solemnly that they would never repeat anywhere any account of the things they heard or saw in the Royal Household, while Ladies and Maids were on their honour not to keep diaries. These promises were kept most loyally. And the result of it all was that the Prince helped to annihilate himself. It is like standing at the end of a narrow avenue—of poplars, say, the abele poplar so beloved by the Prince—and looking for a procession to advance. There are the two rows of trees, one in sunshine, one all shade ; but there is no moving life, there is nothing but the trees. Standing there, is it possible to see the procession mentally, to make its different parts live and walk, take on their motley colours, sparkling with jewels which shine the brighter for the dark velvets that form their background? It may perhaps be possible to recover some presentation of it, but the real procession, which has vanished, is not easy to bring again into the light of reality.

There are still living those who knew the Prince, or who lived in the circle of which he had been the centre, and who believe that the ways of the Court sixty years ago were sacrosanct—people who, if the Prince is mentioned, will echo all the opinions about him which Queen Victoria, with much assiduity, taught her people to repeat. After them comes the next generation, who, having heard all the mischievous stories, and not having had the courage to read Sir Theodore Martin's five huge volumes on the Prince, are inclined to believe the mean things and yet to think he must have been passable because the Queen grieved so long for him. As for the younger generation, those who, tired of pretence, energetically demand, in the words of Ibsen, " My castle on the table, Mr. Solness, my castle on the table," they are busily engaged in looking forward; to them a study of the past is necessary for an understanding of the future. They do not believe in human perfection, and is it likely that they will accept and admire the Prince Consort as a kind of holy guardian angel to the Queen? Will they have patience with the blaze of regretful adulation which shone over his tomb? Will they not rather say, " This is all overdone, he must have had a fault or two; but anyway he appears to have been so dull that he is not interesting ! " The popularity of guardian angels has passed, with many other childlike beliefs; we want a reality in their place.

What was the Prince afraid of when he enforced

this peculiar reticence about his doings? Was it that he dreaded criticism, or was it simply the outcome of an abnormally reserved character? That the Royal household was not such an eternal abode of peace as it has always been described it is but in human nature to suspect; and, again, it is not easy to believe that a person brought up with such undue severity as was little Princess Victoria would give her own children unvarying indulgence; so it is open to surmise that the childish days of King Edward and his brothers and sisters were shaken by occasional troubles. But things like these would not be sufficient reason for locking all the gates and doors and drawing down the blinds. The reason could only have been partly attributable to character; the rest must nave been caused by circumstance.

As far as these causes go, it is worth while to refer slightly to the Prince's young life.

Though, during all his existence in England, Prince Albert was regarded as of no great origin, he was a descendant of a house which was both powerful and famous in the tenth century—the house of Wetten, which later became divided into two branches, the Ernestine and the Albertine. Albert and his brother Ernest belonged to the elder, or Ernestine, branch. During later centuries wealth was not a great attribute of this family, for each descendant took his share of the family possessions, and the Duke of Coburg, father of the two boys, was anything but rich. There is no position which leads so quickly to reticence as an inadequate income. Who of us under a reverse would explain to the world in general that it behoves us to be homely, domestic, economical? Who would wish to set common gossip going about the piecing and patching, the napery of darns and holes, the cheap cigarettes, and the enforced avoidance of wine? No; most of us hide all those things, and feel annoyed with the person who betrays them. Thus it is with a Duke of high degree. That his ancestral castle is small and understaffed with servants, that his income is almost trivial compared with his position, are things that he must perhaps endure; but he does not want them talked about.

The Saxes, the descendants of the Ernestine branch, were distinguished for their half incomes and double names, and early in last century there were—and with one exception still are—the reigning Dukes of Saxe-Meiningen, of Saxe-Weimar, of Saxe-Alten-burg, of Saxe-Coburg, and of Saxe-Gotha. The last two became united in the person of Albert's father. All the children of all these Dukes had the right to the title of Duke or Duchess, which habit forms a really intricate puzzle for the student of the history of what might be called the German Dukeries.

Thus it was evidently out of the question that the increasing total of Dukes and Duchesses could have incomes corresponding with their titles. The Princes Ernest and Albert were comparatively well off, their father becoming eventually the head of the Ernestine branch, and the possessor of at least four houses; yet before his marriage Prince Albert's income was only between two and three thousand a year, a very small sum upon which to keep up any princely state. While England was discussing the probability of the Guelph-Coburg marriage—I would not dare say the Coburg-Guelph, for with all her expressed love for her husband Queen Victoria was extremely tenacious of the superiority of her position over his by birth—England's aristocracy and the English public were unwearied in discussing its suitability, and the whole little array of items of the Prince's income were known to all. Before that, when curiosity about him was rife, when as a student he was staying with his brother in Brussels, the failure of their very careful uncle Leopold to offer them hospitality, the place they lodged in, the amount paid for it and for their board, all petty and unimportant details were published by our delightful newspapers as good morsels for the daws to peck at. Thus before Prince Albert arrived in England it was decided that a youth who had had so little money to play with could not expect to be treated in the same way as all the other consorts, male and female, of royalty, and the whole matter was threshed out in Parliament in a way which made the poor young man exclaim, " But the indignity—the indignity of it ! "

These remarkably frank discussions were accompanied in the Press and in the streets by such pretty verses as—

> "Quoth Hudibras of old, ' a *thing*
> Is worth as much as it will bring.'
> How comes it then that Albert clear
> Has thirty thousand pounds a year ? "

Constantly in the papers of the time were to be found little two or three line paragraphs such as : " We have heard much said about the dear men, but if the wishes of Victoria towards her husband were to be carried out, he might prove the dearest man in the country."

The broadsides about the marriage would contain a dozen or less verses, generally badly written, but all betraying a slighting attitude towards the Prince, generated and fostered by the action of the Duke of Wellington and Sir Robert Peel in the two Houses Here is a verse from one :

> " She says when we are wed,
>   I must not dare to tease her,
> But strive both day and night,
>   All e'er I can to please her ;
> I told her I would do
>   For her all I was able,
> And when she had a son,
>   I would sit and rock the cradle."

Prince Albert had need of all his dignity to enable him to bear with equanimity everything that was said or written about him. Of course, reasons were given for offering £21,000 or £30,000—which were the two sums named in Parliament—in place of the £50,000 which Queen Anne's husband, the queen-consorts except those who had more, and Prince Leopold, had received; but, good as the reasons sounded, none of them was real. The whole fight came from a desire on the part of the scorned and flouted Tories—Tory was then the correct word, and not a term of reproach —to be revenged on the young Queen. It was part of a plan arranged by Peel with the concurrence of the Duke of Wellington—the man who prided himself on loyalty to the Crown whatever happened—which it was hoped would bring the fall of the Whig Government within sight. Those who felt any scruples in the matter smoothed them away with the remembrance that the Prince was but a poor Prince, and with the supposition that £30,000 would seem like a fortune to him. Of course, the extreme economists, then known as Radicals, led by Joseph Hume, who voted with their enemies the Tories, did it from the standpoint that the Prince when he was the Queen's husband had really no need of an income at all, he would just be taken in and done for; therefore they argued that with so much poverty in the City it would be criminal to vote him a penny more than would give him clothes and pocket-money.

How far is the cynical saying true or untrue, that to be insulted through the purse is to endure the deadliest insult of all? I imagine that it is nearer fact than idealists will allow. Certain it is that the Parliamentary squabble about the Prince's religion did not make on his mind such a lasting impression as that concerning his income. The assertion that he was a Catholic, and therefore not eligible as a husband for an English Queen, was the first move in the Peel-Wellington arrangement; and though the assertion was preposterous, though everyone knew that it was a lie, the disaffected party, helped by the extremists, gaily played up to their leaders, and gave Albert a good reason for being prejudiced, before his arrival, against those very men of whom he was likely to see most when settled at the Palace. So keenly did he feel it that, although he never showed resentment, he said, when writing to his friend Baron Stockmar fourteen years later : " Peel cut down my income, Wellington refused me rank, the Royal family cried out against the foreign interloper, the Whigs in office were only inclined to concede me just so much space as I could stand upon. The Constitution is silent as to the Consort of the Queen ; even Blackstone ignores him ; and yet there he was, and not to be done without."

Parallel at that time with the keen Tory feeling against the girl-Queen ran a more general dislike to the Coburg family, a dislike which became active through resentment that this family should be so generally successful in life, and which was helped by the prejudice against Leopold and the suspicion as to the political leanings of the Duchess of Kent.

Leopold when in England had been a most dandified person, regarding himself, as he said, as *de la fleur des Pois* of good manners. By his superior airs, by his keen business instincts, and by his deadly lack of humour, he had managed to get disliked by everyone. He said one day reprovingly to some gay speech of his second wife, Louise of France, " Pas de propos legers, Madame !"—which in ordinary English might be translated " No jokes !" And it is doubtful whether his Queen, who became so beautifully mild and sad, ever uttered another joke while she lived. The Tories hated him for his superiority, and they bitterly resented the somewhat harmless

Whig intrigues of the Duchess; so when a third
Coburg was brought to dominate their society, he was
flagellated unmercifully.

All these things may have combined to set the
Prince against the English people, and make him
desire a privacy which few great people can enjoy,
one which, in fact, is more or less impossible to those
who live under limelight. But there was another
thing. The English people are accredited with a
reserved character which can only be outmatched by
the Germans. This may be true, but whatever reserve
they feel about their own concerns, they show little
about the concerns of others, and for years Prince
Albert was made the butt of the ribald Press, not so
much of newspapers as of the broadsides and the
caricaturists. The great caricaturists, such as H. B.,
Leech, H. H., and others, were sometimes unkind,
but never vulgar; below them came a multitude of
pencil men who depicted the Royal couple in badly
drawn and crude cartoons, seizing upon some real
characteristic and making it food for the mirth of the
streets. Nothing escaped them, and the terror of this
was that there was always just so much truth in the
gibe as would make it sting. The very fact that the
Prince wanted his castle to be so guarded that its
inside should be unknown to the world, made journalists and others doubly anxious to penetrate its
secrets, and so a more than usually alert eye was kept
upon Palace doings, and if anything could be found
wrong it straightway appeared in the papers. This
became unbearable to the Prince, and led, on more

than one occasion, to acts of injustice and oppression, and also made him demand that solemn promise of secrecy from anyone who could by chance know anything of his private acts.

An older man—Albert was not twenty-one when he married—would have probably been more robust, and met his troubles with greater success, but he never was able to break down the barrier which his entry into England built up between him and the English people, for England was fast drifting towards democracy, and he, though liberal-minded for a ruler, clung tenaciously to the ancient rights of the Crown.

Why is it that, putting aside all question of time, King Edward VII. was nearly all his life more popular than his father? No one can attempt to prove that he, as a young Prince, complied with his parents' demand for purity. He got into amorous scrapes before he left college; he gambled at cards to such an extent that he figured in a notorious baccarat case; he gambled on the racecourse and took to debt almost as easily as the fourth of the Georges. The fast folk of the land applauded him; the clean-minded vowed that he should never be king; and the pious pretended that things were exaggerated, and that their loyalty demanded that they should believe that a man in such a position could do no wrong.

Prince Albert neither philandered, gambled, nor played cards. He was so sensitive concerning public opinion that he was never known to go out alone, wherever and however he went an equerry accompanying him. He refused to pay visits in general society. No fair dame could boast of having given his Royal Highness a cup of tea by her quiet fireside, and no man could claim that the Prince had done him honour by supping with him. He deprived himself continuously of the chance of gaining the goodwill of those among whom he lived that he might carry out one of the missions thrust upon him by his wife, which was to maintain and "even raise the character of the Court. With this view he knew (or was taught) that it was not enough that his own conduct should be in truth free from reproach; no shadow of a shade of suspicion should, by any possibility, attach to it." And then we are told that, "wherever a visit from him might advance the real good of the people, there his horses might be seen waiting; never at the door of mere fashion"; that he loved to ride in London where building and improvements were in progress, especially if they were for the benefit of the working classes, &c. The Queen, of course, regarded this futile form of well-doing as a proof of extreme wisdom and virtue, though the general sentiment of that day did not endorse her opinion.

Here was a youth of twenty-one from a small German State, one who up to his marriage had been troubled with no responsibilities, who had been brought up in a wholesome, open-air, middle-class way, knowing little of State affairs, and only just becoming conscious that politics were important enough to need attention. He came from the life of a student at Bonn to a regal position in a great Court in the largest city of the world, the only link between his student days and his new existence being a few months' travelling in Italian cities, where he paid far more heed to antiquity than to life.

This self-complacent young man took upon his shoulders, or found his shoulders burdened with, the gigantic task of teaching a whole foreign nation how to live. This, of course, was commendable enough; it was akin to all other heroic labours; he was young and enthusiastic, and he set himself to slay the hydra-headed dragon of licentiousness. No one would have objected to this if he had thought more of the people to be saved and less about their sins, but in actual fact he showed little real consideration for those people; his actions rather betrayed that he was intent upon proving in his own person the crude fact that it was possible to live without sin, and that he would have nothing to do with sinners. So he decided that his end could only be gained if he held himself aloof socially from everyone. It is as though a man hid from wind and rain because he feared a spot of mud, and disdained the sun because it causes dust.

This superior attitude came as a snub to the aristocracy, and it is easier to forgive a real injury than to forget a snub. In this was another reason why to the end of his life there were many who disliked him, and the public never tired of criticising him, laughing at him, and remembering that he did not really belong to them. If he could only have lost his self-consciousness, have been gracious and friendly with all who made or should have made his surroundings, he and the Queen would probably have heard nothing of the occasional paroxysms of anger which swept the public mind like a fury at the mention of his name. For the character of the man in the highest place is discussed by all, down to the very lowest. Let him get the reputation among those near him for geniality, graciousness, and honourable living, and those furthest off will know it, and rate him accordingly, and so accordingly will he be universally beloved or disliked.

Our late King was almost at the other extreme, for he was certainly genial and gracious. Yet when in that fulness of time, which was becoming distinctly over-ripe, he came to the throne, all alike, the fast folk, the clean-minded, and the pious, welcomed him with open arms; all that he did was in the public eye right; every sign of foreign amity was put to his credit; all people, Conservative or Liberal, idle man or worker, claimed him as their own. He did not try to teach, he did not set himself up as an example, and he had shown quite plainly many times and oft that he did not care what folk thought of him; and so when, after a short reign, he made room for another, the public mind was far more sorrowful than when " The Great White Queen" was laid in her mausoleum.

A cynic might say that he was loved for his sins, but that is not so. He was loved for his kingly manner and his kindly heart. Another king, possessing these qualities in conjunction with the Prince Consort's domestic probity, would have a double chance of national popularity. The English nation loved Charles II., not for his profligacy, but for his hearty

C 2

ways; the sins were condoned because of his laughing face and witty tongue. Were it otherwise, the nation should have loved the Prince Regent, which it did not.

Queen Victoria thought when things went wrong that her beloved was a martyr to a wilfully misunderstanding public, whereas he was but suffering the natural consequences of a priggishness which was mistakenly regarded as a virtue both by himself and the Queen. A man may be a saint and yet be extremely popular, so long as he does not lay stress upon his own character nor show suspicion of those who make no profession of holiness.

However, if frankness has not been accorded about personalities and a household which, if all implication be true, was a perfect home of happiness, the records of the time give many details, now hidden from the reading public under mountains of paper and printer's ink; the pencils of those who could see fun everywhere have left a marvellous pictorial history from which to draw conclusions, all that is needed is a patience that endureth long for seeking, sifting, and translating into words.

CHAPTER II

PRINCE ALBERT'S destiny was fixed almost as soon as he was born; certainly before he had attained the mature age of four years. Up to that time he was a baby cared for by nurses, kept in necessary awe by his two grandmothers Saxe-Coburg and Saxe-Gotha, and spoiled and petted by his beautiful, vivacious, wayward mother. The young Duchess, married at sixteen, was a little thing, full of the *joie de vivre*, desiring gaiety and laughter; but she had married a Coburg, and the Coburgs were chary of fun, puritanical in life, and careful about money. She found relief in parties, balls, theatricals; and an official in the Palace named Szymborski in some way influenced the mutual relations of the Duke and Duchess. Whether he made love to her, or only made mischief between the two, her letters do not say; but the people of Coburg insisted upon a dramatic reconciliation between the husband and wife, and then stormed Szymborski's house, he first taking refuge in the castle and then getting out of the country. However, the Duchess drove away for ever the next day; so by the time little Albert was four, his mother had gone out of his life.   Then the women nurses were dismissed, and there were left the two little boys, their father, a tutor who seems to have been also a nurse and attendant, and Grandmother Saxe-Coburg in the background, a loving, thoughtful woman.   But before this exodus the nurses had begun to conjure with the name of Cousin Victoria.   It was not " if you are good you shall have some chocolates," but " if you are good you shall marry the Queen."

Queen Victoria must have had some sympathy for naughty little children, for she actually allows stories of imperfect manners to have a place in the " Early Life of the Prince Consort," and one feels some gratitude towards the brave tutor who, being invited to send his written memories of the Prince, was temerarious enough to include warlike incidents, doing it with gentle deprecation which yet had a strong tinge of admiration in it.

So whatever Albert grew to in manhood, here we learn that as a boy he was wilful and obstinate, and that he could scream for hours if it suited his mood.

Just before he lost the society of his indulgent mother she gave a children's fancy dress ball, at which her little son, dressed as Cupid, was destined to dance with a certain little girl.   When it was his turn to move on with his partner, nothing would induce him to stir; instead, he lifted up his voice and howled, his screams echoing through the rooms.   At which the Duchess exclaimed ironically to her husband, " This comes of his *good* education."

QUEEN VICTORIA.
From a Print in Mr. A. M. Broadley's Collection

He seems to have found these paroxysms of temper and screaming useful in getting his own way, and on one occasion, when the noise pierced through all the rooms of the castle, the Duke secured a cane, taking the precaution of sending the tutor and Ernest out for a walk that they might not be distressed by witnessing the punishment. After some time they went back, thinking all would be over, but the sweet Albert was still screaming, and the Duke in a most uncomfortable frame of mind was still fingering the cane, not having had the heart to use it! This incident somewhat conflicts with the reply the Duke made to one who wondered how his children got on without a woman about them: "*My* children cannot misbehave!"

Then there is Albert's childish diary to enlighten us, written before he was six, and containing such entries as—

"I got up well and happy, afterwards I had a fight with my brother." . . . "I had another fight with my brother; that was not right." . . . "We recited, and I cried because I could not say my repetition, for I had not paid attention. . . . I was not allowed to play after dinner because I had cried while repeating." "I cried at my lesson to-day, because I could not find a verb; and the Rath pinched me, to show me what a verb was. I cried about it."

The Rath might have given a more humane example of a verb. But we certainly here get a picture of a nice little boy who could be both good and naughty.

The Queen seems to think it pleasing that this unnatural baby felt a great dislike to being in the charge of nurses and rejoiced when the change of attendants took place; but it is open to question whether, if he had been brought up under more natural conditions, his life in England would not have been easier. He would have been better trained in social manners, and he might have been too modest to set himself up as the tutor of the public conscience; besides, he could scarcely have regarded every woman as a snare to his reputation as he did when settled in England.

However, no one thought of these things, and while all those worthy men—father, uncle, tutor, and Baron Stockmar—were seeking round to discover the best education which could fit the child and youth to be the husband of the Queen of England, they were neglecting the great essential—good and easy manners.

As a boy Prince Albert was a sleepy creature, and when about ten years of age his one idea after his seven o'clock supper was to get to bed. If for some reason he could not retire, he would manage to disappear into some recess or behind some curtain, and be discovered later fast asleep. On one occasion—royal sharer of the Fat Boy's somnolence—he not only fell asleep at the table, but fell off his chair without waking, and went on quietly sleeping on the floor!

This sleepiness remained with him all his life; as a young man he went to bed at nine, and we hear of him later gracing parties by his handsome presence and placidly sleeping through the music.

Queen Victoria said that Prince Albert had a wonderful sense of humour, that he delighted in telling

good stories, and in listening to them; but one looks
in vain for confirmation of this in the two books on his
life. The only examples given of Princely levity
show the lowest sort in humour, that of practical joking.
Thus he once wheedled his tutor into filling a number
of tiny glass tubes about the size of peas with sul-
phuretted hydrogen for him, which he threw about the
floor and boxes of the theatre, to the great annoyance
and discomfiture of the audience, at which confusion
he was highly delighted.

Visitors to his home did not escape his love of playing
tricks; and one night he filled the cloak pockets of a
grown-up cousin with soft cheese! When she was
leaving, he went with her to the cloak-room, and
eagerly helped her on with her garment, revelling in
her horror at the mess, and laughing at her scolding.
There is little that can be termed humorous or witty
in such schoolboy tricks, but they are the nearest we
get to examples of the lighter side of Prince Albert's
nature.

Thus to balance the account of his abounding
virtues, we may say that he was sometimes obstinate,
self-willed, and thoughtless of others' comfort; and
to this may be added that he was by no means averse
from imposing his own will upon others. His frequent
fights with his brother did not mean that this elder
brother persecuted him, but that he himself demanded
subservience to his will. This fact is told by the tutor,
but so buried in the words of honeyed praise that, for
laughter's sake, I reproduce the passage:

" Surpassing his brother in thoughtful earnestness, in

calm reflection and self-command, and evincing, at the same time, more prudence in action, it was only natural that his will should prevail; and when compliance with it was not voluntarily yielded, he was sometimes disposed to have recourse to compulsion."

There surely cannot be anywhere a better example of courtier-like language. Albert fought his brother that he might force him to do something he did not like—as commonplace boys will sometimes do; and we have the incident worked up into a dissertation upon his thoughtful earnestness, his self-command, his calm reflection, his prudence!

This sort of thing really pleased the Queen; she could not see through it herself, or if she did she did not think that her people would see through it. As Benjamin Disraeli once said to Mr. G. W. E. Russell: "It is true, I *am* a flatterer. I have found it useful. Everyone likes flattery, and when you come to Royalty *you should lay it on with a trowel*." Flattery in lumps *may* bring good immediate results for the person who uses it as currency, though it goes bad after a time, and does more harm than good.

It was curious that, seeing how certain everyone was of Prince Albert's destiny, more care was not taken to teach him English. It was not that he did not learn it, but every subject was taught by one man until the boy was fifteen, and after that, though he had various masters, there is no trace of any Englishman being included among his tutors.

It was not until 1839 that any effort was made to rectify this omission, and King Leopold, who then was directing his nephew's affairs, sent Albert to travel in Italy. One of his companions was Francis Seymour, whose regiment was stationed in Ireland, and who, going to Brussels on leave, attracted the attention of the King. It was just one of those happy meetings in which the right person is recognised at first sight, so when Lieutenant Seymour should have been going back to Ireland, Leopold used his influence to get an extension of leave, and offered him the post of attendant upon the Prince, saying, "Your duties are to speak and read English with him."

This engagement was soon ratified, and for the first time in his life Albert was allowed to know intimately a man from the kingdom over which he believed that he would reign, perhaps in name, but anyhow in reality.

The attraction between the two young men was mutual; it lasted through their lives, and the Queen paid a compliment to Francis Seymour after the Prince's death which was so worded as to be also a compliment to the Prince. In that later time when the young Lieutenant had become General Sir Francis Seymour, and had been Equerry and Groom in Waiting for many years, the Queen wrote in the "Early Life":

"General Seymour was appointed Groom in Waiting to the Prince, and is now in the same capacity with the Queen. The Prince told the Queen in after years how good a young man he was, and how anxious he had been to keep everything that was bad or impure from approaching him, though, God knows, vice itself would ever have recoiled from the look alone of one who wore 'the lily of a blameless life' ('the white flower of a blameless life'); but still it is pleasing to record such conduct."

Constantly in the Queen's books and in the two devoted to Prince Albert are these sort of passages to be met with, all concerned with the Prince's purity; but it should be realised that it was Victoria rather than Albert who initiated the "purity-of-the-Court" crusade, and that long before she married she had, and with justice, grown up in horror of the things she heard about the lives of the Guelphs, as well as the lives of the European Sovereigns. So she had determined that her Court should set a very different example. Being very young, very impulsive, and relying implicitly upon the advice of the person who had most gained her ear, she made the tragic mistake which preceded the death of Lady Flora Hastings. From that time "the purity of the Court" was a phrase for the gossips, and more than one broadside dealt with the rare atmosphere which was desired at Buckingham Palace and at Windsor. A little while ago I came across a cartoon published just after Her Majesty's marriage, which pointed this fact. The Royal couple are on their four days' honeymoon at Windsor, and on the second morning Victoria jumps out of bed and begins dressing, not noticing in her haste that she has got hold of the wrong garments. The Prince, in nightcap and dressing-gown, stands looking at her helplessly, saying :

"But, mein dear? mein dear, do not de honeymoon

last a mont'? and mein luf, you put on mein trousers! You do not mean that—yet, do you?"

To that the Queen responds, "Am I? ah! Well, I am resolved to go, so you had better dress and prepare. The *Purity* of my Court is of national importance, and without my presence the ladies there will have neither example nor precept."

The Queen's opinions on this subject were so well known that it was reflected everywhere for her benefit. Those who furnished their recollections of the Prince for "The Early Life" laid great stress upon it, Stockmar wrote of it, and it appeared in very definite form in the letter of congratulation written by Albert's brother to Victoria on their engagement.

The Prince seemed to have lived in an atmosphere of adulation all his life, for it was the custom of the time for people to belaud their nearest and dearest, just as now we laugh at them and offer stimulating criticism. To-day a youth of twenty would think his brother deserved a punishment lustily inflicted if he wrote, as Prince Ernest wrote, thus:

"One reads less in his face of knowledge of men and experience, and why? It is because he is pure before the world and before his own conscience. Not as though he did not know what sin was—the earthly temptation—the weakness of man. No; but because he knew, and still knows, how to struggle against them, supported by the incomparable superiority and firmness of his character! . . . Albert never knew what it was to hesitate. Guided by his own clear sense, he always walked calmly and steadily in the right path. In the greatest difficulties that may meet you in your eventful life, you may repose the most entire confidence in him. And then only will you feel how great a treasure you possess in him."

And just at this time Victoria was on her part assuring Albert that he might repose the utmost confidence in her, and in what she planned for him.

The Prince must always have suffered from a certain physical delicacy, for he was never happy either in town or in low-lying lands. The air of the woods, the breezes of the mountains, would at once remove all depression, and Seymour tells how he would exclaim: "Ah, now I can breathe! now I feel that I live!" as soon as he had climbed high above the lowlands.

Though by the time the tour was over the young lieutenant had to return to Ireland, Prince Albert cherished the hope that later on he would again be able to claim his services in some intimate capacity, and when at last the great fact of his marriage was arranged, he was keenly anxious to secure Francis Seymour as his Secretary. However, Victoria and Melbourne had already settled such details, and insisted upon the appointment of George Anson to that post. So Seymour became a personal attendant, groom, and equerry, and was one of those who went to Coburg to bring the Prince to England.

Up to that time Albert was just a pleasant, ordinary, somewhat delicate young man. He was not troubled by any excess of piety, as the Queen wished us to believe, his brother affirming that it was to please the English public that Sir Theodore Martin discoursed about his natural piety, for the description certainly did not fit him.   He could swim, skate, fence, use the broadsword and rapier, shoot, and ride, but of politics he thought very little.   His tendencies were towards a "natural liberalism," such as would obtain in an autocratic State where party politics were unknown.

It was said of him that he only liked shooting for the opportunities it gave him of studying nature, but this assertion received no confirmation in his life in England, for he seemed to shoot with the very express desire of killing.   His riding smacked more of the school than of the field or the Row, and the way he sat his saddle gave many opportunities for chaff and unkind remarks when he joined other riders in this very superior island.   As to the rest, everyone knows that he played the piano and the organ; that he composed music, little of which has, however, been given to the public; that he sang, drew, painted, etched, and liked to dabble in the sciences.   He also enjoyed discussions in metaphysics and philosophy, and tried his hand at literature, writing his Rhine experiences and an elaborate treatise on German Thought.   As a youth he said that life would be very pleasant but for its amusements.   When his father wanted him to go to Carlsbad he was terribly cast down, saying that paying attention to ladies was an occupation he particularly disliked—a not unnatural remark from a youth of nineteen, and one which showed him to be still in the cub stage.   His remark is reminiscent of the story told me by Lady Seymour, of how, when in Florence at a great assembly, the Prince was eagerly discussing some abstruse subject with the blind Marquis Capponi, one of the Tuscan aristocracy; and the Grand Duke Leopold, standing by Lady Augusta Fox, remarked to her : " There is a Prince of whom we may be proud. Lovely partners wait for him, while he is occupied with the learned."

In 1837 the Prince spent six weeks in Switzerland, and wrote to his cousin Victoria that " he had explored every part of that country "; just as later he made up his mind to see all that Rome could offer him in three weeks.

On the whole, the Prince's life abroad and in his father's duchy contradicts the idea that his morbid desire to preserve an impenetrable privacy in England had much to do with custom or habit. At his father's Palace in Coburg, and at Rosenau, the country house where Albert and his brother spent their youth, free access was given to the grounds. About two hundred yards from Rosenau was a small wirtshaus, which was a favourite resort on Sundays for the people of Coburg, who could there rest and take their beer or coffee, after which their amusement was to stroll all over the grounds of Rosenau, for " the system of exclusion which prevailed with regard to English parks was unknown there, and the walks and grounds were at all times freely thrown open to those who wished to enjoy them."[1]

I notice the same custom mentioned in the account of the investiture with the Garter which took place at Coburg a few days before the Prince started for

[1] " Early Life."

England. At the ceremony the Duke sat on his throne at the end of the room supported by his sons and others. The Duchess, Princesses and Court ladies were in boxes on either side, while the back of the room was filled by as many people from the town as it would hold.

Albert's spirits were high during his engagement, but they fell lower as time went on and as he slowly began to understand that England held no recognised position for him. A Queen Consort was well understood, she was head of the Court and was expected to exercise a direct influence over the manners of society and " over her own sex in particular." In Queen Victoria rested both the Headship of the nation and of the Court, for the Prince was allotted no place, no work, no influence, nothing but that he should be a mate for the Queen. So at first by pin-pricks, and later by rough blows, his peculiar position was drummed into the young man's mind. He was told that he could not quarter his future wife's arms with his own; that in that respect he must stand apart; the Garter King at Arms—specialist in the subject— affirmed it and based his judgment upon the want of precedent. But when the Prince, more wide awake than himself, asked him what had been done in the matter when Leopold married Charlotte, he had to admit his mistake and establish Albert's right.

There was the private refusal by the Queen and Melbourne, based upon knowledge of public opinion, to make him a peer, and then there were the other troubles of income, doubts about his religion and

D

precedence, about which I have in an earlier volume written at length. And at last he wrote bravely:

" I will not let my courage fail. With firm resolution and true zeal on my part, I cannot fail to continue noble, manly and princely in all things." " My future lot is high and brilliant, but also painfully strewed with thorns. Struggles will not be wanting, and the month of March already appears to have storms in store."

All English people were glad that the Queen should marry. Each party hoped that it would benefit materially by such an event, though the Tories both hoped most keenly and feared most vividly. If the Queen's husband supported her in her anti-Tory policy they were ripe for revolution, and many conflicting testimonies were offered as to the Prince's leanings; but their general feeling was that a nephew of King Leopold must be their enemy, and so they did their best to frustrate their own hopes by opposing with bitter jealousy every advantage Parliament wished to offer him. Had he not been a man of such fine calibre nothing could have saved the governing class from a prolonged and evil struggle.

The people themselves looked upon the affair with more gaiety, and they expended their sense of humour in the circulation of innumerable broadsides, which were adorned with the crudest and most highly coloured portraits and pictures, sold everywhere for a penny, and sung and repeated in the houses, taverns and streets. Not one of them but emphasised the financial position of the Prince and the popularity of

the Coburgs in the marriage market. The following
verse was a great favourite :

"Vant you a wife, a husband, send
　　To Germany, and in a trice
Coburgs by dozens will contend
　　Which shall be yours, at any price ! "

These two broadsides are amongst the least offensive
of those published :

My German purse is loaded now,
　　So penniless before,
And I've a stock of toggery
　　I never had before ;
And for a spouse for little Vic,
　　John Bull will dearly pay—
Oh ! my heart, my heart is aching
　　For our grand wedding day.

For her I'll shun all other girls,
　　For her be sour as kraut
When Paget or some other sprig
　　May try to coax me out.
With her I'll constant be at church,
　　And likewise at the play—
Oh ! my heart, my heart is aching
　　For our grand wedding day.

She's all that Lehzen painted her,
　　No Queen is so divine,
And her heart is not Prince George's
　　Because I know it's mine.
Few have intrigued as Lehzen has—
　　O'er all she bears the sway ;
Oh ! my heart, my heart is aching
　　For our grand wedding day.

To this the Queen responds :

We will live and love together,
　　Like two young pretty dears ;
We will laugh at party quarrels,
　　And all religious fears.

D 2

> I shall quickly sack my mother,
> When I am wed to thee;
> Lehzen too must also vanish,
> Else mischief there will be.

In the second the Prince's version of the National Anthem was supposed to run as follows :

> God save sweet Vic, mine Queen
> Long live mine little Queen,
> God save de Queen.
> Albert is victorious;
> De Coburgs now are glorious,
> All so notorious,
> God save the Queen.

> Ah, Melbourne, soon arise
> To get me de supplies—
> My means are small.
> Confound Peel's politics,
> Frustrate de Tory tricks,
> At dem now go like bricks,
> God d——n dem all.

> The greatest gifts in store
> On me be pleased to pour,
> And let me reign;
> Mine Vic has vowed to-day
> To honour and obey,
> And I will have de sway—
> Albert de King.

So Prince Albert came to fulfil his inexorable fate. However much the people of England laughed and sang songs over the marriage, they were ready to receive the bridegroom with open arms, and they thronged in thousands to Dover to await his coming. The first time the Prince journeyed to England he was so seasick that he said the voyage had given him such a disgust for the sea that he did not like even to think of it. And again, when coming to his marriage in February, 1840, he was very ill during the crossing, so that it was a white-faced youth who gallantly stood on the bridge of the steamer and acknowledged the shouts of the crowd thronging the piers. From Dover to Canterbury, where he stayed a night, and from Canterbury to London, he drove to the constant accompaniment of huzzas, which only ended with the kiss of his bride in the hall of Buckingham Palace.

In Lord Broughton's " Recollections," edited by Lady Dorchester, occurs the only natural account of the marriage that I have seen. Lord Broughton was greatly pleased with the Prince's appearance, and says that " he was a little embarrassed with his gloves and his Prayer-book, and seemed not to know whether he ought to bow to the Archbishop of Canterbury and the Bishop of London, or to the altar. Queen Adelaide talked a good deal to him, and seemed to be telling him what to do during the service : so, also, did the Duke, his father, a fine-looking man."

The Queen entered the chapel twenty minutes after the Prince, looking "handsome, but pale, and the orange-blossoms in her head shook violently. But she performed her part with her usual propriety and presence of mind, and prompted Prince Albert during the reading of the lessons more than once. She once beckoned him to approach nearer when he put the ring on her finger, and pointed to the finger on which the ring was to be put. She pronounced the responses in a clear, steady voice, and repeated, ' I, Victoria, wed thee, Albert,' in a tone of deep, calm feeling which

I shall never forget. The Prince also repeated his lesson well, but with more emotion than the Queen."

The long ceremony being ended, the bride kissed the near relations round her, including little Mary of Cambridge, and threw a playful smile at Lord Melbourne, who held the sword of state, after which " The Queen and Prince walked down the chapel hand in hand, and even then I remarked that Her Majesty was obliged to prompt Prince Albert. His Royal Highness seemed afraid of being too conspicuous; and there was an apparent shyness in his manner which he never, so far as I observed, entirely got rid of when in the presence of the Queen."

As in her courtship, so in the early part of her marriage, it was evident that the Queen's was the dominant mind. While the young Prince was confused she was calm and self-contained; her voice was clear, Albert's shook with emotion; she even showed him on which finger to put the wedding-ring; while the awkward young man tried to efface himself she greeted her friends, then took her husband's hand and drew him out of the chapel. Prince Albert was, in fact, finding that what one anticipates with such brilliant hope, is sometimes spoiled in its fulfilment by its strangeness. In many ways this was his experience through life. He seemed almost always to give in to the Queen and never outwardly bore malice to those others who had thrown humiliation over his entry into England. But his gentle nature, his studious mind, his quiet domestic upbringing, were generally destructive of any sustained self-assertion against

odds, while the impulsiveness, the decisive autocracy
of the Queen's character made it yet more difficult for
him to find his feet in this strange land. He was at
first overawed, uncertain, shaken with that painful
nervousness which has to be hidden at any cost, and
of which the outward expression is so often a cold
reserve. It was years before the nervousness disappeared or the reserve melted, and so at first he
thoroughly earned the criticism of being stiff, cold, and
haughty. There can be little wonder that he was so,
for he was held in the balance unceasingly, every action
and every word in public being discussed.

The younger men, who should have stood by him
and initiated him into English ways and customs,
jeered among themselves at his failures in small detail,
and were never tired of the cheap judgment of "what
can be expected of a German?" There was absolutely nothing neglected in an unconscious attempt to
spoil the Prince's chances at the outset, and so
apparent was this that both he and the Queen were
for a time more keenly interested in his learning to
ride like an Englishman—she tutoring him in the
Royal riding school—and so gaining the approbation
of the English, than they were in the important art
of ruling.

But, in the exuberance of her desire to do honour
to her beloved, the Queen had committed a very injudicious act in making him Field Marshal on his
arrival in England, the appointment being in the
Gazette two days before the marriage. It was a most
unpopular appointment with the army, for over the

heads of tried, long-service men was placed a mere boy, a dilettante student who knew nothing of war or of army affairs. The Queen may have thought she was honouring both the Prince and the army, but the latter regarded it as an injustice, and so a barrier was raised at the outset between the Prince and his popularity, and a cry was given to those grumblers who during the Crimean War let their indignation rise to a mad height.

CHAPTER III

THE QUEEN AND THE PRINCE

THESE two young people, having consummated their mutual attraction by marriage, had to pay the penalty of Royalty by starting their life together at the wrong stage—that is to say, that they had after marriage to begin to learn each other's natures. There has been so much said about the beauty of the love match which the Queen made that folk forget that a real love match should be based upon something firmer than sentiment and ignorance. Excepting at second hand, what did Victoria and Albert know of each other when they married? Their whole intercourse had been limited to two meetings, one lasting for four weeks in 1836, and the other occupying a few weeks in 1839, in the second day of which the engagement took place. During the first visit of Albert to England he was not quite seventeen, Victoria was three months older, a mixture of wilfulness and obedience, one of her strongest convictions being of the high sacredness of her rank.

During these two visits both young people were naturally "on their good behaviour." What did

Albert know of Victoria's bursts of passion or of her capacity for jealousy, and what did she know of his immovable obstinacy or of his want of affinity for Court life? These things had to be discovered painfully and gradually, and, as Albert's brother said, " the young pair could not yield to each other."

At that time no embargo had been placed upon the pens or voices of their attendants, so that many accounts of domestic friction passed into the world of gossip, and there grew up a strong popular opinion that the Prince had gained, in vulgar parlance, " the grey mare " for a wife. Even before they left Windsor on February 14th the cartoonists were busy drawing pictures to prove first, as we have seen, that the Queen intended to " don the breeches," and secondly that the Prince had designs on the Crown. Before the first month of wedded life was over the Tory Press was criticising " the severity of the Queen's domination over the Prince Consort."

As for the other charge, the French newspapers styled him *Le Roi d'Angleterre*, and one English picture showed him standing before a long glass putting on the Crown, Victoria, surprised and annoyed, telling him he must not do that—the Crown being hers alone, to which he is made to respond that what is hers is also his now that they are married. Another satirist, after Albert had been appointed regent in case of the Queen's death, drew him in shooting costume aiming at a crown, saying, " Ah, hah, mein dear ; I shall see if I can hit you, though you seem to say, ' I wish you may get me, Monsieur Regent.' " What the Prince may have expected on this point is not told in words, but there was certainly continental precedent for his becoming titular King. The husband of Donna Maria of Portugal received the title at the birth of their second son, and later Prince Francisco of Spain, who married his cousin, Isabella, was at once inducted into the outward form if not the reality of Kingship.

The Queen ardently desired that Albert should be made King Consort, which caused Melbourne to respond impetuously :

" For God's sake, say no more about it, Ma'am, for those who can make Kings can unmake them."

But the Prince came among us and lived among us for seventeen years without any English standing, which gave every excuse to the carper, when he wanted to wound, of dubbing him " The Queen's German husband," though the people at large had long called him the Prince Consort.

The difficulty of getting used to each other was emphasised and kept alive by the Queen's " dear, good Lehzen," the woman who from nurse and governess had become Secretary, Counsellor and Chief Adviser to the Queen, who in fact superintended the Royal Household and arranged many details connected with the Privy Purse. This lady, who had been made a baroness by George IV., had done her best at first to promote the marriage, then, fearing loss of power, had influenced the Queen to show continued hesitation, but the marriage accomplished in spite of her she bent her energies to the task of keeping the husband in the place she had allotted him, to wit, that of male in

Victoria's household, a kind of King bee, a person whose only function was to provide heirs to the throne. She decreed that details of the Queen's high business as ruler must not be made known to him; from all discussions, important or otherwise, he was to be shut out. The household—so admirably managed by Baroness Lehzen—was a thing apart from his interference; as to the Queen's letters—was not Lehzen herself a proficient Secretary?—who was this young man that he should dare to ask questions about such things? Thus the Prince had two rulers, his wife and his wife's confidante, and he was made aware of it before he had been married twenty-four hours.

The bride and bridegroom went down to Windsor alone after the wedding, that they might secure two days of quiet in which to start life together. In another carriage, at a different time, Lehzen also travelled to the Castle, unknown to anyone but her dearest charge and Queen. So when the Prince went to breakfast the first morning of his wedded life he had the mortification of finding the Baroness ready to hand him his coffee. And this was only the first of many annoyances and slights from which for two years he had to suffer.

The people of England disliked the name of Lehzen as much as the Tories had once disliked the Duchess of Kent. She was so retiring, so ignored in conversation by her mistress, so thoroughly *behind* the throne, that they had come to invest her with an almost sinister power, and this suspicion, openly commented on in the Press, made the Queen think an even greater secrecy necessary. She was universally regarded as the bestower of privileges:

"Is there a single situation about the Court, from a maid-of-any-work to a Lady of the Bedchamber, or from a Groom to a Lord Chamberlain, that is not sought through the Baroness?" was a pertinent question made by one paper. Yet the secret of her influence lay in her love for Victoria and in the fact that at a time when the Duchess of Kent was following with her daughter a rigid system of repression, Lehzen believed in the opposite method, that of developing the girl's tastes and character; and to this she added a very judicious flattery. The Queen might always be sure that the man who sat next to Lehzen at dinner was listening to the praises of the First Lady in the Land. In memoir after memoir, in one biography after another, I find that the Baroness's table companion was always hearing of the Queen's tastes, her habits, her manners, her reading, her doings as a child, and so forth.

A further cause of friction in the royal dovecot was the Queen's attitude to the Tories, made more bitter by the undignified public squabble that had taken place in Parliament over Albert. So strong was the resentment Victoria felt that she was determined that only one of that political colour, her old friend Lord Liverpool, should be present at her wedding.

"But the Duke! you must have the Duke!"

"No, surely on such an occasion as this I need only have my *friends* with me," was her reply.

In the end she gave way to the great pressure put

upon her, and sent the Duke of Wellington a belated invitation, and his reception could hardly have pleased her, for as he left the chapel—not being one of the bridal procession—spontaneously, without signal, and yet as if with common and universal consent, everyone rose and gave him three hearty cheers, which seemed to gladden his heart.

It had not occurred to Victoria that her bridegroom could possibly ever disagree with her sentiments, and when she heard him voicing ideas which could scarcely be accepted by the Liberals her agitation and anger were great.

On this point she found herself at once standing between the old and the new, the influence, embodied in Lehzen, of the Kensington Camarilla, and the fresher, stronger ideas of the beloved. The Prince had to fight for it, had even to fight for his right to speak on the matter at all, for Lehzen was constant in warnings against interference with the royal position, against combining the husband and the counsellor.

To be angry at a new idea offered by a respected person, then to consider it, and at last to adopt it, is a natural sequence in many minds, and the Queen's prejudices became softened, so that Thomas Raikes in his Diary affirmed that he had news that by April the influence of the Prince had caused the Queen to be more civil to the Tory party, and that she had actually invited some of them to the Palace.

On the third day after the marriage Windsor was invaded by the whole Court, headed by the Duchess of Kent and the Coburgs, which necessitated dancing

parties and other festivities, and then two days later
the Queen and Prince had to return to London to give
themselves up to the doubtful pleasure of receiving
addresses.   A levee was held of which Disraeli wrote :
" The Queen looked well; the Prince on her left in
high military fig, very handsome, and the presence was
altogether effective."   Albert was very nervous, but
the ordeal was rendered easier by his having his father
and brother near him.   To this levee came the Peers
and the Commons in two gorgeous processions, the
peers in their robes, the Commons led by the Speaker
with Lord John Russell on one hand and Sir Robert
Peel on the other, both clad in the Windsor uniform.

Albert's brother Ernest, who stayed with the bridal
pair until April, did not escape the popular criticism
upon the Coburgs in general.   He was, in the gracious
way of the period, taunted with closeness about money
matters, and was supposed to be in league with Albert
to get everything he could out of the English and the
royal moneybags.   I have seen a caricature of the
period in which he leans over the back of his brother's
chair, watching him with great interest as he is feeling
in the depths of a gigantic knitted purse.   Victoria
sitting at the table cries :

"Albert, take your hand out of my purse, I *command* you.   It is too bad, hasn't John Bull allowed you
a good yearly sum for pocket-money without your
filching from me ? "

To which Albert replies : " Really, mein dear, I
know all about it, but Shon Pool, I find, hasn't allowed
me one half enough for my expenses, and if I want

more now and den I shall see no harm in coming to mein wife's purse for it." Upon which Ernest whispers in his brother's ear, "Albert, give me a little while you are about it."

When Ernest went away it was with a very sad heart that the Prince saw him go. It was the last tie with his own country broken, for he knew that never again would any of the old intimacies be resumed; he was being left to a new life among people who were not disposed to accept him too cordially, with one only, a new companion, to uphold and comfort him. So the two young men sang together a German student's farewell song, "Abschied," and they parted, their eyes full of tears and Albert as pale as a sheet. It must have been one of the saddest moments of his life, for the affection between the brothers was very strong.

The poor Prince was horrified at the late hours kept by the Queen. His favourite bed-time being nine o'clock he yet would find himself obliged to stand about and be polite until one or two in the morning. The programme for the evening was generally that the Queen and Prince would enter the Drawing Room at eight, or nominally at eight, and after dinner she would go with the ladies into the long gallery, into which the rooms opened. At the dinner Victoria never omitted the custom of having her own health drunk, and now it was followed by that of her husband, she throwing him her sweetest smile. They thought it all right, I suppose, but the good taste seems questionable to-day. She was anxious to induce the men to discontinue the practice of sitting over wine, but the experiment led to ill-humour and a lingering after dinner in the ante-room, so she modified her wishes, requiring them to remain a quarter of an hour only behind the women. After dinner there was generally dancing, Victoria reserving the waltzes for her husband. From the time of her accession she often wrote out her own instructions as to the placing of guests; such as : " Lord Melbourne will take in the Queen and sit on her left, Lord Ashley will take in the Dcs. of Kent and sit *between* her and the Queen, and Lord Byron will sit on the Dcs. of Kent's right."

When the King of Prussia was staying at Windsor in the early part of 1842, that he might stand sponsor for the Prince of Wales, Madame Bunsen, wife of the Prussian Ambassador, was naturally with her husband a guest at the Castle. The definite impression of the visit which she gave in her " Memoirs " showed the Queen to be one of those delightful hostesses who allow her guests full liberty of action, so that Madame Bunsen enjoyed her stay there for its quiet and independence; it was a rest, not an exertion, and the period of state stiffness lasted only from eight to eleven in the evening. She was enthusiastic over her first evening, and yet a little afraid of being lost :

" When dressed we went to the corridor, where Lord Delawarr and the Duchess of Buccleugh, etc., were waiting, and the former led us through the corridor to the ballroom, where the guests awaited the Queen." The King of Prussia, punctual to 7.30, was there and Prince Albert entered. Before long two gentlemen walking in at a door and then turning and making profound

E

bows towards the open door showed that the Queen was coming. She went directly to Madame Bunsen, the stranger, and spoke her pleasure in seeing her. To the tune of "God save the Queen" Victoria took 'the King's arm, and went in to dinner.

"The scene was one of fairy tales—of indescribable magnificence, the proportions of the hall, the mass of light in suspension, the gold plate on the table, glittering with a thousand lights in branches of a proper height not to meet the eye. When the gentlemen joined the ladies the Queen went into the ball-room and made the King dance a quadrille with her, though he had long ceased to dance. At 11.30, after the Queen had retired, I set out on my travels to my bedchamber; I might have looked and wandered some miles before I had found my door of exit, but was helped by an old gentleman, I believe Lord Albemarle."

In 1840 Guizot—who became Louis Philippe's fatal adviser on the downfall of Thiers—stayed at Windsor Castle, and he wrote to his daughter that he had won over twenty pounds at the Ascot sweepstakes: "Twenty-three sovereigns for me, which will balance the twenty pounds I had to spend in fees to the servants at Windsor Castle."

Of the Castle itself he said: "It certainly is one of the most delightful and picturesque castles in the world; its exterior is a Gothic fortress of the Middle Ages, the interior is a very elegant and comfortable modern palace. The dining-room is splendid. On my left sat the young Queen, whom they tried to assassinate the other day, in gay spirits, talking a great deal, laughing very often, and longing to laugh still more; and filling with her gaiety, which contrasted with the already tragical elements in her history, this ancient castle which has witnessed the careers of all her predecessors.   It is all very grand, very beautiful, very striking."

Victoria in her love of dancing reminds us of Queen Elizabeth, who, according to some pleasant verses, danced and danced and danced, and pranced and pranced and pranced when endeavouring to please the senses of the Spanish Ambassador with the Coranto. Though we are generally told that young wives in the 'forties did not dream of dancing, there is every evidence that the young wife, Victoria, was always ready for that amusement.   But she had little fancy for the stately minuet.   She really most enjoyed a rousing country dance, which gave every facility for romping and laughter.   The Duke of Argyll speaks of a country dance called " Grandfather," in which two take a handkerchief and go down the row and those they pass jump over the handkerchief.   He was taught it at Frogmore, and seems to have been much impressed with the Queen's laughter over the fun.   Lord Campbell also tells of a romping kind of country dance in which the Queen delighted, named Tempêtre.

Pictures were published of Her Majesty and the Prince dancing the Highland fling; dancing the polka with the Princess Royal and the Prince of Wales on board when going to Scotland; engaging in a reel on the *Victoria and Albert*, the vivacious Sovereign crying,

E 2

" Now, Sir Robert, jig away all like the Highland laddie, and I will step and step with you as gay as any lassie." The unhappy Peel murmurs something about his rheumatism, and wishes the Queen had introduced a sliding scale rather than a Scotch reel, but he has to dance ; and while he and the Queen are footing it together, Prince Albert dances with one of her ladies, and, sad to say, the two are tenderly ogling each other. But when it did not suit the occasion, and when it was but a quiet evening that was being passed, Victoria was quite ready for a round game. " German Tactics " was the earliest one the Prince introduced, the name, of course, being seized on by the jokers. On these evenings 11.30 was the bed-time, but this was still too late for the Prince, and the breakfast was at first put off to ten o'clock to allow him to get sufficient rest. Later it was fixed for nine, which gave an opportunity for an after-breakfast walk before the business of the day began.

One hears so much of the extraordinary amount of work which Albert did that the Queen's own description of the routine of the day takes one quite by surprise— there was so much more play than work in it. After the nine o'clock breakfast, the walk, and the business, they drew " and etched a great deal together, which was a source of great amusement, having the plates 'bit' in the house. Luncheon followed at the usual hour of two o'clock. Lord Melbourne came to the Queen in the afternoon, and between three and six the Prince usually drove her out in a pony phaeton. If the Prince did not drive the Queen he rode, in which case she took a drive with the Duchess of Kent or the ladies. The Prince also read aloud most days to the Queen. The dinner was at eight o'clock, and always with the company. In the evening the Prince frequently played at double chess, a game of which he was very fond, and which he played extremely well."

Later on, when the Prince had greater interest in political work and his unremitting toil is mentioned, the *Court Circular* reports a removal from Windsor to Osborne, then a few days at Claremont, followed by six weeks at Balmoral, and a day or two at Buckingham Palace, just to satisfy London. Each of these places seemed to have its own particular amusement to offer, but the record of changes does not give an impression of sustained work.

The marriage had caused jubilation in some Tory papers, it being inferred that not only Melbourne but some of the Court favourites would be weeded out, and there is little doubt but that the Prince felt some discomfort at the constant presence of various friends of the Queen. In June *The Times* declared that Victoria was received rapturously at Ascot because Lord Melbourne was not in her train; and public references to Lord Alfred Paget were continual, such as: "He is always making some courtly blunder, as he is the most 'miss-taking' individual at Court"; or, "The Royal attention will no longer be monopolised by the Pagets and the Melbournes. We are glad that its fitting reward is awaiting Paget interferences, and that it will be found possible for the Queen to move amongst her subjects without Lord Alfred haunting her." "The word 'to clear the Palace' of its family-club officials will ere long be passed by Prince Albert."

As there were, it was said, nine Pagets about the Court at that time, there was some excuse for a popular belief in favouritism. Matilda and her sister Laura were maids of honour, Lady Sandwich was a lady in waiting, the Earl of Uxbridge was the Lord Chamberlain, Lord Alfred Paget was equerry, and Lady Constance Paget was also at Court. These are six which I have traced, and it may be true that there were three others. But Lord Alfred remained equerry for many years, being given also, in 1840, a captaincy in Prince Albert's Own Hussars, under the charming Lord Cardigan !

For some time after the marriage Melbourne still sat at one side of the Queen at table and Albert on the other. The Prince had, with the zeal of the young, fully intended to displace his lordship altogether, but he found that things could not so lightly be carried out. There were some sharp disagreements between the Royal pair over the kindly Melbourne, and then the Prince began to fall under the fascination of the genial, fatherly man, who was one of the cleverest and most learned, if also the laziest, of courtiers and statesmen, one who, though not a great party leader, was certainly a good Queen's Minister.

It is reported in the " Early Years " that the Prince —knowing Melbourne better as time went on—wrote of him : " He is a good, upright man, and supports me in everything that is right." The Queen annotated this with : " The Prince does not add, what would have been the truth, *that it would have been impossible for him to ask or wish for support except in what was right.*" The italics are mine. If it were not for the circumstances which brought it forth, this sort of expressed idolatry of the Prince after his death would be very shocking. But the reason for it was that Victoria hoped, by a constant singing of his praises, to ensure Albert at least posthumous admiration. It has, I fear, had rather the opposite result.

It is true that the Prince was not admitted to discussions upon State affairs, any more than he was admitted to those upon household matters, but then Melbourne not only paid him every deference, but showed a growing and genuine respect for his abilities, as well as a sympathy for the difficulties of his position. Thus it came to pass that when the Prince felt things going wrong, either domestically or otherwise, he went to Melbourne for help, and received every assistance which that astute counsellor could give. It was Melbourne who urged upon the Queen that her husband was something more than just her husband, that he was a man of ability, capable of giving her signal assistance, that she had not only the right, but the privilege of asking his help in great matters as well as small; and Melbourne as well as the Prince blamed Lehzen for her interference. It is no wonder that Albert hated the woman who stood in the way of his independence; yet he was powerless, for if he openly showed his bitterness his dear little wife, while believing she loved her dearest, most angelic Albert better than anyone in the world, would hotly defend her old friend. It was said, however, that when matters grew too difficult, Victoria gave Lehzen some timid hints—for she was as much in awe of as in love with that lady—that she might like to retire on a pension and resign her secretaryship into the hands of the Prince.

From this and other causes there were many quarrels, echoes of which got abroad. There is that well-reported violent quarrel after which the Queen rushed from the room. Returning after a time she found the door locked, and knocked imperiously for entry :

" Who is there ? " called the Prince.

" The Queen of England ! " was the haughty reply. And all remained quiet in the room behind the door.

Again and again Victoria knocked, and again and again came the same question and answer, until at last the Queen, conquered, responded :

" Your wife, Albert."

Upon which the door was opened and the weeping Queen was comforted.

Another quarrel which also had to do with a locked door occurred over the question of the Prince going out when the Queen wished him to remain in. To ensure obedience to her own wishes she turned the key of the room he occupied. As she stood outside expecting all sorts of angry protests, only silence fell on her ears; Albert did not even beg to be let out, so, somewhat piqued, she softly opened the door to see what he was doing. The philosophic Prince had got out his paint-box, and was calmly making a sketch of the view from his window.

Another time the disagreement was over the tea-table, with the result that she-of-the-passionate-temper flung the contents of a cup into her lord's face.

"What do you think of that?" murmured the Prince to his attendant, as he rose to change his clothes.

These reports caused more than one wag to affirm that to Victoria and Albert was to be awarded the Dunmow flitch of bacon, and H.B. had an elaborate drawing of a great procession, the Prince and Queen riding on one horse, and the flitch being carried before them; H.H. publishing an even more amusing cartoon of the royal pair demanding the flitch of John Bull.

The Prince's misogynist tendencies were put severely to the test at his wife's Court, for Victoria liked pretty people about her, and was said to have ladies "who were in appearance ideal attendants upon an ideal Queen." There was the young Marchioness of Douro, wife of one of the Wellesleys, for whom the Queen had a great liking, and who was beautiful enough for *Punch* to compliment her through the lips of a stoker on the N.W.R. :

"But, Lord, Jem! that there Marchioness Douro's a bewty,
(Wich Princesses and Princes to nuss it's her dooty,)
And sez I to myself—' Bless your sweet face, sez I, ma'am !
If I goes off the line with *yer,* blow me sky high, ma'am ! ' "

There was Miss Pitt, who had the reputation of causing the Queen active jealousy : not that she wanted to, but Victoria could not bear the Prince to talk much to anyone, Melbourne once remarking with kindly amusement that she seemed jealous if he talked long even with a man. There was Miss Spring-Rice, who could gladden him with her fluent German, Miss Devereux, Miss Cocks, and the older and statelier ladies of the Bedchamber. The constant presence of such a number of elegant, highly-bred women could not fail to rub off some of the priggishness and roughness which a callow youth so often mistakes for manliness, and Albert grew easier in his manners, and with the active if sometimes indignantly expressed help of his wife he began to learn to hand a lady out of a carriage, and not to get out first and walk off, to open the room door for the Queen, and otherwise become more courtly. But this cut both ways, and the Queen suffered acutely in watching his greater politeness to ladies. She could not bear to hear his laughter, which was generally both loud and unmusical, in unison with that of some fair conversationalist, and it was said that he had to pay the penalty for his new polish in many a *mauvais quart d'heure.* One joke went the round that he was anxious to arrange and attend a dramatic performance, at which the two plays should be " The Jealous Wife " and " The Taming of the Shrew." He was also accredited with the desire to watch the evolutions of a famous dancer too often, a desire which was not allowed to be gratified, and many other skits and jokes were published which aimed slyly at the Queen's failing of jealousy.

An American, after visiting England in 1844, gave his opinion of the Queen and Prince in his local paper in the following words :

"While I could not undertake to say that the Queen is handsome, I was much struck with her whole manner and appearance. She has a very intelligent face, with eyes and mouth indicative of the firmness and courage which belong to her race, and she is certainly one of the most graceful creatures I have ever seen. There is much dignity in her carriage, and her whole air is more grave and matronly than usually belongs to women of her age. She is not, I should judge, entirely free from her temper—on the contrary, if I am not much mistaken, she would not hesitate to give even her *cara sposa* the very—jessy, should he happen to displease her. I should say that she would be an admirable hand at a curtain lecture. Albert is good-looking, very tall and well made, but his countenance is quite inexpressive—in fact, somewhat vacant and hard. He would not 'take on' much, in my opinion, at the dismissal of a favourite or the death of a friend. There is rather a melancholy air about him, but whether this results from the death of his father, or, as some say, the constant *surveillance* of his Royal spouse, I will not venture to guess. He is altogether what we should call in our country 'a nice young man,' and, seeing that he receives some £30,000 a year, besides 'board and lodging,' we may safely conclude that he is well satisfied with his situation, even throwing in the curtain lectures."

The married people who never disagree even in the first days of their companionship are generally those who know each other so well that they have already learned the intricacies of each other's characters.

Those who marry first and have to pursue the character study afterwards are bound to find points of difference, and, if they are impulsive, to put their finding into words. Thus Victoria really loved her husband as passionately and sentimentally as she felt it her pride to do, and their early life held many idyllic periods, especially in the country. The Queen had had little education; French, German, and a smattering of Latin were her nearest approach to intellectual attainments; music, singing, drawing, and painting were, of course, her accomplishments, accomplishments considered necessary to every girl at that time and for many years later.

Of the world and its wonders, of Nature with its inexorable laws, its beauty and its cruelty, she knew nothing. Lady Lyttelton, whose privately printed and but recently published letters have been so much quoted by every Royal biographer,[1] said that the Queen did not at the time of her marriage know an oak from an elm, and scarcely knew a rose from a thistle. She gives pictures of the Royal pair, he cantering up to his wife's carriage to point out a swarm of bees, and to add some information about the Queen bee, etc., Victoria answering, "How curious!" and making pretty little remarks. Then again the Queen would point out some new plant imported into the garden, adding half shyly the information she had received about it from the Prince.

It is an interesting aspect of the two chief people

[1] "The Correspondence of Sarah, Lady Lyttelton," edited by the Hon. Mrs. Hugh Wyndham.

SARAH, LADY LYTTELTON.
From a Pastel by Swinton, in the possession of Viscount Cobham.

of a great Court. The Queen, a charming *ingénuc*, though three years a Queen, the very young husband, gradually finding his level and inducting the untaught girl into some of the delightful simplicities of the natural world.

So far London, late hours, dancing, had given Queen Victoria the greatest delight, but she was so malleable that she soon began to accept her husband's dislike of the town as her own. She had always been miserable when she left London; now she began to believe that she was miserable when she went there. It was simply a matter of imitation, which gradually she carried into everything, for the impulsive nature generally in the end gives way to the cautious one. During his first year in England the Prince wrote to his grandmother: "We came here the day before yesterday to spend a month at stately Windsor, and I felt as if in Paradise in this fine fresh air, instead of the dense smoke of London. The thick, heavy atmosphere there quite weighs me down. The town is also so large that without a long ride or walk you have no chance of getting out of it. Besides this, wherever I show myself I am still followed by hundreds of people."

Years later Victoria said in excuse for avoiding London: "London became positively distasteful to the Queen, and was only made endurable by having her beloved husband at her side, to share with her and support her in the irksome duties of Court receptions and State ceremonials. It was also injurious to her health, as she suffered much from the extreme weight and thickness of the atmosphere, which gave her the headache."

Another and an amusing piece of imitation was commented on at the time that the Duke of Norfolk entertained his Sovereign. Prince Albert had a peculiar dislike for mutton, and the Queen had acquired the same distaste, so it was announced that no mutton was to appear on the board at Arundel!

The Prince showing a disposition to be quite polite to the Tories, some of them began to feel a little conscience-stricken when they thought of the recent Parliamentary debates, and they in their turn tried to work out some means by which they could gracefully hold out the olive branch; so they invited him to speak at an Anti-Slavery meeting at Exeter Hall. It was an astute method of killing two birds with one stone, for curiosity about the Prince would safely ensure the filling of the hall. The invitation was at once accepted, and Albert learned his speech by heart, repeating it before the Queen in the morning. It was, of course, a success, and Sir Robert Peel, who presided, made a laboured and fulsome return of thanks for the Royal condescension, upon which John Russell remarked:

"The Prince would much rather Peel had not cut off £20,000 a year from his income, than that he should be asked to make a fine speech and give £100 to the Anti-Slavery Society."

Peel followed up his first advantage by appointing the Prince President of the Royal Commission which was to consider the best means of promoting Art and Science; and a further honour was offered, in that of Director of Ancient Music, the duty of the directors being to take turns in arranging concerts in Hanover Square Rooms.

All these endeavours to give work to idle hands was one method by which the English statesmen hoped to fit the young German into a little groove, to point the way of opportunity for him in one direction, and to close it in another. He might play among the pretty-pretties of life as much as he liked, fill the graceful part of figure-head, patron, and lover of the *beaux arts*, but he was to be headed off from any interference with English politics. As Baron Stockmar, the Prince's hypochrondriacal tutor, had laid great stress upon the necessity for Albert to study law and politics, and as Albert himself had a strong idea that Kingship went with his position, he took the offerings made him with a very decided feeling that they were only the promise of greater things to come.

When Queen Victoria married, she had but two houses, for St. James's Palace had long been abandoned as a home, and both of them were Royal residences—that is to say, they were dwellings which had no hint of private ownership about them—Windsor Castle, the Sovereign's country residence, and Buckingham Palace, the town house. The latter has always been one of those failures which might have been such a splendid success, for enough money has been spent on it several times over to have built a new palace, and yet it remains ugly, sordid, and inconvenient.

In 1825 Buckingham House was turned into Buckingham Palace for George IV. by partly pulling down, by altering, and patching to the tune of £300,000. On Victoria's accession it was done up, and a conservatory turned into a chapel; on her marriage many rooms were altered and redecorated, and less than a year later additional alterations were again made, doors were let into walls, staircases thrown up to the rooms above the Queen's and the Prince's suites, and the nurseries made by filching the servants' bedrooms, said to be the attics, and stretching floors across their loftiness so as to make two rooms where before only one had existed. Then in 1847 these were found inadequate, while the Queen's rooms, being over the workshops, were rendered odious by the noise of sawing and hammering and the smell of glue and paint. So stone was imported from Caen, and a whole new front, with suites of rooms built, the nurseries fitted up in the north wing with kitchens and everything needful, so that there was no need for communication with the rest of the house; alterations which cost £150,000.

The only really noble thing about the exterior of the Palace had been the Marble Arch, built by John Nash for George IV. of Carrara marble, on the model of the Arch of Constantine at Rome. It cost £80,000, and the bronze gates were designed and cast by Samuel Parker at a further cost of £3,000; they are said to be the best and most dignified gates in Europe. During the first part of the nineteenth century England was at one of its lowest ebbs in art, and the clever

Government officials who were responsible for the moving of those gates thought themselves sufficiently careful if the carting was done in a common stage waggon, with the result that the most beautiful piece of the ironwork which should have crowned the gates was smashed to pieces; thus London lost a treasure, the artist's heart was broken—and no one seemed to care.

By 1850 the Queen decided that the Marble Arch was in her way and unnecessary, and so the poor thing went begging for a situation, suggestions being made that it was only a nuisance, and should be demolished. When we are all dead, the generations who come after will begin to prize this beautiful thing, and even we know that it is worth all the Buckingham Palaces that can be built. It is a blessing that some-one had the fine idea of planting it down at Tyburn, for its influence has spread all round it.

Like all her forbears, the Guelphs, Victoria had but little eye for the chaste in beauty, and so whenever Buckingham Palace was redecorated, it put on new and brighter tints of crimson and purple and gold. The hue of the precious metal plastered the ceilings and walls; it covered the woodwork of the chairs and sofas; it glittered in the ornaments, and sparkled from the hangings. One room was decorated in yellow satin, and every article in it was overlaid with burnished gold. The Throne Room was hung in crimson satin and velvet with gold on every available spot. The State ball-room, which was not finished until 1856, and at a cost of £300,000, had its gold ceiling

F

upheld with gold-topped Corinthian columns of porphyry scagliola,[1] while one of the drawing-rooms, abounded in columns of purple scagliola in imitation of lapis lazuli. It was these columns which Charles Greville sneered at as "raspberry-coloured pillars without end, enough to turn you sick to look at," adding that the costly ornaments in the State rooms exceeded all belief in their bad taste and every kind of infirmity. These sham marble columns rose from the palace floors in every room and in every direction, being in addition to mirrors and vivid colour the chief things in the scheme of decoration of the interior. Though it is comforting to be told that the Queen's private rooms were more simply furnished, it is difficult to realise a home in such surroundings.

When Parliament was asked in the mid-'forties to vote the large sum for the rebuilding of the Palace front, *Punch* published a cartoon on the subject. It showed Prince Albert, a very worn and lined paterfamilias, his famous hat in hand, with his pretty, dainty Queen by his side, accompanied by four children and a fat nurse carrying a baby—and followed by soldiers and footmen, wandering through the streets of London, uttering the following prayer:

"A Case of Real Distress.

"Good People, pray take compassion on us. It is now nearly seven years since either of us have known

[1] Scagliola is a mixture of gypsum, isinglass, alum, fragments of marble, and colouring matter, which, being beaten to a paste, is laid on to imitate marble of the sort desired.

the blessing of a comfortable residence. If you do not believe us, good people, come and see where we live, at Buckingham Palace, and you will be satisfied that there is no deception in our story. Such is our distress, that we should be truly grateful for the blessing of a comfortable two-pair back, with commonly decent sleeping rooms for our children and domestics. With our slender means, and our increasing family, we declare to you that we do not know what to do. The sum of one hundred and fifty thousand pounds will be all that will be required to make the needful alterations in our dwelling. Do, good people, bestow your charity to this little amount, and may you never live to feel the want of so small a trifle."

Lord John Russell demanded the money from the Commons, saying that unless it was forthcoming the Royal children would have to live permanently at Windsor, and so be often separated from their parents. He added also that he thought it would be a handsomer plan to commence a new Palace altogether, which drew a chorus of protests from all sides. Verses and songs were written deprecating such a course, such as :

> "Oh ! do not build for me
>   Another palace, pray,
> I have already three—
>   And sure enough are they.
> Besides a country seat,
>   All in the Isle of Wight,
> Another build not, I entreat;
>   I've houses plenty ! quite ! "

In his *Weekly Newspaper* Douglas Jerrold commented as follows on the idea :

" Lord John Russell thought it would have been ' a handsomer plan '—that is, we presume, had John Bull been very full of cash—' to commence a new Palace.' Another palace !—and that, of course, too big or too small—or too high or too low—or too damp or too smoky for the next tenant. It is so difficult to accommodate all the glories of royalty. Happy are the snails ! for *their* king—as the poet says—carries his house on his back."

Lady Eastlake, who with her husband was much favoured by the Queen and Prince, went into ecstasies over Buckingham Palace after the alterations were made, writing in a letter : " It is superb. The hall and staircases are regal, and Devonshire House, Apsley House, and all the houses I have seen sink into insignificance in comparison," adding that marble and gilding were on all sides, with sheets of mirrors, and every nook and alcove was full of the loveliest flowers. However, Lady Eastlake was subject to passing enthusiasms, for a year later she wrote of Stafford House that it " surpasses in splendour anything that can be imagined. Buckingham Palace is nothing to it."

Of Buckingham Palace garden there could be no two opinions. It covered nearly forty acres, and was more like a park than a garden. It must have been a delight to weary Royalty, in spite of, or perhaps because of, the fact that formalism was then the highest ideal in gardening. It contained—and still does contain—a lake, and a summer-house on a mound, consisting of several rooms, which the Prince had decorated with frescoes by the best-known artists, and which was —perhaps—as good for the children as a simple, unassuming structure would have been; and Albert introduced into the fields and alleys all sorts of animals and aquatic birds, that he might have the pleasure of feeding them and studying their ways.

It is curious in these days of sanitation to look back to the time of our grandmothers, and realise the abominations under which they lived, Queen and courtiers as well as humbler folk. Thus during the 1847 building operations a shocking report of the sewerage around the Palace was given. All the houses forming the streets to the south were entirely without drainage, though there were occasional cesspools hidden among the houses, into which the sewage passed. There it lay until the pool was full and its contents putrid, and those happy conditions being attained, the whole contents were pumped into the open gutters, diffusing miasma around as the stream passed through the streets, until at length it found its way into the sewers. The only alternative to this operation was for the inhabitants to let the flood percolate into their dwellings. I have seen within the last twelve years the same method pursued in a French fishing town, and the occasional release of the sewage was not even made to synchronise with the high tide. Such happenings as these under the Palace windows might well give both the Prince and the Queen "the headache."

After the Prince Consort's death an examination of drains was made at Windsor, and it was found that beneath the Castle and the wards were about fifty cesspools and that the drains were very defective.

CHAPTER IV

THE QUEEN'S CHILDREN

ALTOGETHER the Queen at this stage of her career must have possessed considerable charm. She was impulsive, generous, loving and passionate, generally thought the best of people, and was very frank and sincere. On the other hand, she had so ingrained and lofty an idea of her great position that she was to a certain extent blinded about herself and by herself, and she never did come anywhere near comprehending that she was self-centred and selfish. Thus all through her letters her love for her husband, so readily expressed, is rather an appreciation of the satisfaction it gave to herself than any realisation of the good it should confer on him. She always stood first, occupying the centre of the picture; he was always there, but a little behind, a little in the shadow, one upon whom she could shed her light and who would naturally be overwhelmed with joy.

Yet he was much greater than the Queen in character. He possessed the strength of the Christian virtues; he could suffer and be kind; he could work cheerfully and give all the credit of his labour to his wife; he was thoroughly unselfish, and had firmness, strength, and intellect. Still he remains a shadow in the train of one whose greatest claim to greatness was a long and temperate life, upheld and protected by exceptionally able Ministers, and passed in the fierce light which beats upon the Throne. Such a statement will not find favour with those who, accepting judgments ready made without thinking them out, are persuaded of the superlative character of our late Queen; but all unprejudiced study and thought on the subject points to this conclusion.

However, I am dealing with her now as a woman just entering her third decade, when all the circumstances of her life made her interesting; when she was looking forward, as healthy-minded young married women do, to rearing a family, and making great preparations for the first event which should contribute to that result. The public seemed to know what was about to happen almost before she did herself, and as early as April and May there were newspaper comments about an important event which would occur in November.

The Queen accepted the prospect of the trial before her in the happy spirit with which the inexperienced look forward to giving birth to their first child. There are many women who, after that first time, have not the bravery to face such an agonising episode again, and there are others in whom the love of children is so deep that they forget the pain in the joy of possession, and gradually secure the proverbial quiver full; happily, the Queen—who never wanted pluck—was of the latter class.

Among the many announcements made as to the Queen's health before the event occurred was one which alluded to a weakness of the little lady's, that of having her portrait painted or her bust modelled, one process of this sort succeeding another with fair regularity. "To our gracious Sovereign herself, the natural prospect of her accouchement, we are happy to state, appears to furnish anything but grounds for misgiving or alarm. Her only consternation seems to lie in the temporary interruption which the circumstances of the case may impose upon her ability to sit for her portrait."

On November 10th the Princess Royal was born with the usual royal publicity, the Prince remaining in the room all through the Queen's labour and witnessing the birth of the child. In the next room, within earshot, were gathered the Archbishop of Canterbury, the Lord Bishop of London, Lord Melbourne, Viscount Palmerston, the Earl of Errol, Lord Steward of the Household, the Earl of Albemarle, Master of the Horse. In another room waited the Countess Sandwich, Lady of the Bedchamber; Colonel Cavendish, Equerry-in-Waiting; Sir Frederick Stovin, Groom-in-Waiting; Colonel Wylde, Equerry to Prince Albert, and Captain Seymour, Groom-in-Waiting on Prince Albert. All of them waiting there for hours for the last effort, the first cry.

Is it not a disgusting custom? Think of a very difficult birth—in a time when chloroform was not used —and a poor girl, weakened by hours of atrocious pain, losing her self-control and screaming, with all those old and young men of the world, married and un-married, feeling it their duty to remain and listen to every sound, to every moan. And then later on, when it was all over, and things were again normal, this victim of folly and suspicion would have to meet all these people, with the knowledge that they had made the willing audience at the tragedy which attends motherhood, a tragedy which all nature demands shall take place in the deepest seclusion. This alone is sufficient to console the most ambitious woman for the fact that she does not wear a crown.

Though the sufferings of the Queen were not abnormal, and the birth was rapid, so that a few hours completed the whole trouble, she may have felt how outrageously her right to privacy was shocked, and tried to arrange differently in the following year, when the Prince of Wales was born, for I find that stickler for etiquette, Charles Greville, grumbling that "from some crochet of Prince Albert's they put off sending intelligence of Her Majesty's being in labour till so late that several of the dignitaries, whose duty it was *to assist at the birth*, arrived after the event had occurred, especially the Archbishop of Canterbury and the Lord President of the Council." He goes on to say that: "At two o'clock a Council was held and the usual thanksgiving ordered. Last year the Prince took the chair, which was all wrong; and this time I placed him at the top of the table on the left, the Archbishop next him." He further added that the Queen commanded Peel and several others to dine at the Palace the night before, though it was Lord Mayor's Day and she must have known it, so they all had to break their engagement with the Lord Mayor. "Melbourne," said Greville, "would have gone to the Mansion House, but the new people had to stand more on ceremony with her."

This last allusion needs some elucidating, for it was the second snub the Queen had offered the City, and one which was believed to have been intentional, though the object of her anger was not the City, but Sir Robert Peel. To the agonised distress of Victoria, the Whig Government had at last fallen, and she found herself forced to accept Sir Robert Peel as her Minister. As she felt a distinct dislike for him, consequent upon his act in 1838 about the ladies of the Bedchamber, she was not inclined to extend to him too much consideration, and wilfully "commanded" him to dine at the Palace on the ninth of November, the night on which he was engaged to make his great manifesto at the Lord Mayor's banquet in the City. Sir Algernon West tells in his "Recollections" how Peel said to Sir James Graham : "You must now make the Ministerial Speech." Sir James protested, and as Peel went out of the room, added : "The only thing I can hope for is that the Queen may be brought to bed on that day."

Perhaps Sir James's prayer had force enough to move Heaven, for the Queen was certainly unable to entertain Sir Robert Peel or anyone else, and the Prime Minister joyfully went to the City and gave his speech.

The other and rather earlier snub was of a more

serious kind, because it succeeded. The Prince, having become a member of the Goldsmiths' Company, was presented with the freedom of the City and made a member of the Fishmongers' Company on the 27th of August, 1840, ceremonies which were to be followed by a great banquet, arranged entirely as a compliment and expression of goodwill to the Queen's husband.

We all know how easy it is to arrange to attend some public or private function, and then how easy it also is when the time has arrived to wish one had not accepted. Such was the case with the Prince, and even more so with the Queen, who, not having been asked to take part in the function, and being unable to do so—at least with grace—had she been approached, did not wish her *cara sposa* to spend so much time away from her in the company of the City men.

However, the Prince had accepted, and the City magnates surpassed themselves in the preparations they made to entertain him; then at the eleventh hour the Prince repented. On the evening before the ceremony he had written a long letter to his father, in which he said :

" To-morrow I shall have to encounter much fatigue. I go to the City, first to the Corporation of the Fishmongers, into which body I am to be received as a member, and thence to the Guildhall, where, besides addresses, I am to receive the freedom of the City. After that I have to attend a banquet of four hours' duration at the Mansion House."

Yet an hour or two after writing this he summoned the Lord Mayor to Windsor, and informed that chagrined personage that though he would be very pleased to be made free of the City, he would be unable to attend the banquet. So on the day which had been anticipated as forming history in the City the Prince went to the Guildhall, received the freedom, apologised verbally to the Lord Mayor, and then drove straight to Buckingham Palace, where he had a comfortable dinner with his attendants before going back to Windsor, the great company at the Mansion House dining meanwhile in an irritated frame of mind. The next day the Lord Mayor received a letter from George Anson, giving no reason at all for the Prince's absence, but saying that he was commanded to repeat the very great regret with which the Prince felt himself compelled to decline the hospitality offered, and " begged him to appreciate the true motives of delicacy to which he felt imperatively bound to yield, and to give up what, under other circumstances, would have given him so much pleasure."

The affair was much canvassed, the Queen being generally blamed, a truer judgment than people knew, as she had been sorrowing over the fact that the day's absence was more than she could bear, the longest parting since their marriage !

> "They say that Albert's clever, yes,
>   With wit and talent he's imbued :
> But then to Vic he, so we guess,
>   Indebted is for being shrew'd."

So sang the City wags.

Sir Theodore Martin, in his biography of the Prince, does not think it even worth mentioning that the freedom of the City was conferred on him, and it is not unlikely that he avoided this subject because of the unpopular ending to the ceremony.

During the weeks in 1840 that the Queen remained in her rooms, Baroness Lehzen was given entire authority in the Palace, and she was both mistress and master of the establishment; it would have pleased her to be able to keep the Prince out of his wife's room altogether, but in any case she was determined that there should be no interference in those matters which had hitherto been arranged by the Queen and herself. So the Prince felt his position doubly, though he forebore to express any hint of his annoyance to his wife. Later on, when the Queen was herself again, the matter was talked out, and Lehzen found herself in disgrace.

But she still had great influence over the Queen, still impressed upon her the distinction between a queen and a wife, and tried to keep her independent of her husband. On the other hand, Her Majesty had grown to rely so utterly upon her Ministers, that, though she went through the farce of listening to all Melbourne told her, she did not trouble to exercise her mind. It was sufficient that her Government should advise this or that course for her to follow it. Thus, though she responded to Lehzen's tuition admirably, she was, by a defect in her own nature, losing her real position as an active head of the State. Lehzen did not realise this, and she fought quietly for her beloved pupil's regality, watched over her health, rejoiced and sorrowed with her, and retained a passionate love for the girl whose happiness she was unwittingly spoiling.

So it had to be war between her and the Prince. He dared not rebel openly, as a word against Lehzen was sufficient to provoke a scene of anger with his wife, though the birth of the child quickened the Queen's love for her husband, and she sometimes grew indignant at the assumption of the humble German woman; but the quarrels were smoothed over, and things went on as usual, with perhaps more sub-mission from the dependent, but no lessening of the Prince's dislike. In the autumn of the following year, when he knew that another child was coming, and a dissolution of Parliament was imminent, he consulted Melbourne as to Lehzen's banishment, "expressing the constant state of annoyance he was kept in by her interference." [1]

Talking it over with George Anson, who was in the Prince's confidence, Melbourne said that it would be more difficult to remove her after the change of Govern-ment; because, if a Tory Ministry pressed such a point, the Queen would immediately resent it upon them; to which Anson replied that, though the Prince would be able to carry his wish if he decided to get rid of the Baroness, his affection for the Queen would prevent him from pressing a painful point, one which could not be carried without an exciting scene. And the thoughtful Secretary finished the discussion with "People are beginning much better to understand the lady's character, and time must surely work its own ends." So, for a little, a very little longer, the Baroness remained in the royal household.

[1] *Letters of Queen Victoria.*

The birth of a royal child was a windfall to a great number of people. There were generally three doctors, Sir James Clark, Dr. Locock, and Dr. Blagden, while Stockmar, being also a doctor, was in the Palace at the time. At the birth of the Princess Royal Dr. Locock was paid one thousand pounds for his services, and probably the others received proportional sums. The royal wet-nurse, who was the wife of a professional man, was also paid one thousand pounds, besides taking various emoluments and a pension of three hundred pounds a year. Mrs. Lilly, the monthly nurse, must also have found her connection with Royalty a most fortunate one; she certainly became a well-known character in England through the verses and cartoons which were published about her. Indeed, no one concerned in the royal events, of what at that time was called "the gander month," escaped the pencil of the caricaturist, and few escaped the gibes of the versifier :

"Doctors Locock, Blagden, Clark,
  They made the great discovery,
And having brought the goods to town
  Were paid upon delivery,"

is only saved from coarseness by its touch of wit.

It was also announced—not, it need scarcely be said, officially—that Prince Albert intended to present Dr. Locock with a piece of plate, bearing the inscription : "To the great deliverer of his country."

The wise men of the Empire, who waited on the threshold of the royal lying-in chamber, that they might pretend—all this clinging to effete custom is but pretence—to be guarding against another warming-pan scandal, did not go away until the baby, having been washed, was brought in to them, naked on a cushion for their inspection. Quite a refined and delicate little ceremony! And one caricaturist drew the Duke of Wellington as a nurse handing the cushion about for his fellow statesmen to inspect its occupant.

The Duke was always at these interesting gatherings, and must have gained quite an experience of what a new-born baby should be. At the birth of the Duke of Connaught the Prince managed so well that not only the Archbishop and President of the Council, but nearly all the officers of State, were too late for the ghoulish period of waiting, for they only arrived after the birth had taken place. When Mrs. Lilly entered with the usual flannel bundle, the Duke asked a question and received a reproof, which Thackeray has crystallised for the ages in the following lines:

"Lord John he next alights,
  And who comes here in haste?
The Hero of a Hundred Fights,
  The caudle for to taste.

Then Mrs. Lilly, the nuss,
  Towards them steps with joy;
Says the brave old Duke, 'Come, tell to us,
  Is it a gal or a boy?'

Says Mrs. L. to the Duke,
  'Your Grace, it is a *Prince*.'
And at that nurse's bold rebuke
  He did both laugh and wince."

The Queen said that after the birth of the Princess Royal, Albert only regretted for a moment that it was not a boy, and the fact that there were lamentations in

G

the Press over the sex of the babe produced plenty of warm defenders of the Queen and the Princess. As one writer pointed out: "It is a poor compliment to Her Majesty that people regret the child is not a boy. Surely we may anticipate that some day she might become almost as popular a Queen as her mother." But England was supposed, on the whole, to be sorry, and one of the sketches known as *Political Hits*, showed Melbourne as the nurse holding the baby, and offering to a somewhat shabby John Bull a taste of the caudle, saying, "I hope the caudle is to your liking, Mr. Bull, it must be quite a treat, for you have not had any so long." To which John answers, "Why, to tell you the truth, Mother Melbourne, I think the caudle the best of it, but why was it not a boy?" Whereupon Prince Albert, who is present, cheerfully promises "one leetle poy" next year. A promise faithfully kept.

Melbourne came in for a great amount of chaff, his constant presence at the Palace being attributed to the supposed fact that he had become one of the attendants upon the baby. Under the title of "Old Servants in New Characters," we see him as a nurse with the babe in his arms, sitting in a little car drawn by two ponies, with Lord John Russell as outrider, and Lord Morpeth as a footman walking alongside, the Queen and the Prince following, blandly smiling. Again, we get him bending to kiss the infant, but looking in adoring fashion upwards at the Queen, who holds it.

When the Prince of Wales was born there was a long succession of caricatures of Melbourne and Peel as rival nurses, each thinking his own baby the best, until

Peel ousts Melbourne entirely out of the nursery. For in the last one Melbourne proudly holds up the Princess Royal and says: "Look at my babby, there's a beauty for you!" To which Peel, holding up the Prince of Wales, who was born in his time of office, responds: "And look at mine! Why, your nose is quite out of joint now."

The birth of a baby revived temporarily all the suspicions about the King of Hanover which had somewhat died away, and he once more appeared as the subject of English cartoons. In one drawing he—a horrible old man—is dreaming in bed, his sword on the chair by his side; convulsively he clutches the sheet, while Queen Victoria, with a baby in her arms, is wafted through the room on a cloud. A more pointed reference to him was made in December, 1841, and was prompted by the theory, so widely accepted, that the early attempt by Oxford on the Queen's life was made at the suggestion of the King of Hanover. In this skit Nurse Lilly brings the newly-born Prince for the statesmen's inspection, and the King of Hanover puts his head through the doorway, grasping a dagger and hissing in good melodramatic style: "Interloper! a young Popish crucifix! an unbaptised apostate! not a thread of genuine orange colour about him, an unconsecrated heretic. If it were not for that villainous Press, I'd show England that I'd do my duty as a son of the Constitution."

At the present day, when we pride ourselves on our high ethical standard, it is hardly credible that the Queen's uncle could have given cause for anxiety or distress, but there really was a strong suspicion that this son of a line of Kings would go to great lengths to clear his way to the throne of England. He had been accused of trying to win the position through the Orange Lodges of which he was the Grand Master; he hoped to win it from his brother George by proving that William Duke of Clarence was insane. When William IV. was ill he sounded Wellington and the men about him as to the possibility of snatching the crown by a struggle. Soon after, when he was on the eve of going to Hanover as King, for even he thought half a loaf better than no bread, a report went through society that he was plotting to dethrone his niece; and many people believed that he was always on the watch to work her mischief. One cartoon showed him as a vulture in the branches of a high tree, gazing fiercely down upon a doe beneath, the doe having the face of Queen Victoria, and John Bull parting the branches reminds the would-be depredator that all England is watching him. His portrait, with a face like a walrus, great bushy eyebrows and moustaches, was being constantly published by the side of the young Queen, to keep people in mind of the contrast between them, while pictures of his stealing into her bedroom to assassinate her were not uncommon. I have one such in my study now. He had, in fact, made such an indelible impression for evil upon the majority of people that there was nothing of which he was not suspected.

The Duke had got his bad name many years earlier. But whether he was wicked, or whether he was misjudged, his niece Victoria had a lively feeling of dislike for and suspicion of him. He was very angry that the King of Prussia had been invited to stand sponsor for the Prince of Wales in preference to himself, so the Queen, on the birth of her third child, Alice, asked him to England to be godfather. He arrived several days too late for the ceremony, and showed an almost consistent bad temper, which was not improved—indeed, it may have been partially caused—by the fact that his royal niece had managed to give precedence to the King of Belgium. It was scarcely fair, seeing that King Ernest was the son and brother of English Kings, but she had consulted Wellington before his arrival upon the possibility of doing this, and the Duke had replied that the only way was by giving preference in alphabetical order. Her Majesty's suspicion, if not fear, of him was so great that she gave up having a party for Ascot, and stayed away from it herself, rather than invite him to Windsor.

Lady Lyttelton speaks of the precautions taken by the Prince for the safety of his infants : " The last thing we did before bedtime was to visit the access to the children's apartments to satisfy ourselves that all was safe. And the intricate turns and locks and guard-rooms, and the various intense precautions, suggesting the most hideous dangers, which I fear are not altogether imaginary, made one shudder! The most important key is never out of Prince Albert's own keeping, and the very thought must be enough to cloud his fair brow with anxiety. Threatening letters of the most horrid kind (probably written by mad people), aimed

directly at *the children*, are frequently received."
There is nothing published to connect the extreme precautions in the Palace with the ambition of the King
of Hanover, but rumour had much to say on the
subject.

While Hanover was in England the Whigs unsuc-
cessfully moved that his pension as a Prince of the
blood should be withdrawn, which had the effect of
making the Tories befriend him and give great parties
for his benefit; so, for the first time in his life, Ernest
of Hanover was a popular man, and London woke
from its despairing torpor of resignation induced by
the Queen's absence to realise joyfully that a Season
was still possible. Though Queen Victoria would on
occasions speak of an anxiety to foster trade, she rarely
made efforts in that direction at any expense to her own
comfort or whim; that summer, for instance, she spent
almost entirely at Windsor, and the London people
did not fail to blame the Prince for their loss.

It was generally stated that Prince Albert was
anxious that she should be in London as much as
possible, for the convenience of communication
with her Ministers, but even more did he wish it
because he was firmly convinced "of the influence
for good which the presence of a Court, so looked
up to and respected as was that of England under
the Queen and himself, could not fail to exercise
far and wide—far, indeed, beyond the circle of its
immediate neighbourhood."

This is quoted from the " Early Life of the Prince
Consort," the Queen's book as has been said, and yet

she allowed a sentence such as the above to stand. The lamentable lack of humour, the comfortable self-content, the conscious raising of themselves into an example for the whole country, all this helps further to explain why Prince Albert was never heartily accepted as an Englishman. The boy or girl who is most disliked at school is not the naughty or even the vicious one, but the one who is consciously good, who regards himself or herself as a good example; and grown-up folk are but children of a larger growth.

But to return to the King of Hanover. He, becoming at last convinced that the crown of England was finally out of his reach, revived his claim, and quite justly, for the return of the Hanoverian jewels. When George I. combined the Kingship of the two countries he brought over these jewels, worth from £59,000 to £60,000, and they had been so absorbed in, so often reset among, the English jewels, that it was difficult to say which were which. A person who follows simple ethical laws would decide that the restitution should be made as nearly as possible, but "possession is nine points of the law" is a real English motto, and so the matter was referred to a Commission of three, who managed to spin out their enquiry for thirteen years, when the decision was given in favour of Hanover. The Prince and Queen were reported to be so extremely anxious about the jewels that someone remarked that "probably the Queen thinks the Salic law was never meant to apply to diamonds."

The rumour that King Ernest hoped to bring about

the Queen's death by assassination also died down, though for long Victoria feared it, as is evidenced by her green silk parasol lined with chain mail which may be still seen at the London Museum. Oxford's example was, however, followed the next year by several other silly youths, who presented pistols at Her Majesty. In the cases of Francis and Bean the pistols were without bullets, and there was no proof that Oxford had used bullets either. In all that has been written on these incidents no one notices that the Prince was in as much danger as the Queen; indeed, the danger was more threatening to him than to her in 1840, for he sat between her and Oxford, and was within six feet of the pistol. He alone remarked upon that when he described the event as endangering "my life and that of Victoria." One of her ladies said that the Queen looked very pale and anxious on arriving at the Palace after this event, and had a fit of crying in her room, but such things as these were not allowed to be repeated, for the Sovereign must even be above agitation.

Francis, the second aspirant for notoriety, made two attempts. The first day the Prince saw the pistol evidently pointed at him, for he told Victoria that, had it gone off, "he must have been hit in the head." The next day, many plain-clothes policemen having been stationed along the way, and "the two Equerries riding so close on each side that they must have been hit if anybody had"; the Queen and her Prince bravely drove "very quickly" over the same route. Francis let off his gunpowder pistol, the smoke of it covering the face of the Equerry, Colonel Wylde, and was promptly seized, drawing the remark from the Queen, "We felt both very glad that our drive had had the effect of having the man seized. Whether it was loaded or not we cannot yet tell, but we are again full of gratitude to Providence for invariably *protecting* us!" Without belittling Providence, I may honestly comment that the Prince and Queen had followed the fundamental idea of religion, and while imploring God's aid, had thoroughly arranged their own protection themselves. It was Colonel Wylde who must have been genuinely grateful that Francis had omitted the bullet.

The Queen's danger and the Queen's bravery were lauded to the skies, but the words quoted about the Equerries are from her own letter to the King of the Belgians. Francis, whose real crime was a silly desire to know himself talked about, was sentenced to death, and he was in despair at the sentence, saying that the pistol was not loaded with ball, that he only wished to get notoriety, and a home such as Oxford had secured, where he could not fear poverty and hunger. Her Majesty could not bear the thought of a man losing his life through such folly, and he was transported. The evening after this attempt she went to the Opera to hear *Le Prophéte*, and was enthusiastically cheered.

The third attempt by the witless Bean was made with a mere toy pistol costing three shillings. After he had bought it he took it back to the shop, complaining that it would not go off, and had a flint put in.

This he pointed at the Queen, but could not discharge, as the lock was not strong enough, and later the undisturbed rust showed that it had never been used; the hammer clicked, however, and he got deservedly for his folly eighteen months in Millbank.

In 1848 a man named Hamilton went through the same farce with a bulletless pistol in the same place, and was transported for seven years. However, after the first sham attack on Her Majesty no one said anything more about the King of Hanover's complicity in these affairs.

But to return to the babies, it was so long since a direct heir had been born to the throne that the people seemed to imagine that such a matter could not possibly be carried through successfully, and it was rumoured of the Queen's first two children that they were born blind and deformed. This being contradicted and re-affirmed, led to the facetious suggestion that the Princess should be displayed under a glass case for so many hours a day and the crowd allowed to file past and assure itself that she was normal.

It is curious to note that those papers which went in for the very serious, divine origin of the infants seemed so often to be weak in grammar. Here is a gem! "The care bestowed upon the Princess Royal by its nurse and various attendants are only to be equalled by the great anxiety manifested by its royal parents for its health and welfare."

The Christening of the Princess Royal caused the circulation of many skits; one of which—highly coloured—gave a continuous picture of the people in the long procession who went to the chapel, each with a verse beneath. The Bishop was represented pouring hot water from a little black kettle into the font, being described thus :

"This is the Bishop so bold and intrepid
A-making the water so nice and so tepid
To christen the baby, who's stated, no doubt,
Her objection to taking it 'cold without.'"

Just before the birth of the Prince of Wales, London City shook with laughter over what it considered a big joke, for the news ran like wildfire through the streets that the Queen had given birth to twin boys :

"Among the City, 'twas said, one morn
That to the Queen two boys were born.
On which our friend Sir Peter Laurie
Expressed himself exceeding sorry.
'Tis grievous, sir, I must aver—
Such deed should not be done ;
Two boys ! it is too bad of Her
Who won't mind number one !"

The last line is an allusion to the fact that the royal babies were brought up by hand, as the Queen's position demanded that she should not give the time necessary to nursing an infant. It is said that she much regretted this, and would have loved to fulfil the full functions of a mother, yet she urged married Continental cousins not to take the burden and responsibility of doing so. She herself probably never really realised how much she had lost by it.

When the Prince of Wales was born on November 9th, 1841, there were, the papers say, still greater rejoicings. Theatre audiences sang themselves hoarse, candles and paraffin flickered behind glass on the house fronts, women gossiped and men got drunk, and there was everywhere a pleasant feeling that now at last England was all right. John Bull, more shabby than the year before, is drawn upon again to make fun for the million. In one cartoon he enters the Queen's bedroom, where the nurse shows him the infant with : " There, Mr. Bull, what do you think of our new *Annual*, is it not a splendid specimen?" and he, scowling, answers : " Splendid indeed ! and a precious sum I expect it will cost 'me annually ! " Victoria, smiling on her pillow, whispers to her husband, " How delighted he seems, Al, I daresay he will make the nurse a very handsome present."

Mrs. Lilly ought to have been a very paragon of a nurse, for Stockmar, that man of detail, laid many injunctions upon the Prince about the engagement of such a necessary person. " Impress upon Anson the necessity for conducting this affair with the greatest conscientiousness and circumspection; *for a man's education begins the first day of his life*, and a lucky choice I regard as the greatest and finest gift we can bestow on the expected stranger." One nurse was known as Mrs. Packer, but her real name was Augusta Gow, a native of Edinburgh who had been studying music at the London Royal Academy with a view to becoming a public singer. The choice seems to have been rather a peculiar result of " conscientiousness and circumspection." What could a musical student know of babies? However, in those days children's nurses were no more trained than were sick nurses, so probably the only things that mattered were character, aptitude, and of course, purity. And why was she called Packer?

Another nurse, who rejoiced in the name of Ratsey, was found to be a most undesirable person to attend on a little Prince, for Albert entered the nursery one morning and heard some such so-called conversation, interrupted by gurgles and crows, as this :

" Now, what's my little popsy-wopsy laughing at? Did nursey tiddle her iddle, iddle toes, then?"

Such talk could only be regarded as perverted education, so Nurse Ratsey was invited to resign her post. The comic draughtsmen fastened on this, though they heard of it somewhat late, and placed the indiscretion upon Mrs. Lilly. H. H. drew the good lady dancing the Prince of Wales up and down and singing " Hey diddle diddle, the cat and the fiddle," etc. Prince Albert is entering the room at the moment, and says sternly, " Fie, fie, Madam Lilly; vat you talk such nonsense to mine son for? Tell him he be Prince of Wales and de Duck of Cornwall, den he will understand you much better."

However, another cartoon made a much more serious affair of the delinquency of the nurse, for under the heading of *Royal Dry Nursing Extraordinary*, the Prince of Wales was shown lying on the knees of a young and comely but drunken woman, who is holding a long black bottle over his mouth, saying, " What! do *you* want a drop? Hic—why, you little Toper! Hic—I wonder who you take after?

Not your—hic—Daddy, I'm sure! Hic—I'll make you a spirited Heir Apparent. Hic—ha, ha, ha!" The horrified Queen and Prince are just entering the room, the former crying, "Teaching His Royal Highness to drink, as I am alive!" and the Prince responding regretfully: "Ah, mein loof, I was mean him to be one temperance Prince of Wales!" Which was also a sly hit at the Prince's approval of the campaign of Father Mathew, a popular temperance reformer of the time.

"Political Hit" number seven gave a more intimate view still of the royal domestic felicity, for it showed poor Prince Albert walking about the bedroom, with the baby, attired in nothing warmer than a royal shirt and nightcap, grumbling : "Ah, ha, by Gar, dis is cold work, Madam Lilly! to walk about all night in de shirt dis veder." Plump Mrs. Lilly stirring some baby food over a fire is made to respond in a way to delight those who did not love the Prince : "Drat the man! why, you do little enough for your living, and ought to be thankful you've got a shirt to wear at all."

The Prince of Wales was not born until after the first steps in domestic economy had been made at the Palace, and some impertinent person had the quickness to use that event to raise a laugh against the Queen in a cartoon, which showed an enormous uncut christening cake upon the table, the Queen arm-in-arm with the King of Prussia, turning away from it; Prussia, however, murmurs : "I should like a piece of that cake." Peel, on the other side, is whispering in the Queen's ear, "It is my duty to advise your Majesty the strictest economy, so if you keep the cake whole it will do for next year!" To which the Queen replies with unction, "It shall not be touched, Sir Robert."

If the whole country rejoiced over the birth of the Prince of Wales, there was one little person who entirely objected to his presence for a time, and that was the Princess Royal, who shared her mother's jealous temperament, but had no desire to share a baby princess's privileges with an unknown brother. "Pussy is not at all pleased with her brother," wrote the Queen, three weeks after the little son arrived, and this attitude must have remained for some time, as the caricaturists crystallised it in their pictures.

Thus we get an absurd picture of the Queen admonishing Sir Robert Peel on his famous sliding scale, while two nurses, each holding a baby, stand near. From the arms of one the Princess Royal is aiming a right sisterly blow at little Albert Edward, her nurse saying, "Bless the girl, what a temper she has shown since young Master came." Poor Prince Albert, the picture of a harassed, distracted father, is turning to them fiercely with the familiar parental command of "*Do* keep those children quiet!"

Another cartoon depicts Peel and Wellington as nurses, each carrying a baby, and Wellington expostulating, "Bless me, how the dear little girl has been crying ever since the month of November."

Of course, it is quite easy to say that these are only skits, and have no real reference to truth; yet, apart from exaggeration, I find this sort of domesticity well authenticated in books which make genuine history. As a matter of fact, the two young people were for several years even more foolish about their babies than are most affectionate young parents, and in spite of public demands on their time, they spent a large portion of each day playing with their human toys. They also regarded the dignity of the little creatures with the most deadly seriousness, planning their coats of arms as soon as they were born, and heaping titles and posts upon their boys, especially upon the eldest, with lavish hands.

In this matter Victoria showed great anxiety to do honour to the German birthplace of her husband, and determined that the arms of Saxony—Prince Albert being Duke of Saxony—should be quartered with those of England for the little Prince; then, having made up her mind, she wanted it done at once, seeing no need for the usual forms. Peel considered that this haste was lowering to the dignity of the Crown, and that the Privy Council should adjudge upon it and advise it, *if it were right*, and not just because the Queen wanted it. So he wrote letters and saw statesmen and gave more time to this insignificant affair than many an important national matter received. Melbourne would have estimated the thing at its real value and assented at once; and after all, the result of Peel's careful work was the decision that it really was not worth squabbling about and might as well be done as not. So "Duke of Saxony" was not only added to the infant's honours, but given the precedence of the English titles, much to the disgust of those people

H.R.H. PRINCE ALBERT.

(From a Painting by Sir W. C. Ross, R.A.)

From a Print in Mr. A. M. Broadley's Collection.

who cared about such things.   These much-discussed
Saxon arms were horizontal bars in yellow on a black
ground with a wreath of rue across it, and I find the
Queen commenting on her baby girl that she bore
"her Saxon arms in the middle of her English coat,
which looks very pretty"—and sounds decidedly
ambiguous. Why does not Heaven allot a better
sense of humour to Kings and Queens?   It must be
the only quality which could make their position a little
better than endurable, and yet since Charles the
Second no monarch has displayed it.   Prince Albert
had none of it and the Queen had none of it, or she
would never have allowed him to be called from his
most—as well as least—important work to carry her
from her bed to her sofa, whenever she wished it.   Of
this the Queen boasted that to the end of his life he
would come whenever she called, no matter what his
occupation; and she showed not the slightest consciousness that she was exacting and imposed a great
strain upon him; she only told herself—and others—
how strong was his love for her.   But those about the
Prince realised how very trying he found it that, no
matter what he was doing, he was liable to be interrupted at any and every moment to consult with his
wife or attend her in some way.

In 1844 Prince Albert was made happy at the birth
of a second son, Alfred, and he, having been preceded
by Princess Alice, was followed by Helena, Arthur,
Louise, Leopold and Beatrice.   Long before the last
arrival consternation had risen and had swept through
newspaper and political circles.   In 1841 the Queen

H

had thought a large family would be of the greatest inconvenience to the country, but it was an inconvenience which had to be faced, and it is not wonderful that attempts were made to lighten it by jests, sometimes grim enough, sometimes merely facetious. Of the former kind were those that included John Bull. In one sketch, clothed in darns, the thin old man leaves his dinner—a bloater—to jump for joy, shouting : " Birth of another Prince ! Huzza, what a fortunate old dog I am to be sure. Huzza, what do I care for income tax ? "

" The Scene in Perspective, 1850," one of the " Political Hits," published somewhere towards the middle of the 'forties, shows Bull, still thinner, more starved and tattered, receiving the Queen and Prince, both of them fat and looking middle-aged, while behind them come seven couples of children, getting smaller and smaller the further they are from their parents. Victoria introduces them characteristically with : " Our family, Mr. Bull, I quite envy the pleasure you must have in contemplating them, what a happy man you must be ! " The Prince, with very complaisant air, adapts the words of William III. : " Ah, ha, Mistare Pull, I tell you, one, two, three, four, ten year ago, I come to dis country for your Goots," to which John Bull mutters : " Goots, indeed ! You have had money and goots too with a vengeance."

Less venomous and more humorous is the picture of Prince Albert as a gardener putting a glass frame over a flower-pot, from which the head and shoulders of a baby rise, two larger frames holding the Princess

Royal and the Prince of Wales. The Queen stands smiling by the hedge, watching nine other flower-pots dated in consecutive years awaiting their covers. John Bull, outside the garden and leaning over, says : " Hullo, hullo, young fellow ! Come, come, I shall have such a stock of them sort of plants on my hands, I shan't know what to do with them."

The Queen was so happy domestically that she could hide her satisfaction from no one, and indeed was only too ready to express in words her deep-seated belief that she was especially favoured by Providence. so that all the cartoonists caught at this quality and made their drawings turn upon it. Thus someone would represent the children in Windsor Park, every face wearing a beaming smile, the footmen turning their eyes up to Heaven in gratitude for their chance of dragging a perambulator or leading a pony, and the nurses also betraying their pious delight at carrying Royal babies in their arms.

Other pictures gave news of the nursery, a nursery in which a prolific mother keeping only one general servant might spend her time. In one of these the Queen, grown stout, is sitting by the fire nursing two babies, the Prince, also well covered with adipose tissue, crawls laboriously, yet delightedly, on the floor with a child on his back, another dragging him by a cord, and a third whipping him; two or three others are playing leapfrog in the corner, while another falls off a rocking-horse as the door opens to admit Sir Robert Peel, and he receives the little one's head just where his portly figure is best cushioned.

H 2

Any woman who loved her children must have adored a man of such an upright character as the Prince, who had so much devotion to give to his little ones. Their high position, and the strong contrast in this respect between them and those who had occupied the English throne for the previous hundred years, made such parental love on the part of Royalty a very remarkable thing. If some were too ready to turn this quality into a joke, there were others, more sycophantic, who did worse. There was published, for instance, a steel engraving, dedicated by permission to H.R.H. Prince Albert, of "The First Prayer of H.R.H. Prince Albert Edward, Prince of Wales, Duke of Cornwall, etc., etc." In this the smiling, complaisant baby sits on immense gold-corded cushions; the crown, the feathers, his coat-of-arms, every worldly proof of his rank being heaped around him, as he looks up to a blaze of light supposed to represent God, and prays:

"O Lord God Almighty, graciously condescend to hear my first prayer; may old England, my beloved and noble country, be always powerful and happy."

The exhibition of rank and wealth, the commendation of his country, and the prayer for power, surely puts the condescension on the side of the infant and not on that of God. And an enlightened Queen and Prince allowed this atrocity to be published and sold everywhere!

It reminds me of the fact that some years ago, if not at the present time, the pronouns used to denote the Queen in the prayer-books at St. George's Chapel were always printed in capitals, while those alluding to the Trinity were in small letters.

As for the Prince of Wales's titles, they ought to have been numerous enough to overburden his small person, and were much caricatured.

Victoria and Albert clung to form and ceremony and saw no absurdity in making such announcements as the following when the Prince of Wales was only a few months old: "His Royal Highness Albert Edward, Prince of Wales and Duke of Cornwall, has appointed George Pearse, of Brandwinch, to be His Royal Highness's Gamekeeper for Brandwinch, Duchy of Cornwall." *Judy* held the fact up to derision by showing us a nice, fat, befeathered baby in a high chair, blowing a tin trumpet, who leans forward and thrusts a paper inscribed "Royal Letters Patent" towards the kneeling gamekeeper; the Queen, Prince Albert, Peel and the nurse looking on with interested gravity, the lines beneath being:

"Of 'intellect's march' the young prince is partaker,
St. Pearse is game*keeper*, and Albert game *maker*."

When he was two-and-a-half the little boy was appointed a Governor of Christ's Hospital and "exercised his influence in that capacity in favour of a meritorious young gentleman"; just as his younger brother Alfred was made a Governor in 1848, upon which occasion the Queen sent a donation of £500 to the Hospital. For such fees it is believable that the Hospital would be ready to draw all its Governors from the nursery.

When in 1844 it was rumoured that the Prince of Wales, who could hardly talk, for he was very backward in this respect, was to have a separate staff of servants, not in any way connected with Her Majesty's House-hold, the levity was general, and the child was drawn in many absurd positions, generally in a high chair, flourishing a rattle, with twenty servants bowing around him, begging for posts. *Punch* gave the domestics as Master of the Rocking Horse, Comp-troller of the Juvenile Vagaries, Sugar-Stick-in-Wait-ing, Captain of the Tin Guard, Black-Rod-in-Ordinary, Master of the Trap Ordnance, Clerk of the Pea Shooter, Assistant Battledore, Lord Privy Shuttle-cock, and Quarter-Master-General of the Oranges.

The little ones began lessons at a very early age, and alarming accounts of the precocity of the Princess Royal were given. She could speak German, English and French fluently when she was three years old, and was able to read short words and spell out long ones. It is a relief to remember that a three-year-old child's vocabulary is a very small one.

The Queen's view of education was said to be both serious, liberal and comprehensive, with a distaste for formalism, but she gave in entirely to Prince Albert in such matters, and he was guided almost entirely by Baron Stockmar, who believed that he had dis-covered the secret of success in the way of education. For Prince Albert he laid down the rule that the educa-tion should be truly English and truly moral, with the condition that only the thoroughly moral, intelligent, well-informed and experienced should come in contact with the children, and that the parents must have full, implicit confidence in the tutor. He was very insistent that the education should begin from the day of birth, and would have liked to point to George III. as a model character because he was believed to be domestically a model man, only he could not do that, as the result in the behaviour of that monarch's six sons proved that, however much and however well they were taught, they turned out scamps. Yet some of George III.'s methods were reproduced by Prince Albert, notably that of isolating his boys from all companions.

Stockmar's two essential conditions were too limited and too vague. It is not possible to make morality and Englishism subjects for teaching without destroying both, for by talking about them and explaining them one of two results is attained : either speculations and arguments are raised in minds too immature to deal with them wisely, or the delicate mind is biassed towards hard and fast rules and creeds which, when maturity is reached, are crude and narrowing. The best Englishman is the best man of the country, not the one who has learned other people's ideas of what an Englishman should be. Englishism, like morality, is an atmosphere, and we cannot imprison an atmosphere in words.

Stockmar became more concrete when he added that : " The beginning of education must be directed to the regulation of the child's natural instincts, to give them the right direction, and above all to keep the mind pure." This was well enough if it had all been accomplished without words, but the idea of purity was so often verbally expressed by the Queen that it would hardly have passed unused in the education of the young people. In those days the power of suggestion was not recognised; it was not realised that an insistence upon purity would at once start a consideration of impurity; and before he died the Prince had to garner some of the harvest of the early educational mistakes in the ready way in which his eldest son took Venus as his guide, philosopher and friend by the time he was twenty.

The Princess Royal was at first neither judiciously fed nor well regulated, but when there were three children in the nursery all this was altered; a governess, about whom there had been long and serious discussion, was secured in the person of Lady Lyttelton, and other tutors and governesses engaged; Mr. Henry Birch (most appropriate name) becoming responsible for the Prince of Wales. It is told of him that when Prince Albert desired that the boy should not be taught the catechism so early this gentleman resigned his post, but graciously resumed it on the Prince yielding the point. Also a new household system was instituted, the food given being plain and good, such food as children need.

Prince Albert never forgot Stockmar's tuition on education, and went to the schoolroom nearly every morning to superintend things; nothing escaped his vigilance, for he said: "It belongs to parents rather than to tutors to make children religious, pure-minded and affectionate." As time went on and the children dined when their parents lunched, "on the plainest of plain fare," Albert carried his supervision to a pernicious extent, for he made a habit of asking the tutors for their reports before luncheon, and going through them while at table, administering the scoldings or praises which he considered just, though the former would to-day be considered extremely severe. So it was no unusual thing for all the juveniles to be reduced to tears before the meal was over, and to rise from the table hungry. Truly a good educational system!

CHAPTER V

THE QUEEN AND SIR ROBERT PEEL

In the autumn of 1841 Sir Robert Peel attained his desire and came into office as Prime Minister; only, however, to spend the five most disturbed, most strenuous and most heart-rending years of his life, and to go out with a mere handful of men at his back, execrated by almost all those who had been so jubilant at his accession of power. To him and his then policy we owe that new party, first known as Peelites and then as Conservatives, a party which was more enlightened and more advanced than that of the violent, autocratic Tories, who could not believe that manners and customs participated in the universal law of change.

Peel had bitter enemies and warm friends, who among them said he was shy, reserved, unfair, appreciating fun, honest, dishonest, cold, kindly—in fact, disagreeing about him generally, though they all agreed as to his reserve.

The Queen did not want him, and when Lord Broughton said that Peel had spoken well of her in his address she remarked: " That is all very well, but he and I shall never love each other." She felt then that she could not forgive him for his early opposition to the Prince, nor could she forget the bitter quarrel over her Bed-chamber women.   There was also the remarkable difference in manner between himself and Lord Melbourne.   Through very nervousness Peel was pompous in his talk and given to lecturing in a prosy fashion, and he dared not use the decision which Lord Melbourne would express when the Queen proposed anything he thought undesirable, for he had not the influence of his predecessor.

Melbourne and Peel were the subjects of many criticisms when offices were being changed; the former was said to continue occupying the Devil's Tower at Windsor, having been engaged in a game·of chess for the last three weeks; and "his opponent not having been able to take his Queen, the castle was still fortified."

Judy advised him thus :

> "Fly and roast, my Melbourne dear,
>   Prepare for Christmas use
> The usual dishes, all save one,
>   For Peel has cooked *your* goose."

Among H. H.'s "Political Sketches" is one of the Queen leaning back in her chair and saying to her doctor, Peel, "I think, doctor, the present system of diet does not agree with my constitution; I prefer Lamb[1] to anything else."   "Yes, but your Majesty seems to forget that Lamb is out; try a little minced veal with lemon Peel."

When the change of Government had become a certainty the Tory leaders began to marshal their men,

[1] Lord Melbourne's family name was Lamb.

and found themselves at once faced with a difficulty. Many of those who had formerly held office or who might naturally expect to hold office now, were scarcely of a character to fit in with the new ideal of purity so dear to the Queen and Prince, and as it is a well-known fact that in such cases it is often the culprit who is the last to think he has done wrong, most of them stood expectantly waiting, having already selected their various posts. Both *The Times* and *The Standard* published leaders praying the *roués* and the most notorious members of the Tory party not to force themselves just at the moment into the most conspicuous places in Her Majesty's Household, as they would not be acceptable at Court. And when these gentlemen were eventually passed over there was much heart-burning, envy and malice.

On the whole, the Queen-Prince were right, though even to such a rule exceptions should be allowed in cases of great ability, for the country should not on any excuse be deprived of signal services.

Who is to decide truly as to the moral standard of other people? Rumour may always be wrong, and the most discreetly seeming person may be the greatest sinner. There were stories afloat about the great Duke himself; Lord Melbourne and his sister Lady Palmerston were generally believed to be the children of the many-loving Lord Egremont; and Melbourne himself had twice—once most unjustly—been made co-respondent in a divorce suit; Lady Conyngham, received by the Queen, and whose husband was Master of the Horse for some years, had been mistress to George IV.; the then Duke of Buckingham, whom the Queen elected to honour with a four-days' visit, had no good reputation, and Palmerston had not been held impeccable. Even Queen Adelaide herself had at one time been the subject of wanton scandal. Of course, the demand for personal purity in all those who filled public or palace posts was a counsel of perfection, one which could not accurately be fulfilled, but it did to some extent raise social and public life from the degradation into which it had sunk through the example of George IV. and his friends; and it gave the first impetus to that saner, healthier standard of living which has waxed through the years, though it has by no means yet come to perfection.

However, the many troubles about offices and posts were eventually settled, and Peel also began to form friendly relations with his Sovereign. By a certain deferential treatment, by an open expression of admiration for the Prince, and by the tact and courtesy which he was quite able to use, the Prime Minister began to remove the strong feelings of dislike which animated the Queen towards himself. The papers gradually moderated their language; *The Times*, which had hastened to insult Victoria the Princess and her mother while William IV. lay dying, and had repeated the insults as soon as the Princess became Queen, now went to the other extreme, condescending to publish flattering articles, and assuring its readers that Her Majesty was superior to Elizabeth and

Anne as a model for female sovereigns. As in matters of this sort reason is seldom shown, it was soon rumoured not only that Victoria was friendly with Peel, but that she had thrown herself as completely on to his side as she had recently been on the side of Melbourne. So that when Peel opened the subject of Bank Charters in the House, a lampoon described him as extending his hand and asking: "What is this I have in my hand?" To which a Member replies: "A sovereign," drawing the remark from Peel: "The honourable Member is perfectly right. (A laugh.) He might perhaps be pardoned the expression when he said that he had a sovereign under his thumb. (Loud laughter.)"

This was not true when it was uttered; in fact, it was never quite true, though Victoria's youthful habit of leaning on the man in power made it largely so before Peel finally went out.

From the first Peel's position was difficult, for at heart he was neither Whig nor Tory, or perhaps he was both; in any case, once he was in office circumstances forced his views until they became too advanced to please his own following, and not advanced enough to please the Opposition. He found himself called upon to face an awful situation, and had the courage to look at it steadily, make up his mind as to what should be done, and do it. His Premiership was a martyrdom, for he was howled at by every party in turn, and stung almost to death by Disraeli, who was appropriately drawn by one caricaturist as a wasp.

In all the attacks upon Mr. Asquith or Mr. Lloyd George there has been nothing so wanton and so bitter as those upon Peel by a number of his own men known as the "young England party," led by Disraeli, who was at that time ready to back any policy which would help him to prominence.

Victoria opened the Session of 1842 personally, which showed that she was determined to make the best of a bad matter and give her uncongenial Minister every public support. The distress in England was so acute at the time that her Speech was awaited eagerly, and was found very disappointing from its vagueness and want of promise. In the words of one grumbler :

> "When Victoria went to Parliament,
>   The deuce a word she said
> About the state of England,
>   The Corn Laws or the bread.
> They did expect she'd something say,
>   To smoothen out the bother,
> But the speech was full of nonsense
> From one end to the other."

However, the first thing that Peel did to mend matters was to bring in his Bill for the "Sliding Scale," which provided for taking off half the duty on corn. As this was regarded as a direct blow to farmers and to the landed interests, a murmur rising to a roar was heard all over England, except in those cities and places where "chalk and alum and plaster were sold to the people for bread," or where they were living on potatoes, for the English as well as the Irish had come to that. All over the country bonfires were built and

Peel's effigy burned, which was quick work, as he had only been in office a few months.

When an income-tax of sevenpence in the pound was introduced—as a temporary tax—and at the same time a revised Customs tariff abolished or lowered the duties on seven hundred and fifty articles out of twelve hundred, both parties began to think the heavens were falling. Yet for a time Peel's party remained fairly pliable in spite of its grumbles, and the popular opposition to his measure was loudest among the newspaper and song writers, voicing, as many of them did, the complaints of the more well-to-do. In 1839, when the marriage of the Queen was in contemplation, and the Whig Government, horrified at the yearly deficit, tried to convert it into a balance by taxing all sorts of things, the popular cry was:

> "They will tax the periwinkles,
>   They will tax the children's toys,
> They will tax the German sausages,
>   Black puddings and saveloys,
> And for to raise some money
>   For the wedding of the Queen,
> They will tax old maids and bachelors,
>   That are turned seventeen."

But now, though the sentiment of resistance to taxation remained, the song dealt not with periwinkles and children's toys, but with the great of the land, and, because of his secession from principles which would have been acceptable to such, Peel was dubbed a "rat."

I quote the following broadside in its entirety, as it shows by whom the Prime Minister was held in reprobation, and further, by satiric intent, takes no account of the submerged tenth to whom it was hoped that some escape from their destitution would be ensured :

"To political critics who pore o'er the news,
And all Cabinet measures approve or abuse;
Has not Bobby, the rat, found the way to clink 'em,
By placing the long-dreaded tax on the income.

Poor Bobby, your foresight was sure in a fog,
Or your senses bewildered and muddled with grog;
What folly, what madness, the rich to cut down,
To take gilt from the mitre and wealth from the crown.

Our Queen and Prince Albert are maddened with rage,
And hint pretty boldly you should sit in a cage;
'D——n my plood,' says Prince Albert, 'is this my fine marriage,
Am I almost a King, and must part with my carriage?'

E'en the young Prince of Wales, as being heir to 'the nation,'
By means supernatural, holds conversation——
'Oh, naughty Sir Bob, you and I von't be cronies,
How dare you to tax my nice phæton and ponies?'

The Bishops, those lights of the world, too, are kneeling,
And pray for your fall—with a good deal of feeling;
Yes, even the Judges declare that they're danged,
If you had your deserts you would surely be hanged.

The Lawyers and Doctors have held consultation,
And declare one and all you have ruined the nation!
And Daniel[1] declares as he casts up the Rint,
That post-haste to the divil you ought to be sint.

Old annuity Maidens and Widows with pension,
With rancour and hatred your name daily mention;
Yes, even the clerks you have helped to get places,
When they dare, put their hands to their nose and make faces.

---

[1] Daniel O'Connell, the Irish leader.

Poor Bob, what a scrape you have got into at last,
You are paying at present for sins that are past,
And well you deserve it—such ratting acts, sink 'em,
The Corn Tax on one hand, on the other the income.

Refrain:—

You have put all the great little folks to the rout,
And they cry one and all in a rage ' turn him out.' ''

Over the income-tax rose a little domestic trouble in the Palace. The Queen, being by nature generous and just, announced her determination to claim no exemption from this tax; which by no means met the view of Prince Albert, who was most anxious that no precedent should be created in acknowledging any obligation to the country in money matters. So the offer was withdrawn.

Punch gave a graceful cartoon of the Queen, standing on her doorstep and handing money to the tax-collector, a benevolent-looking Peel with his pen in his mouth. Prince Albert, hat on the back of his head, hands tightly clenched in his pockets, and evidently uttering angry protestations, stands behind the Queen. Other and slightly later caricatures were not quite so complimentary to Victoria. At this time the Duke of Wellington—perhaps to pay off past favours—loyally backed up Peel, so we find him as doctor's assistant holding a basin when Dr. Peel goes to bleed Her Majesty. She receives him with : " You see, Doctor, I have not the least objection to lose a little, but why did you not stick entirely to Mr. Bull ? " To which Peel answers : " I do not intend to forget the old gentleman, who, by the way, at all times bleeds very

freely, but I think it necessary to extract a little of
the surplus from about the Court." The Prince,
standing by the Queen's chair and backed up by
various frightened people, is saying in fear : " Doctare,
it is of no use to try and bleed me, I have not noding
to spare."

In the end the Crown lawyers were called in, and,
as might have been anticipated, decided that any
idea of their sovereign paying the income tax was a
mistake and that she was fully and honourably
exempt.

One incident which happened at the end of 1842
raised much amusement, and was the cause of endless
gibes at the Prime Minister. He received as a New
Year's gift two rolls of velveteen (then a new invention)
of a green colour, from the manufacturer, a Mr.
Barlow, of Ancoat Vale Works, in Lancashire. Peel
accepted the velveteen and wrote as follows :—

" I am much obliged by your kind attention in sending a specimen of the beautiful manufacture which
accompanied your letter. Lady Peel admires it so
much that she will convert one of the pieces into a
cloak for her own wearing; the other I shall apply to
my own use."

Punch says that Peel ordered it to be made into
trousers. Early in January a paragraph appeared in
the *Manchester Guardian* advertising the velveteen,
announcing the fact that Sir Robert Peel had been
good enough to accept a short length of it, and that
the design represented a stalk and ear of wheat,
grouped, or rather thrown, together very tastefully,

"with a small scroll peeping from beneath bearing the word 'Free.'"

Peel, who had not examined the details of the stuff, indignantly gathered together the velveteen, cut and uncut, and sent it back. He was at that time being attacked by the Whigs for not deciding at once on the total repeal of the Corn Laws, a policy which the Queen in the end strongly favoured, and it is most likely that he was beginning to vacillate on that point, so *Punch* rubbed in the affair of the velveteen. "We have no doubt whatever that, as far as a cloak might have been got out of the stuff for himself, Sir Robert would have had no objection to retain the velveteen as a provision for future accidents, keeping it on or putting it off as the wind might blow, or the sun might shine; but when once the velveteen was made into trousers, when once the Minister had donned so succinct a garment, it must become to him a sort of tight-fitting principle, not under any circumstances to be put aside, with the least respect for usages of honourable society."

As soon as the belief that the Tory leader had found favour with the Queen gained ground, popular Tory sentiment towards the Sovereign began to change; and with the birth of a Prince Her Majesty's virtues as a Queen and a wife were assured—for a time at least. Hitherto it had been the custom to drink the health of the Dowager Queen with musical honours, which was really an expression of the anger of the Tories against the Queen Regnant. For Adelaide, though drawing £100,000 a year from the Exchequer, kept no Court, gave no entertainments, and had always been unpopular, excepting with those few who, knowing her well, appreciated the sweetness which her narrowness of mind could not stifle.

One paper gave the following sarcastic advice to the wild Tory generally : "*That* when the health of the Queen is drunk at Tory dinners, a certain quantity of 'ironical cheers' shall be thrown in in order to keep up a show of loyalty, convenient at the present season to be ostensibly maintained.

"*That* whenever the health of the Queen Dowager is proposed on similar occasions, the guests shall be requested to 'bottle up' their extra admiration for that illustrious personage, and so 'moderate the rancour' of their applause, as to avoid the appearance of an invidious and just now most impolitic distinction.

"*That* notwithstanding the intense veneration felt by every true Tory for her Dowager Majesty, Conservative orators are forbidden to dwell at any length on her marvellous virtues, lest it should be imagined that our gracious Sovereign, whom it is particularly, for many reasons, desirable to flatter and conciliate, possesses no virtues at all."

In fact, old Tories were advised to smother their feelings on this point, and, however strong their preference for the Dowager, to see the need of being "preciously hypocritical."

Public interest in the Dowager waned in proportion as Victoria recognised that she was Queen of both parties and of all her subjects. It was a hard lesson for her to learn, for, in addition to past matters, she could not get over Peel's awkward manners, and she thought him strikingly ignorant of character, which made it difficult to respect his judgment. Some idea was raised, towards the end of 1841, of asking Parliament for an increase in the allowance made to the Prince, but the Queen was firm in refusing to have this suggested; she said nothing should induce her either to send Peel to the House with such a message or to accept such a favour from those Ministers; Peel might now be regretting his action concerning the grant, but it was, and was intended to be, a personal insult to herself, and was followed by opposition to her private wishes on the precedency question, in which latter Wellington took the lead, as Peel had done in the Commons against the grant. She never could forget it, and no favour to her should come from such a quarter. Thus did she deliver herself to George Anson.

The last favour that she had received from the Whig Parliament was a grant of £70,000 to rebuild the stables at Windsor, which housed one hundred and twenty horses; the extravagance of this grant provoking much discussion at a time when such a large number of her people were in want of the necessaries of life.

Of Peel's supporters, the Duke of Wellington, who loathed the Corn Law repeal, was in the end one of the firmest, for he generally first considered the dignity of the Crown. On the admittance of the Tories to power, the Duke had the pain of finding that he had more or less lost his prestige in the House; a younger race had come to the fore, who knew him not as a leader, and they were inclined to think little of the old giant. Disraeli, of whom some one has said that he was "genius without conscience," with his dyed curls, his dandy ways, his superficiality, his radical training and instincts, his ready wit and direct method of abuse, took the place of leader to these younger men, and he had little use for one whom he considered worn out. So Wellington found his advice disregarded, his wishes forgotten, and grew irritable and moody. Yet he was popular enough with the public, for once, on his going late to a concert, the singing was stopped, while the audience rose *en masse*, wildly cheering.

When the Queen begged him to uphold Peel in passing his measure on Free Corn he consented, but with regret and suppressed anger; indeed, from the autumn of 1845 to the summer of 1846, he lived constantly in an almost uncontrollable state of irritation. As he said, "Rotten potatoes have done it all; they put Peel in his d——d plight." He was not quite so severe as Lord Alvanley, who declared that "Peel ought not to die a natural death." Alvanley did not live to know of Peel's tragic end.

During the violent debate on the measure, some great landowner asked the Duke to allow a Committee of Enquiry to be formed on the burden the Act would put upon the land. He refused the request, but, being worried again and again, at last said: "Well, my good fellow, you must have it. I will not oppose it; I am quite of your opinion on the subject; it is a d——d mess, but I must look to the peace of the country and the Queen."

That many people hated the Prime Minister for his change of view was amply proved when, at the beginning of 1843, his private secretary, Edward Drummond, was fatally shot in Whitehall by a Scotchman named Macnaughten. Peel, when in Scotland on Her Majesty's first visit there, drove much with the Queen, leaving his secretary to drive alone in his carriage, so Macnaughten, who declared that the Tories had ruined him, came to London, watched Peel's house, and, seeing Drummond go in and out, assumed that he was Peel and murdered him. He was acquitted on the plea of insanity, and confined in Tothill Fields Prison, a verdict which raised intense indignation in the country, as everyone was convinced that the man was not insane.

No Government could ever have had a more distressing period of power, for starvation stalked the land; severe rains had spoiled the harvests for several years, the heavy tariff on foreign corn made it prohibitive, and the only way of meeting the difficulties had been to impose fresh taxes on other foodstuffs and create preposterous Poor Laws. The Hungry 'Forties is well known as a phrase at the present day, though few now really realise the acute distress which then spread, not only over the British Isles, but over the whole European Continent. The high price of bread, the want of work, the enslaving of women and little children in factories and workshops, raised intense public bitterness and anger against the rich, and it was not easy for a woman in such a prominent position as Queen Victoria ever to do right in the opinion of all people. All sorts of curious recommendations were made her in the interest of the poor, which, if followed, would sometimes have had no effect at all. Joseph Hume, for instance, made the absurd demand during the Income Tax discussion that the gold lace should be stripped from the clothes of the Queen's servants.

The Queen was contemplating the issue of a personal letter authorising the clergy to make an appeal to the public on behalf of the distressed; and by the irony of things it was at that very same time—June, 1842—that the gold coinage was found to be light, and a Royal proclamation relating to it was issued. Thereupon a panic followed, not on the Stock Exchange, but in all the poor streets of London. The workman who was so fortunate as to take a pound on Saturday discovered that some of the shopkeepers would not accept it as current coin, others would only give nineteen or even eighteen shillings in exchange, and a report quickly spread that the Queen had called in all gold sovereigns at nineteen shillings each, and that after July only fifteen shillings would be given for them. Everywhere was anger, rebellion, and confusion, for if gold had lost its value what was there to depend upon? and at last eighteen shillings was eagerly taken as a fair exchange for a golden sovereign. So keen was the distress at this time that Peel actually had half farthings issued, that the very poor might have facilities for buying the smallest of small quantities.

During this trouble, the words "light sovereigns" were caught up, and applied to reigning people, and—in spite of the discontent—generally with compliments to Queen Victoria. A clever cartoon was done at the time, in which the Queen—a delightful figure—weighs down the scale, though the other side is crowded with Louis Philippe, the King of Hanover, the King of Austria, the King of the Belgians, the King of Prussia, and a shadowy sixth, who from the insecurity of his position ought to be Pope Pius IX.

The *Comic Album* probably expressed the feeling of the country—for, bad as England was, the other European countries were then in yet more parlous state —when it said :

> " Examine the whole regal bag,
>   And weigh out the Sovereigns in lots !
>   There's Harry the Eighth, who was *heavy*,
>   And Mary the *light* Queen of Scots !
> And while over History ranging,
>   Both ' heavy ' and ' light ' there may be,
> I've one that I'd never be *changing*,
>   Victoria's the Sovereign for me."

A little later Ireland being in a flame, Dan O'Connell, that wonderful orator, having been very active, was put on his trial; the Church and the Puseyites in England, and the Church and the Seceders in Scotland, were at war; the stalwart Rebecca was fighting grotesque abuses in Wales, and behind it all was the

"Light Sovereigns."

From a Print in the Collection of A. M. Broadley, Esq.

knowledge that a blight had fallen upon the potatoes, which gave Peel the fear of a terrible famine. But to this latter calamity the public gave no thought. Absurd pictures and still more absurd lines circulated, making fun of most things, though whether these troubled Peel it is not easy to say. He was depicted as the master of a corn-grinding machine, which ground poor people and Irish folk into high rents for the landlord. He was a doctor, Dr. Sangrado Peel-'em-bare, with little labels hanging all round him from innumerable pockets :

> "Dr. Sangrado Peel-'em-bare
> Requests once more a trial fair,
> If relief my patient ' axes '
> Of Corn laws, Tariff, Income-taxes,
> I've still a large supply on hand
> To meet the popular demand."

In caricature Peel was the butt of all sides; in the House he was being looked on as the general enemy. Lord John Russell, " that cunning little fox," was ever ready to attack; the heavyweight, Lord Brougham, who always thundered against those in power because he could not regain the Chancellorship, was also on the watch to harass him.

> "There was an old Broom of St. Stephens,
> That set all at sixes and sevens,
> And to sweep from the room
> The convictions of Brougham
> Was the work of this Broom of St. Stephens,"

was *Punch's* witty way of summing him up.

Brougham's lasting disappointment about office is

indicated in the following lines, as well as his great success as a law reformer :

"Since I first came from Scotia, *sans* shoe or shirt,
I've been chiefly engaged in the carting of dirt,
Trying to clear it, and trying to thin it,
(When there's been any dirt, I was sure to be in it).
I've clean'd out the Courts, and clean'd out the lanes,
But now they have turned me adrift for my pains."

Disraeli's second-in-command was Lord George Bentinck, "the most ignorant man that ever led a party," said Lord Broughton; and these two, with Lord Malmesbury and the Duke of Richmond, did all they could to make Peel's life impossible. They were all at him, the terriers, the retrievers, the mastiffs, the mongrels; while Peel, like a bulldog, hung on to his task, and never let go till he had completed it. It is not necessary to follow all that happened through the process of the struggle; what is important here is that the Queen and Prince were soon heart and soul in it, for, following the course of events as they did, they could see nothing but the free importation of corn to relieve the people.

That Peel was up against a very awkward corner, and that he was honestly convinced that Free Trade in Corn was the only possible course if he would avoid prolonged public suffering and revolution, is unquestionable. Behind him, he had the Anti-Corn-Law League, the most powerful league—not excepting the old Orange league—ever initiated in the country; he had the Whigs, many of the Tories, the Queen and her Court, and against this overwhelming majority in numbers and influence stood the monopolists alone, Peel felt that only pertinacity and bravery were needed to ensure success.

A sign of the universal trouble and the doubt of Peel was a cartoon of the Queen, the Prince, and Peel looking over London from a balcony of the Palace, up the columns of which Melbourne and Russell are trying to shin. Great buildings are falling, crowds rushing about in a mad state, and O'Connell as a comet is speeding to Dublin, crying, " Here's all St. Giles at my tail, St. Paul's going down and whiskey's going up." " Do you feel assured, Sir Robert, that we are perfectly secure here?" asks the Queen. " Believe me, Madam, I do not feel the least shaky," he replies.

Another cartoon, from the Tory side, shows him acting the part of thimble-rigger on the green with Lord Brougham and another standing irresolutely by, while the Queen in high cap and cloak, acts as tout for her confederate, with a basketful of wigs, coronets, ribbons, and George collars, singing :

"Come, buy my pretty trinkets, my collars, jewels, garters,
  Bishop's wigs, Chancellor's wigs, coronets, and charters,
  Any honest lad at Bar or Church may suit his mind,
  If so be he can win of the thimblerigger behind."

John Russell, a small boy, looks on with derisive grin.

In 1844 the Government were beaten by a majority of twenty on the sugar duties, a majority which included some of Peel's own men, and he was so angry, so disgusted at the personal animus shown against him, that he determined to resign. The Queen was in a panic, dreading such a course desperately for fear of having to "send for the friends of her youth," as one cynic put it. In a letter to King Leopold she wrote that "we were in the greatest *possible* danger *without knowing to whom to turn*," and that Peel's resignation would have been for the whole country *a great calamity*; "we have been quite miserable and *quite alarmed* ever since Saturday."

Nothing could exceed the exasperation against Peel, nor the exasperation under which he laboured; but the Queen begged him to remain by her, the Cabinet met several times, and then on the Monday following agreed to adhere to their measure, and to resign altogether if again beaten. Peel's speech in the House rather increased than lessened the annoyance, yet the second trial brought him a majority of twenty-two, and the former amendment carried against him was rescinded. This is an incident which was repeated, with some differences, in the House during the autumn of last year, 1912, on an unimportant amendment rushed through in an hour by the Unionists upon the question of Home Rule.

When the Queen opened Parliament in February, 1845, some one wrote that she was pleased to go down to Westminster and treat her Parliament to a dish of pancakes, which were prepared by that great and careful cook, Peel, while Her Majesty supplied the sugar and Brougham the lemon.

Almost the first business of the Session was a question as to the truth of the assertion in the *Chronicle* that the title King Consort was to be conferred on the

Prince. This assertion was a *canard*, but it was one
that the Queen would have liked to make the truth,
for by that time the Prince *was* King, guiding the hand
that held the pen, and the Queen did nothing without
his advice. So long as nothing was said about it no
one cared, but as soon as it was mentioned publicly
Englishmen first pretended to feel afraid of Germany,
and then determined to snub a presumptuous marion-
ette Princeling, who was exceeding the antics pre-
scribed for him by his employers, the British Public.

The Queen in writing to Peel was quite fair in the
matter : " The title of King is open assuredly to many
difficulties, and would perhaps be no real advantage
to the Prince, but the Queen is positive that something
must at once be done to place the Prince's position on
a constitutionally recognised footing, and to give him
a title adequate to that position."

She had to wait for that desired result just as long
as the King of Hanover had to wait for the return
of the Hanoverian jewels.

Then a Bill was brought in to help the Irish by increasing the grant to the Roman Catholic College of
Maynooth, and all England went into a fine frenzy
over Catholic persecutions and Protestant virtue; the
Bishops put on all their secular armour, and half the
Tory party flung scorn at their leader, who carried the
measure in their teeth. Victoria was a good Churchwoman, and she showed a real sense of her position and
of her responsibilities to all classes of her subjects,
whether Protestant or Catholic, on this occasion, while
being roused to wrath on " the bigotry, the wicked and

blind passions" shown. "I blush for Protestantism," she said, "as a Presbyterian clergyman said very truly, 'Bigotry is more common than shame.'"

Then the terror of the potato blight fell upon the Isles, appearing all over them, also in Sweden, Belgium, and Holland, where at once steps were taken to see that the people had food. But the first piteous results of it were apparent in Ireland, and Peel could foresee what was to come; famine, complete disorganisation, social war, for which the English, on being asked for bread, were to give the stone of coercion. Peel wanted to pass a measure for the temporary free import of corn into Ireland, but the idea was received with such a tumult in the Cabinet—for it was felt that to let go of Protection temporarily was to let it go for ever—that he dropped it. Even his attempt to *reduce* the duty on imports so as to give starving people more chance was bitterly opposed by the landlords in the Cabinet.

Then as Lord John Russell publicly announced a scheme for Free Trade, and as Peel, sent to Parliament as a Protectionist, had been by stress of events convinced that Free Corn was the only course, he resigned, promising the Queen that he would support Russell as Prime Minister, and use all his influence with the House of Lords to prevent their impeding the new Minister's progress.

Queen and Prince were again miserable. Now they did not want the Whigs in power, they did not want "Johnny," they wanted Peel, and they hoped to keep him. Perhaps Peel was so distressed at his Queen's distress that the keeping of his word was too difficult, but certain it is that when John Russell said that he would be in a minority unless he had Peel's support, the retiring Minister gave an evasive and guarded answer, in which he left every door open to allow of escape. Russell pressed for a more definite reply, but did not get it. A further hitch in the arrangements was that Lord Palmerston must be included in his Cabinet, and would not take any office but that of Foreign Secretary.

In 1840 Victoria and Albert had had their feelings so worked upon against Palmerston by King Leopold that they were in great fear of him. It was a family matter; Leopold had married Louise, daughter of King Louis Philippe; Palmerston, fully appreciating the French King's character, had sternly refused to yield to him over the Turkish-Egyptian war of that year, and Leopold, taking the side of his father-in-law, accused Palmerston of being the personal enemy of Louis Philippe, of wantonly frustrating his schemes, and of being eager to rush England into war. It had frightened the two young people, and they naturally felt an affinity for Kings which led them to believe that Kings could do no wrong; indeed, the one and only compensation for losing Melbourne had been that they also lost Palmerston.

Now, in 1845 he was to come back to his old office, in which he would certainly cause war with France, break the entrancing friendship between themselves and the *dear good* King, Louis Philippe, and plunge all Europe into a conflagration! Could not Peel,

K

really, couldn't he save them from these terrible calamities?

When Lord John went to Victoria she told him definitely that Palmerston must be given the Colonial Office and not the Foreign Office, and she begged Lord Aberdeen to support her objections to Palmerston in political circles. Lord Grey also refused to act with Palmerston, and so Lord John, after being kept dangling a week by the irresolute Peel, declared that he could not form a Government, and Peel slid automatically into place again; as Disraeli said in his flamboyant way, " Russell handed back with courtesy the poisoned chalice to Sir Robert."

The Queen was filled with joy, saying jubilantly to Peel when he came, " So far from taking leave of you, Sir Robert, I must require you to withdraw your resignation and to remain in my service." The Prince asked Wellington if he did not think Russell had behaved very badly in keeping Her Majesty a week without a Government, and Peel solemnly assured his Royal mistress—what he would have died rather than have said to Russell—that had the latter taken office he would have acted towards him with the most scrupulous good faith and have done everything to give him support. The fact was Peel wanted to do the work himself, but for form's sake had to pretend to give the originator of the idea first chance. Witty *Punch* published a cartoon of Peel as the Artful Dodger, saying to Oliver Twist (Lord John), who sits on a doorstep with his bundle by his side : " Oh, how green you must be to think you could form a Ministry."

On the reassembling of Parliament, the majority of the Tories went over to the Opposition, the Whigs supporting Peel, and there was no end to the songs made about the great transaction. Some of the pretty words current in the debate which followed are indicated in the following lines from " old Mrs. *Morning Post* to her naughty, naughty boy " :

"That Robert there will be my death,
    He will, as sure as fate.
Come here, Sir, come, don't answer me—
    You ' loathsome ' reprobate.

You nasty, gross, ' plebeian ' boy,
    I saw you, little pigs,
You and Dick Cobden in the dirt,
    Running all sorts of rigs.

' You thought? ' why, bless the boy ! what next?
    To scrunch his pretty toy—
What business, Sir, have you to think?
    You naughty, naughty boy."

Punch also made a parody of a certain nursery tale : " There was a little Lady who had twenty-four million babies, and she wanted to get cheap bread for them, but she could not because of the Corn Law. So she went to the Lords and she said : ' Lords, Lords, repeal this law, or I cannot get cheap bread for my babies.' Then the Lords said to her ' Pooh ! We are the landed interest; what do we care for your babies ! The Tories to a man will stand by us ! ' So she went to the Tories and she said, ' Tories, Tories, desert the Lords; the Lords won't repeal the law and I cannot get cheap bread for my babies.' Then the Tories said to her : ' Madam, we have no objection to eat dirt; we do it

K 2

every day; but at present we are under the orders of the Duke.' So she went to the Duke and she said—" etc.; the final result being that " Cobden began to reform the League; the League began to become a Fact; the Fact began to frighten Peel; Peel began to speak to the Duke; the Duke began to order the Tories; the Tories began to desert the Lords; the Lords set to to repeal the Law; and so the little Lady get cheap bread for her babies."

Dizzy and Bentinck had plotted together to destroy Peel, and Bentinck began the game by accusing Peel of persecuting Canning, "hunting him even to death," in 1828, when that statesman had died through over-work as Prime Minister. He accused Peel of treachery, lying, and inefficiency, attacking him with a coarseness and violence which disgusted all but those to whom scurrility and insolence were really palatable, and doing everything he could to ruin Peel's character. When Peel, astounded at the unexpected and absurd charge, answered Bentinck successfully, Disraeli launched it in a new and bitterer form, using every trick of his peculiar rhetoric to drive his equally peculiar charge home, " in this House the vulture rules where once the eagle reigned!" He hacked and mangled Peel with most unsparing severity, positively torturing his victim. Charles Greville, who was a Tory, said that it was a miserable and degrading spectacle. The whole mass of the Protectionists cheered Disraeli with vociferous delight, making the roof ring again; and when Peel spoke they screamed and hooted at him in the most brutal manner. When he

vindicated himself, and talked of honour and conscience, they assailed him with shouts of derision and
gestures of contempt.   Through the speech Peel sat
white, wretched, reduced almost to tears, and when
at last the false sentiments and resonant sentences
stopped, asked the House to suspend judgment, and
went out.

Three days later he made a most complete refutation of all that had been charged against him, of which
Disraeli himself said: " There never was a more
successful explanation."

Among Peel's last words were these : " I shall leave
a name execrated by every monopolist, but it will be
remembered perhaps with gratitude by the poor, to
whom I shall have given untaxed food."

When he left the House after this speech about
a hundred people stood in the street awaiting him,
who raised their hats as he appeared, and then at a
short distance followed him as a bodyguard to his
home.   Whether it was a mark simply of respect or
an attempt to protect is not recorded, though the
authorities in those days considered it needful to care for
their prominent politicians.   When Sir George Grey was
Home Secretary in Lord John Russell's Government
from 1846 to 1852, he sent for the Sergeant-at-Arms
one day and said : " I don't think it quite safe for Lord
John to walk home from the House to Chesham Place
in the middle of the night.   He is a small and feeble
man, and there are bad characters about in Birdcage
Walk and Pimlico.   You had better tell the Superintendent of the House of Commons police to have him

watched home." The Sergeant did so, and the
Superintendent cheerfully replied: "Oh, that's all
right. Lord John is always watched home—and so is
Sir George Grey. But we don't let them know, because
we don't want to frighten them."

The very day that the Corn Law Bill passed the
Lords, the Protectionists and the Whigs—who had no
longer any use for the Prime Minister—combined to
defeat the Government on the Coercion Bill, and Peel
went down to Osborne to give in his resignation,
begging of the Queen, as a reward for what he had
undergone, that she would never again ask him to take
up office. She accepted his resignation with deep
regret, knowing that now there was no hope of escaping
from Lord John and Palmerston. "We have felt so
safe with Sir Robert . . . knowing that he would
never let monarchy be robbed of the little strength
and power it still may possess."

Peel represented a middle party, a progressive
Tory, such as suited Royalty then, but for the old
crusted Tory the Queen still had no partiality, and the
wild men among them gave her fresh cause for dis-
pleasure, for on the day that Peel made his speech
declaring that he would support total abolition of the
Corn duties, Prince Albert went to the House hoping
to listen to a fine debate; with the result that Sir
George Bentinck, in verbose language, accused him
of "allowing himself to be seduced by the First
Minister of the Crown" to go there and give
the semblance of the personal sanction of Her
Majesty to a measure which it was believed by

LORD GEORGE BENTINCK.

the majority of the landed aristocracy would ruin them.

So the Prince never went to a debate again, which was a deprivation to him, and, I think, one also to the public, as it prevented this show of interest on the part of the Court.

CHAPTER VI

THE QUEEN AND IRELAND

ONE of her subjects for whom Victoria was erroneously said to have a liking was Daniel O'Connell, the brilliant Irish patriot who, according to Cyrus Redding, was one of the few men who dared bid defiance to a world in defence of a great principle. It was he who, seeing one of his attackers in the House reading his speech under cover of his hat, parodied Goldsmith in his reply :

> "And still they gazed and still the wonder grew
> That one small hat could carry all he knew."

Early in her reign Victoria had been drawn to him, for, like a true Irishman, he was extravagant in his praises and professions of loyalty to his Sovereign. "A Little Blarney" was the title of a drawing of O'Connell sitting smilingly by Victoria holding one of her hands and gently patting it, Peel and Wellington behind the Queen's chair gloomily looking on. O'Connell himself thoroughly believed in the Queen's friendship; and when the Irish Lord Chancellor declared publicly that Her Majesty was determined to prevent repeal, O'Connell promptly responded that it was a lie, whereupon Peel was forced to admit that Victoria would do all in her power to retain the Union.

After her marriage, when Albert impressed upon her how dangerous to the Empire he considered the Irish repealer to be, she no longer felt any favour for him, and heard of O'Connell's influence over his country-men with uneasiness, realising with anger that at his word a crowd of ten thousand, fifty thousand, on one occasion a quarter of a million people would gather to listen to him. At this great meeting two followers presented him with a cap of green and gold, which the *Illustrated London News* said was not less *outré* than the infantry cap invented by Prince Albert. At O'Connell's trial the Attorney-General persisted in calling this his crown.

In 1843 and 1844 O'Connell was tried for seditious conspiracy with all the cleverness and judgment which England has ever extended to Erin. That is to say, that every Catholic was struck off the jury list, a pro-ceeding regarded in England as an act of madness, and in Ireland as one of brutal injustice and insult.

This trial was definitely between O'Connell and the Crown, and in spite of the popular and righteous indignation at the packing of the jury, Queen Victoria's only desire about it was that he should be condemned, so it was a foregone conclusion that the verdict should be against him; though in his desire to please the mighty the Chief Justice went too far. He imposed a year's imprisonment and a fine of £2,000, in addition to which O'Connell was to enter into securities—himself in £5,000 and two sureties in £2,500 each—to keep the peace for seven years. And Victoria had either the ignorance or the callousness to write to her uncle, " O'Connell being pronounced guilty is a great triumph ! "

At the trial Judge Barton shed tears over the sentence, and the members of the Junior Bar applauded the accused. Popular belief still, however, regarded the Queen as his friend, and believed in the spirit of a cartoon by H. H., in which Daniel kneels in a den surrounded by lions wearing the heads of Wellington, Brougham, Peel, Melbourne, and Russell, while Victoria looks down at him from a hole in the wall, a shaft of sunlight going from her to him, and he looking smilingly up at his young Sovereign.

The sentence was so indecently unjust and such a mortal weight upon a Government which was trying to reduce dissatisfaction in Ireland, that the House of Lords reversed the judgment on the grounds that " the whole Protestant jury, the partiality of the Chief Justice, the division of opinion between the judges themselves, and the political character of the judgment, all pointed to a biassed decision."

So O'Connell was released, but his power was gone; and three years later he died in Genoa on his way to Rome, all the Consuls—except the English—being present at the funeral service, the representative of the United States wearing his official robes.

Those who wished to save Ireland from disaffection, rebellion, and treason uttered the prayer : " Let the Queen come to Ireland ; let her show her sovereignty

there as she has done in Scotland. She can visit
France, Germany, and Belgium; she can go again and
again to the Highlands; then let her also come here,
and prove that the Irish are her people."

The Queen's abstention meant the withdrawal of
the nobles and landlords from the island. Ireland
was not to them a place to live in, to work in, or to
spend money in; it was not worth while there to foster
trade or agriculture, for it was remote and despised; its
only use was that money could be drawn from the stone
huts in the fields and from the farmers who struggled
to live by the needs, not of the rich, but of the poor.
So the cry rose incessantly about the throne, " Come
to Ireland," and the Queen feared to go, her husband
feared to let her go or to go himself, and the Queen's
Ministers feared yet more to let her go or to go themselves. Like the great sea serpent, the report rose
every year that she was going, and every year until
she had sat on her throne a round dozen of them the
report proved false. Deputations waited upon her
from Dublin, and in 1845 the Lord Mayor of that city
headed one such, declaring to her that the mere rumour
that she was coming to Ireland filled every heart with
gladness. To him she replied with compliments,
saying : " Whenever I may be able to receive in
Ireland the promised welcome, I shall rely with confidence on the loyalty and affection of my faithful
subjects." In 1846 the report was so fully believed
that it was decided to fit up in a superb manner the
Chapter Room of St. Patrick's Cathedral, the work to
be completed in three months, because it was thought

that when she came she would hold a Chapter of the Order of St. Patrick as George IV. had done in 1821.

But she did not go, though it was quite evident that she realised she ought. She wrote to Lord John Russell, saying : " It is a journey which must one day or the other be undertaken, and which the Queen would be glad to have accomplished, because it must be disagreeable to her that people should speculate whether she *dare* visit one part of her dominions." Lord John shelved the matter on the score of expense, and the inadvisability of encouraging Irish proprietors to lay out money on show when the misery and distress of the people were so acute. His economy was well meant, though it was wrong, for the presence of the Queen in Ireland would have taken over so many people and so much money that the island would have gained, not suffered.

By then the creeping evil of famine had got its grip on the country, and what it effected in Ireland it is impossible to describe. England was bad enough. Some newspapers published weekly columns showing how to mix beet with flour, how to make soup with vegetables, and in general how to get blood out of a stone. The most wild-cat schemes were publicly advised to a bitter people. Several hundred scientists met to discuss what they called " famine bread," and among their recommendations were the use of yams, turnip-bread, sugar-beet, mangold-wurzel, carrot, red beet, parsnip, artichoke—all of which would have been dearer than flour. But the very crown of their ideas was Icelandic moss, ground and mixed with half flour, or hay treated in the same way. Moss-bread was bitter, they allowed, but the hay was sweet and high-flavoured, though of a dark and repulsive colour.

The Prince made use of this meeting, and *The Windsor Express* published the following paragraph about his kindness and liberality : " Kind Consideration of Prince Albert.—At a time when the potato disease is employing so much of public attention, *it cannot be otherwise than gratifying* to know that His Royal Highness Prince Albert has, with the kindness which is so prominent a feature of his character, caused the distribution, by the resident clergy, in several districts, of *extracts from a speech* delivered by Dr. Buckland, Professor of Geology, at the Town Hall, Birmingham; wherein the proper treatment of the potato under existing circumstances is set forth. The usefulness of these extracts will be generally acknowledged, and His Royal Highness will receive the thanks which his meritorious conduct so highly deserves ! "

The Duke of Norfolk made a suggestion which caused his name to be cursed from one end of England to the other, one which in the recent agitation over the Veto Bill was brought up again and again in speeches to prove that the Lords were villains. He advised hungry people to throw some curry-powder into water and drink it if they wanted to appease their hunger. This advice was caught up in almost every paper and bandied about in every circle of society :

"Confound those Dukes for saying, what the world will ne'er forget,
That with curry-powder, beans, and starch poor folks might manage yet."

One does wonder whether this advice was a stupid attempt to point a way to alleviation of pain, or whether it was pure cynicism; in any case, coming from a tremendously rich man and offered to the destitute, it *was* asinine.

In Ireland disease went hand-in-hand with famine, and crime came to complete the terrible trio. So that in the end no fewer than two million people were lost by starvation, disease, the law, and emigration.

Then Victoria tried homœopathic treatment by ordering a day for national fasting, humiliation and prayer, which order was announced as follows in the Court Circular: "At the Court at Osborne House, Isle of Wight, present the Queen's Most Excellent Majesty in Council, Wednesday, 24th March, 1847, was appointed for a General Fast. A splendid entertainment was served up after the Council to the Ministers, Nobles and Bishops who attended."

Evidently the decision had to be fortified with a good feed, and the Bishops and others thought that sufficient unto the 24th of March was the misery in Ireland and elsewhere.

So England's little Queen was prevailed upon to order her subjects to shut their shops, to refuse to eat, to go to church and to pray, because their brethren in Ireland were starving. They were to humiliate themselves and so turn away the wrath of God. It is so easy and comforting to make God the scapegoat of our own sins and follies, to throw our moral responsibility upon Him! As some cynic once remarked : " To lay our wickedness on God is the very monkey trick of piety."

The order was obeyed, by some in spirit, by most in form. The Queen and Prince went solemnly to church, after which they probably ruminated upon events, or perhaps Prince Albert explained to his Queen the utter folly, the irreverence and the economic stupidity of the fast, for he had more thought in his little finger than a whole half-dozen of the wise counsellors who proposed the idea had in all their complicated brains. But whatever he did there was that two o'clock dinner lost to him, *the* meal of the day, from which no other inducement in the world would have kept him.

Then think of the Palace kitchen, cold and empty, no joints roasting for the servants' dinners ! Think of the pages and housemaids, the—no, I won't say the cooks, they kept the keys of the larders—the ladies-in-waiting and the equerries, looking furtively at each other and each wondering how everyone else felt. Think how they all waited and waited until the dread—in this case the blessed—midnight hour struck ! and then with what joy they sat down to a delicious, hot supper. Why ! that supper was worth all that had gone before, only some were so hungry that they gobbled—the Queen and Prince did, I am sure, for neither was delicate in table manners.

All these people were, it is true, put to a little inconvenience, which mattered to no one, but there were those other people who had to pay twice over for the royal luxury of fasting. The food shops were shut and the baker's man, the butcher's man and all the other men and women engaged in other shops, not only went fasting but lost their day's pay; the labouring man, already face to face with want, had to be idle for a mere sentiment, not only he but his babies had to fast for two days to please the vagaries of Her Majesty's Bishops and Her Majesty's own complaisance with those vagaries.

If there had been more sense and less nonsense talked at the Council, the wise men might have hit upon the plan of asking for a day's income from the Queen and from the Prince, from the nobles and the Bishops, from the sinecurists and the millionaires, and so down through every grade of society, until they came to the poor. That would have done good to Ireland and an injustice to Providence would not have been perpetrated; though probably Providence did not mind.

The matter was, of course, not overlooked by the wicked satirists of the time :

"*Beggar-boy:* Teacher, what is a General Fast?
    Teacher: A day, boy, set aside
        By holy Church for sinful men,
        To mortify their pride,
        By never eating all the day
        Of meat, boil'd, roast, or fried.
      Boy: Is that it, teacher—then ain't me
        And poor old mother pious?
        For days and days a bit of meat
        Has never come anigh us :
        And since to starve is to be good,
        Why let each well-fed sinner,
        Just suck his thumbs on General Fast,
        And give the poor a dinner.''

Really, the poor young Queen—who was old enough, however, to have known better—was most horribly ill-advised, for her next attempt to meet the case only plunged her people further into distress. It is not stated that this new idea was carried out for the health of the people, and it may just as likely have been another of the good, judicious Prince's domestic economies.

Two kinds of wheat, "firsts" and "seconds," were in use, the first being Essex White and the seconds Baltic Red. Naturally, the inhabitants of the Palace were fed on the best wheat, which cost twenty-five per cent. more than the other. But now that the time of stress had arrived the following order was issued by the Queen and Prince, though only Her Majesty's name was used: "Her Majesty, taking into consideration the present high and increasing price of provisions, and especially of all kinds of bread and flour, has been graciously pleased to command that, from the date of this order, no description of flour, except seconds, shall be used for any purpose in Her Majesty's Household, and that the daily allowance of bread shall be restricted to one pound per head for every person dieted in the Palace. By Her Majesty's command, Fortescue, Board of Green Cloth, May 12th, 1847." No wonder "Famine in High Places" became a favourite headline in the papers, and sarcastic paragraphs appeared under the title of "Palace Bread." Think of the Marchioness of Douro and the Duchess of Sutherland, Lady Jocelyn and the Hon. Miss Stanley, each beautiful

L

enough to live on a lemon ice for a twelvemonth—in poetry—being told that they are not to have more than a weekly couple of quartern loaves apiece until Baltic Red was down to 56s. and Essex White had fallen to about 70s.!

That the remarks were not always "quite nice" it may well be believed:

> "Our loving Queen it may be seen
>   Has ordered, I confess,
> Her home no other bread shall eat
>   But what is second best.
> She sent Prince A. the other day
>   Into a baker's shop,
> For a stale three-farthing penny roll,
>   To make the children's sop."

As must have been expected, other people followed their Sovereign's economic example, the Carlton Club, other large establishments, and many of her nobles, with the result that the poor were doubly deprived, for the price of seconds flour rose until it equalled that of the best, and the want grew more bitter. It is not incredible that that being so, interest in Royal functions took an inquisitive turn, that notes were made of the extravagance which went hand-in-hand with parsimony at Court, and that the papers commented on such happenings as the following, guilelessly published in the "Court Circular," the information in which was passed by Prince Albert. At this time the Grand Duke Constantine of Russia was a guest of Her Majesty, and one dinner at Windsor Castle was thus described: "The magnificent St. George's candelabrum was placed in the centre of the table, which

LADY JOCELYN.
From a Painting by J. Hayter.

was brilliantly illuminated with candelabra of large size, richly sculptured in gold. Rows of gold dishes were ranged the entire length of the table, the larger sort resting on eagles of silver gilt, and on the plateau among the different centre pieces were arranged several beautiful plants in flower inserted in vases of silver gilt. A buffet of gold plate was erected at each end of the hall, that at the eastern extremity containing a number of racing cups, including the Lincoln Cup and Two Goodwood Cups, won by Fleur-de-lis, the property of George IV. Among the remarkable articles on the buffet was the brilliant huma composed of pure plates of gold closely inlaid with precious stones, with pearls for eyes, and suspended from its beak a large and valuable ruby." In such surroundings seconds bread, and that limited in quantity, was eaten!

Lord Campbell tells in his "Life" that he went to dine with the Queen, but whether his account was simply facetious or really exact it is a little difficult to know. "The greatest delicacy we had was some very nice oatcakes. There was a Highland piper standing behind Her Majesty's chair, but he did not play as at State dinners. We had likewise some Edinburgh ale. The Queen and the Ladies withdrawing, Prince Albert came over to her side of the table, and we remained behind about a quarter of an hour; but we rose from table within the hour from the time of our sitting down. A snuff-box was twice carried round and offered to all the gentlemen: Prince Albert to my surprise took a pinch. On returning to the

I. 2

gallery we had tea and coffee." It certainly gives a very homely idea of a royal dinner.

That confidence in the Queen's justice was shaken, particularly among the very ignorant, is shown by the following paragraph clipped from the *Bedford Times:* "Great consternation has pervaded certain classes at Luton from the belief in a rumour that the Queen had ordered all children under five years of age to be put to death if the scarcity of provisions continued. One poor woman was seen to weep bitterly at the contemplation of the probable calamity. . . . !"

Lord George Bentinck was simply brilliant in a speech he made in the House over the famine, when he affirmed that to suit Peel's policy a *sham cry* had been got up about the failure of the potato crop a year earlier. Now he was sorry to say that that pretence had become a reality. This time there was no sham, but he greatly feared that this sad reality was the just vengeance of Providence for the great ingratitude which had been displayed in needlessly complaining of his bounty.

What a royal panacea a day of fasting and humiliation must have been to such a mind!

In spite of mistakes and a too ready acquiescence in an unnecessary domestic economy, Victoria was warm-hearted and compassionate. She felt festivities to be out of season, and talked of giving in charity rather than spending on herself. At which idea Peel remonstrated: "I am afraid the people would only say that your Majesty was returning them change for their pounds in halfpence. Your Majesty is not per-

haps aware that the most unpopular person in the parish is the relieving officer, and if the Queen became relieving officer for all England she would only find her money go a very little way, and get more grumbles than thanks."

Then Victoria expressed a wish that all ladies attending her Drawing Room should wear dresses of English manufacture, and to encourage trade she gave a great fancy dress ball. That so frivolous a proceeding should much annoy a section of the community was inevitable, and apropos of it one sour preacher declared from his pulpit that "When Charity took to dancing it ceased to be Charity and became a wanton."

The first of these balls was in 1842, when the guests were respectively Knights and Dames of the time of Poictiers. The gowns were described in a gorgeously illustrated volume issued afterwards, some of the pictures of which are given here, representing the costumes which were worn by the Queen and the Prince on that occasion. Her Majesty founded her gown upon that of the effigy of Queen Philippa on the tomb in Westminster Abbey. Her hair was encased in a network of gold, embroidered in precious stones, and the crown was formed of graven gold, ornamented with a single jewel, which cost the enormous sum of £20,000. The underdress was of blue and gold brocade of Spitalfields manufacture; the surcoat was of ponceau velvet bordered and faced with ermine; down the centre of the stomacher was a band of jewels laid on gold tissue, and the girdle, only visible at the sides, was studded with jewels. A mantle of gold and silver brocade lined with ermine completed the Queen's costume.

The Prince, who also copied his clothes from the tomb in Westminster Abbey, wore a long tunic of blue and gold brocade, the collar, fitting closely round the neck, being embroidered thickly with jewels; this tunic was slit in the centre up to the knee, and was embroidered at the edges to match the collar and wristbands; scarlet hose, scarlet shoes embroidered in gold; over the tunic a mantle of scarlet velvet, bordered with gold lace set with upwards of one thousand large pearls. This was lined with ermine and fastened across the breast with a band of purple velvet studded with diamonds, rubies and emeralds, a turquoise of enormous size in the centre. The whole of the materials were of British manufacture.

In considering this description one wonders what people were made of seventy years ago, to be able to drag about such a weight of clothing. Think of the little Queen dancing in several garments of velvet, one lined "throughout" in ermine! Of course, in ordinary life women then wore a much greater weight than they do to-day in cotton garments and petticoats, and so they were somewhat trained to it, but what a waste of strength and energy it implies. I wonder if the small size of women at that period was caused by this burden!

The *Illustrated London News*, which had not long come into being, reported this ball very fully, and

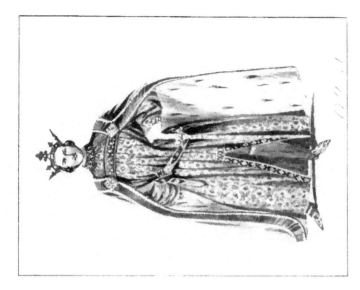

QUEEN VICTORIA AND PRINCE ALBERT IN FANCY DRESS.

From Prints in Mr. A. M. Broadley's Collection.

wishing to embrace the whole family, added the following nonsense : " Besides, there were our future King—*Ich Dien*—and his pretty sister, who had got a glance at the Royal Edward and Philippa on their way to the *bal masqué*. As they lay in their cradles of state the sound of revelry temptingly broke in upon their gentle repose, conjuring the lively *mille et une nuit* dreams of infancy." As "our future King—*Ich Dien*" was only just six months old, I fancy he was scarcely impressed either with the costumes or with the music.

One of the most amusing and graceful skits upon this ball showed the dancers on pantomime horses, the Queen and Prince in the centre, Palmerston as Cupid behind them, Melbourne in cap and bells looking triumphantly at Peel, as though saying : " I am still the favoured one"; Brougham as a Scotch warrior; O'Connell as Bacchus, holding aloft the shillelagh of Repeal and led by his page " Johnny"; Peel in the dress of a leech, dubiously watching the Queen from a corner; and Hume the economist holding up a slate which announces that two and two make four. This was while Peel was still uncertain of his standing with Victoria, and Melbourne was writing frequent letters—quite innocent of politics—to his beloved Sovereign and pupil. It was a neat and witty summing-up of the political relations with Royalty.

Concerning this event two young men, Richard Monckton-Milnes (later Lord Houghton) and Charles Buller, wrote a *jeu d'esprit*, which was taken with enormous seriousness by the people generally. They fabricated a debate in the French Chamber of Deputies and sent it to the *Morning Chronicle*, which published it as "by express." M. Berryer was supposed to have asked in the Chamber, "Whether the French Ambassador (M. de St. Aulaire) in England had been invited to the *bal masqué* to be given by the haughty descendants of the Plantagenets for the purpose of awakening the long-buried griefs of France in the disasters of Crecy and Poictiers and the loss of Calais"; and, "Whether M. de St. Aulaire was going with his *attachés* with bare feet and halters round their necks, representing the unfortunate Burgesses?" M. de Lamartine was supposed to follow, and reproved the speaker for talking of the vilification of France, saying that France could well afford to leave to each people its own historical traditions : "Ah ! let them have their splendid *guinguette*—that people at once so grave and frivolous. Let them dance as they please, as long as the great mind of France calmly and nobly traverses the world." Other members of the Chamber added to this fictitious debate, and M. Guizot closed it with the announcement that the Queen gave the ball because she wished to educate her people by a series of archæological entertainments; but that, in deference to the susceptibilities of France, M. de St. Aulaire would represent the Virgin of Domrémy—he would go as Joan of Arc.

The really funny part of this published joke was that everyone took it seriously. Lord Houghton tells in his "Monographs" that Sir James Graham rushed into Sir Robert Peel's room, crying : "There is the devil to pay in France about this foolish ball!" It was discussed at the Clubs, and translated into the French papers, among which the *Commerce* indignantly protested against allowing the dress of "a woman so cruelly sacrificed to British pride to be worn on such an occasion." Another French paper suggested getting up a ball in Paris at which the Duke of Orleans should be William the Conqueror. The *Irish Pilot* said how strong an evidence of the bad feeling in France against England was this discussion; and the *Dumfries Courier* spoke of the debate "as one of the most erratic and ridiculous scenes that ever lowered the dignity of a deliberative assembly."

Mr. Broadley, in his "Boyhood of a Great King," points out that at this time the French paper *Le National* had a little joke of its own against England, one which the English papers, notably *The Times*, took seriously and reproduced. It was to this effect: "The Government of Queen Victoria, and even her dynasty, have, at this moment, to contend against a kind of opposition which was unexpected, and which in France would appear exceedingly droll. The greater part of the Anglican clergy pretend that the young Prince of Wales, having been baptised by a dissenting Minister, is therefore incapable of ever becoming King of England. In England the head of the State is at the same time head of the Church, and the clergy therefore think that the National Church would lose its priority and even be destroyed if at the head of its hierarchy were to be placed a Prince who had not received orthodox baptism. The Bishop of London and his clergy have already protested against the legitimacy of the succession of the Prince of Wales to the throne; the Bishop of Winchester has followed the example, and not a single clergyman of his diocese has failed to sign his protests. The whole University of Oxford has expressed itself in the same way, and it is announced that the Bishop of Exeter is earnestly and successfully getting up a similar demonstration."

Upon reading this, some wag asked through the papers if the Church was not in danger, seeing that a dissenter had made the Prince of Wales's first pair of breeches.

Lord Campbell complained, in reference to the Poictiers ball, that the Queen's ball was not managed so well as her balls had been when the Whigs were in power—" they were more miscellaneous, and all parties were invited"! It *was* rather sad that he should be called upon at last to meet the despised Tories in Her Majesty's drawing-rooms.

In May, 1845, another fancy ball was given at the Palace, which was distinctly less picturesque than the first, for it illustrated the period from 1740 to 1750, and our proud British aristocracy saw themselves tricked out like Pantaloons, in the ugliest and most absurd costume that ever was invented.

This time the Queen borrowed her clothes from among those of old Queen Charlotte, and appeared in hoop, puffs and frills, powder, and high-heeled shoes. The dress was of gold tissue, brocaded in coloured flowers, green leaves, and silver. It was trimmed with point lace over red ribbon, and looped up with red satin bows, but the bizarre effect of gold and scarlet was spoiled by the broad blue ribbon crossing the mass of colour. The Prince was in crimson and gold, with his Spanish Order of the Golden Fleece as well as the George, and both Queen and Prince put as many brilliants and diamonds as possible upon their garments. At such a ball, which is a spectacle first and a dance next, it seems to me that jewels in number are admissible. It is like a pageant or a pantomime, and the more colour and sparkle the better.

This ball, which included among the guests the Duke and Duchess of Nemours, son of Louis Philippe, was much more criticised than the first, to which people had gone with as much curiosity as pleasure, for now both political and social affairs were more critical. *Punch's* cartoon was entitled, " Children at Play ': Come, dear Nemours, and look at my dolls," in which the Queen was represented with her chief doll, Prince Albert, in her arms, while she is pointing out a number of others in the armchair : Peel, Johnny, Wellington, Lyndhurst—winking over the clothes he is wearing— and others.

George Daniel, the author of " Democritus in London," paid Her Majesty the doubtful compliment of calling this ball a "galvanised resurrection of Monmouth Street masquerading." His description was not quite correct, for the balls he meant were given by the notorious Mrs. Cornelys in a house on the east side of Soho Square, which was sometimes known as Monmouth Square. At this lady's "ticket" balls all the celebrities, including the Prince Regent, used to appear. Old Q. was often seen there, as well as the Duchess of Kingston, who went one night as Iphigenia, "in a state almost ready for the sacrifice," to quote Horace Walpole.

In the same satiric volume are to be found the following lines on this ball :

> "Me a merry Andrew you may
> See at fancy Bal Costumé,
> Figuring with fantastic groups,
> Antique stomachers and hoops,
> High heel'd shoes and stockings roll'd,
> Rouge and diamonds, grease and gold !
> Such as à la mode were reckon'd
> At the Court of George the Second."

But Democritus was right in using the word "galvanised." It was just the spontaneity of youth which was lacking, for the Queen's pleasure was law, and a number of quite respectable and elderly people had to dress up in absurd clothes and pretend to like it. Think of the dear old Duke of Wellington getting hold somehow of a Field Marshal's costume made a hundred years and more earlier, and being announced as the Duke of Cumberland. That he rummaged out the clothes is evident, for the scarlet coat hung loosely about him, and the other things were so baggy that his thin legs seemed lost, and he looked more shrunken and decrepit than anyone had ever before seen him look.

Sir Robert Peel hated dancing with all his might, but he had to dance and try to seem pleased, his one

satisfaction being that the plain Georgian Court dress
which he had chosen made him appear most stately.
Lord Lyndhurst solved the trouble of clothes by
wearing his Chancellor's robes, and being twitted with
the fact, replied : "The Lord Chancellor never dies;
he is always the same."

For some reason Lord Brougham received no invitation, and was in consequence furious, and Brougham
angry was always Brougham talkative.   So on the first
opportunity he attacked the Prince in Parliament concerning Barry, the architect of the new House of Lords,
who would not or could not say when the Lords could
take possession.   As the Prince was Chairman of the
Royal Commission of Fine Arts, Brougham hinted
that Barry was sheltering under the Royal influence, &c.

The Prince had no desire to let any man think he
had a grievance against him, so as an olive-branch Lord
Brougham received a Royal invitation to dinner.   He
accepted and went, but either he got bored or he did
not realise what was expected of him, for, the dinner
over, he calmly left the Castle instead of going with
the rest of the men into the gallery, as everyone was
expected to do, that the Queen might talk with each at
her leisure.   This, of course, annoyed Victoria, who
regarded it as an affront.

Then it was Brougham's turn to be repentant, and
he tried to condone his action by graciously appearing
at the next Drawing Room.   Lord Campbell says that
at this function " again he was unfortunate (although I
really believe he wished to be civil and respectful) by
speaking to the Queen *ex mero motu* as he passed her,

and telling her that 'he was to cross over to Paris in a few days, where he should see Louis Philippe, and that if Her Majesty had any letters or messages for the King of the French it would give him much pleasure to have the honour of being the bearer of them.'" One can imagine Victoria's haughty surprise at this familiarity.

The Polka, which had been working a lively passage from Bohemia through St. Petersburg, Berlin, and Paris, was danced into London by Carlotta Grisè and M. Perrot. Its appearance at Her Majesty's Theatre in 1844 was quickly followed by its adoption in the drawing-room, and though at first Victoria refused to countenance it, she could not resist it long, and it was danced at a State ball in this year. Silly as it sounds, Society went mad over it, and there were polka hats, polka jackets, polka boots, and polka ties. Its praises were sung in the streets and its steps practised at the street corners :

"Oh ! sure the world is all run mad,
  The lean, the fat, the gay, the sad—
All swear such pleasure they never had,
  Till they did learn the Polka.
    First cock up your right leg—so,
    Balance on your left great toe,
    Stamp your heels and off you go
    To the Original Polka O ! ''

My desire to describe the Queen's way of alleviating national distress has put Ireland—the subject of this chapter—in the background, and it is as well to return to it in conclusion.

In 1848 a Galway paper announced that the Queen

had passed Port Patrick on her way to Scotland, and that it was the first sight of Ireland she had ever had. "Have we not reason to complain that Her Majesty will not honour us with a visit? Are we not as loyal and as good as the Scotch? Oh, but then we are the mere Irish! Well! the Queen has actually looked at Ireland; next time we hope she will land on our shores."

In 1849, twelve years after her accession, Victoria and Albert actually did go to Ireland in state, taking the Prince of Wales and the two eldest Princesses with them. They landed in the Cove of Cork that its name might be changed to Queenstown, then went to Waterford Harbour and to Kingstown Harbour. Everyone has heard of the wild enthusiasm, the fervid loyalty, which this visit brought to light in the Irish, who are a people who neither suffer nor rejoice in silence, and everyone has heard of the old lady who cried out: "Och, Queen dear, make one of them Prince Patrick, and all Ireland will die for ye!" Indeed, so hilarious was the joy that it was impossible not to see in it the frantic endeavour of a misjudged and hot-tempered people to prove that at heart they were staunch, though long years of neglect had made them outwardly rebellious. Lord Houghton spoke of it as "idolatrous, utterly unworthy of a free, not to say ill-used, nation." But then Ireland was not and is not free. No dependent country which has to exist under conditions so unfavourable to its agriculture, its commerce, and its social standing as Ireland is a free country.

On re-embarking at Dublin, the Queen sealed her victory over the Irish people by jumping on to the paddle-box of the steamer to wave them a last farewell, and by having the Royal Standard dipped three times that she might do them honour. Thence the Royal party went to Belfast; thence to Loch Ryan, the passage being so rough that the Prince said "the sea was positively unpleasant to look at." Perth, Glasgow, and Balmoral finished their travels.

The visit was, of course, celebrated in song, as in the following, which I have never seen in print, but jot down from oral tradition :

> " When the Queen she came to Dublin,
>   Sure we wished her health to thrive,
> So the darlint Duke of Leinster
>   Thought he'd trate her to a drive.

> "So she got on his outsider,
>   And before they had gone far
> Says she, ' I likes the joltin'
>   Of your Irish jaunting car.' "

After this there was no end to the expressions of affection for their Sovereign from the Irish, who claimed her as a native of their country, saying that Queen Victoria was but another way of writing *Coinne Vochtara*, which in the old Irish meant " chief woman," sovereign, or governing lady. The Irish also declared her to be a descendant of Kenneth MacAlpine, one of the elder dynasts of the Scotic line of Ireland, and that she was indeed Irish enough to have a palace in that green island of her forefathers, among a people always disposed to be as loving and as loyal as the Scots.

The Queen herself had earlier discussed the possibility of having a house in Ireland, but the matter had always been shelved, generally on the score of expense, and Peel had impressed upon her that a house there would turn her into an Irish landlord, and she would in justice have either to exact rents or evict. He did not add that the difficulty or ease of that matter would somewhat depend upon whether she was a good landlord or a bad one, and that Royal good example in that way might do much for the reformation of both Irish landlords and Irish people.

In 1853, the Queen and Prince repeated their visit to Ireland, and again in 1861, when they were received with the same loyalty and goodwill as by the Scotch or any other inhabitants of their dominions.

M

CHAPTER VII

QUEEN VICTORIA AND LOUIS PHILIPPE

UNDER the fatherly guidance of Melbourne the Queen's relations with her Ministers had been cordial and untroubled, but with the advent into her life of Prince Albert a new influence was introduced, and there arose the bitter feeling on the Royal side concerning the Minister for Foreign Affairs—Lord Palmerston, who had in 1840 married Melbourne's sister, the widowed Lady Cowley.

In a way Palmerston was both a great reformer and a great Imperialist, and these two qualities governed his foreign policy. His reforming zeal extended to all countries; his Imperialism was restricted to his own, his eyes being ever upon Europe to guard against any encroachment upon British rights or British prestige. He was also a man of bold methods, one who never willingly let a quarrel get beyond his grip, or waited for an enemy to threaten him. Thus he kept England at peace.

While in power and until 1852, when Pam was dismissed by Victoria,—moved to extremity by her fear and hatred—the only two men in Europe who

really counted were Nicholas of Russia and Lord
Palmerston. For a while after 1852 Nicholas was the
only one—and we had the Crimean War.

The Prince was a very different person from the
Minister. He was intellectual, a student of books
rather than of men, his foreign interest absorbed in
the conglomeration of German States, his outlook
restricted from many causes, temperament, youth,
inexperience, and his bad genius, Baron Stockmar.

All through the two books inspired and revised
by the Queen, Stockmar is mentioned with a fulsome-
ness of praise which by its very irrationality provokes
question. He was an honest, thoughtful, learned,
dilettante politician. He loved the Prince deeply,
and never ceased trying to build up his character.
Like the old-fashioned monthly nurse, he was always
endeavouring to mould his brain by pressure here and
massage there. And the Prince's lack of humour
made him not only take all Stockmar's admonitions
and praises quite seriously, but raised him in his
own estimation above the heads of other men—for
Albert was a doctrinaire rather than a live politician
—and these two got into the habit of thinking that
philosophic conclusions were the only correct conclusions, and when they would not work on current
events, it was put down to the inferiority of those
other men who had to do the labour. In fact,
Stockmar set up with the Prince a small mutual
admiration society, which pronounced itself superior
to the House of Lords and all the politicians in
the Commons.

Thus from the outset it was impossible for the Prince either to like, understand, or even try to understand, Lord Palmerston, for the statesman hid determination under a jest, implacability under wit, and force under a gay manner. "Palmerston is sweet as honey. There is a storm brewing in the Cabinet," said the Prussian Ambassador one day. The Prince was horrified at the statesman's speeches, he could not imagine how laughter could be associated with dignified politics, and he was scandalised at his bold ways.

So it was foreordained that the Minister and the Prince should fall foul of each other, and also that the Queen should uphold all her husband's decisions with her written name, her sympathy and the wonderful strength of her emotions.

Palmerston on his part had always played the courtier to his Queen, though with a touch of irony when discussing serious matters, and he looked upon it as a comedy of State to which he conformed for the sake of convenience, laughing in his sleeve each time that he asked her approval of a despatch, feeling that she would not dare to refuse it.

As well as the royal leaning towards Germany, there were friendly complications with France and with Leopold of Belgium. Thus in considering foreign affairs our Royal pair could never avoid also considering whether an action would hurt Louis Philippe, Leopold, the King of Prussia, the King of Saxony, the Duke of Coburg-Saxe-Gotha, and a fair number of other Saxes. It was quite natural that the two

young people should be loyal friends rather than
astute statesmen; that they should rage when some
cousin felt himself aggrieved by one of their own
servants, that they should be credulous when amity
was offered them, and be ready to swear eternal friendship to the monarch next door.   But when they were at
the most beautiful age of life their quick-brained and
hard-headed Minister was nearing sixty, he had
studied Europe for several decades, he knew its inside
workings better than he knew England, and he had
learnt how to manage it.

At that time what is called the English Constitution
was in a far advanced stage of change.   William IV.
was the last King who arbitrarily dismissed his
Ministers.   The mental incapacity which marked the
later part of the reign of George III., the laziness
of George IV., and the erratic actions of William
IV., had all combined to shift decisive power from
the Throne and place it in the hands of the Government.   Palmerston and his predecessors had quietly
ruled foreign affairs with the help of the Cabinet.
And now came two young creatures, barely grown
up, declaring that the old order must return, that *they*
must decide all that England did, that not a letter
—despatch is the right word—should be sent abroad
before they had seen it, and either approved or
altered it.   As Palmerston once pointed out, twenty-
seven thousand despatches went out from his office
each year.   To which Albert blandly retorted that
those despatches had also to pass before the Prime
Minister and the Queen.   It meant that five hundred

letters were sent abroad each week; these had to be considered, thought out and written in the Foreign Office; sent to Windsor, Osborne or Balmoral for Royal scrutiny, then returned endorsed or altered, some to be again returned to the Queen and sent back once more; a very unnecessary proceeding for the majority of these documents, and one which must have made the work almost impossible. That was, however, but the lightest of the troubles. A worse one was that for years Pam had been practically sole dictator in the Foreign Office, and now the young rulers demanded that he should on all occasions bend his will to theirs and follow their policy, which was often monarchical and Tory, while he was a member of a Liberal Cabinet. The Prince had a slow and ultra-cautious mind, which would let an opportunity slip while considering possibilities, whereas Palmerston knew what to do at once. So when a quick decision was needed Pam often made it without waiting for Victoria-Albert.

As a young man Pam had been so handsome that his college friends dubbed him Cupid, and he always was a dandy, being vain enough, it was said, to rouge when he was old, though this scarcely fits in with the fact that when out of office and in the country he would spend two or three hours in the early morning rowing on the Thames, having first had a long swim in its waters. He was also very keen on horses, and considered the Derby as a sacred institution, and that it was an unwritten law that Parliament should rise on Derby Day. He always rode to Epsom, and it was not until the last year of his life that he had to drive. Watching that last race, and seeing Gladiateur going ahead, he whispered to a friend :

" If the foreigner wins I shall not live through the year."

The foreigner did win, and in a few months Cupid was no more.

His social manners were as charming as were those of his wife, who was the best hostess in London, as well as one of the most beautiful women, and she knew exactly how to support Pam through any difficulty, her parties being famous for the way in which inimical people would—through her sweetness and kindness—become reconciled.

For some years not only Palmerston, but the Queen and Prince, were so engrossed in French affairs that they must have a place here, and really they offered a pretty little comedy, one which turned, however, to tragedy for the French King.

Louis Philippe, the July King, the King of the Barricades, the Citizen King, the " Pecksniff of France " (as Mr. Broadley aptly names him), in fact, the man of many undesired titles and of definite ambitions, felt it a very important matter that his neighbour, the young Queen of Spain, should marry someone who would strengthen his power, say the Duc d'Aumale, his fourth son. On the other hand, the Queen of England felt a distinct interest in the Spanish Queen's marriage, and the question was whether France and England should agree or disagree.

Spain's nominal ruler was Isabella, who had been born in 1830. The actual ruler up to 1840 was her mother, Christina, who had no talent for governing, and who occupied herself in bringing up a large family of illegitimate children. By the time she married their father, Munoz, and gave him the title of Duke of Rianzares, her quiver was full with eight. It was Christina who gravely declared, when she was forced to resign her responsibilities as Regent, that she had done as much as she could to be the mother of the Spaniards.

Before she was banished in 1840, like a far-seeing mother, if not like a good woman, she had been making a nest warm, for which she had stripped the Royal Palaces of their most valuable furniture. The Crown jewels had disappeared, some having been carried away in twelve bottles labelled Old Madeira, and others having been tied in sheets and packed up as parcels. The gold and silver lace had been taken off all the Court liveries and melted down, while carpets and things that could not well be taken away had been sold.

The chief possessions Christina had left her little Queen-daughter, to judge by those mentioned in the report of the commission of inquiry which duly followed, were "eleven chemises of very ordinary linen" and six pairs of darned cotton stockings which hurt her legs, for Isabella suffered from eczema. The Queen had not a single *parure;* in all her Royal residences she could count but three silver inkstands, and with the exception of a few forks and spoons, not only all the silver, but all the plate had disappeared, so that the Queen had to be served on varnished tin.

Isabella was not what in England would be described as a "nice child," for at that age she knew more of primitive human life than many respectable old women, and one of her Court ladies said :

" There is not perhaps a child in Spain more inclined to lying and dissimulation."

However, this infant was declared of age and became Queen in her own right at thirteen, and long before that people were discussing her future husband. Louis Philippe gazed longingly beyond the Pyrenees, and sounded far and deep for indications of the possibility of marrying his son, the Duc d'Aumale, to the Queen of Spain. However, no one approved of it, absolutely no one but himself and his family, and he was so far convinced of this that though the plan was not dropped until six months later, he assured Queen Victoria in September, 1843, that he would not dream of marrying one of his sons to Isabella. He added, though, that it would please him to see another son of his, the Duc de Montpensier, betrothed to the Infanta.

While the King of France had had his finger on the pulse of Europe in regard to settling the Spanish Queen in safe domestic bonds, Queen Christina is credited with hoping that her daughter would marry a Coburg. Various members of that family were suggested, Prince Ernest, Albert's brother, was the first, and when he married someone else, Prince Leopold,

cousin to our Saxe-Coburg and youngest brother to
the King of Portugal, was considered the most
eligible. Thus while Louis Philippe was dreaming of
a crown for Aumale, Prince Albert was having his
cousin on a visit to Windsor, and discussing his future
castle in Spain. So it was honestly rumoured and
believed in Paris that "the most illustrious personage
in the British Isles" was personally very anxious to
promote this Coburg marriage, with the result that the
Tuileries was in a flutter of anger, which was not
rendered less when Leopold of Belgium, on being
applied to, sided with his blood-relations against his
father-in-law.

It is curious in studying the ways of Royalty to see
that crowned heads have their little methods of
administering to each other a snub or a social
insult which cannot be resented. Thus the then three
great Powers, Russia, Prussia, and Austria, did not
for years recognise the Queen of Spain; they looked
over her head, trying to believe she was not there.
Louis Philippe, too, and after him his successor, knew
that they were not thought respectable enough to be
admitted to full European society.

For this reason the Citizen King was ever casting
about to secure allies, thinking that the best way to do
this was to marry his children judiciously, and if the
big people would not have him, surely it was better
to seek the friendship of the small ones than of none.
So his daughter Louise married Leopold of Belgium,
his daughter Clementine married Prince Augustus of
Saxe-Coburg, his son Nemours married Princess

Victoria of Saxe-Coburg, and de Joinville married Francesca, sister of the Queen of Portugal. But he hungered for the support of a great Power, such as England, a friendship which would be powerful enough to put stability into a throne which had never ceased trembling since he had occupied it. To obtain his desire he induced his daughter Louise of Belgium to urge Queen Victoria to make the advance, and though it took time, at last the aloofness of England gave way, and the two princes, Aumale and Joinville, were invited on a visit to the Queen in August, 1843.

Once having moved, the natural impetuosity of our Victoria carried her away, and she and her husband decided that there was nothing so satisfactory as a talk, it was better than fifty letters; and that they would run over to France and quietly discuss the relative merits of a Coburg and a French bridegroom. But it was only to be a kind of unpremeditated friendly visit, a nice little holiday with no idea of State about it. As Gilbert A'Beckett wrote at the time :

> "Prince Albert is a famous prince,
>   Of honour and renown,
> The worthy husband eke is he
>   Of one who wears a crown.
> Prince Albert's spouse said to her dear,
>   ' Though wedded we have been
> Three years and something more, yet we
>   No holiday have seen."

The Queen wished for no fuss over this visit, but she discussed it with Peel, who had to report the matter to the Cabinet, and she put a hypothetical case to the Duke of Wellington. The latter said that she could not possibly go out of England without appointing a Regent, for precedent was too sacred to be ignored; so she turned to the Law Lords, who reported that there was no law upon the subject, and that she was free to do as she wished. Melbourne, to whom she confided her plans, gave her fatherly advice, fearing what her impulsiveness might do.

"Do not let them make any treaty or agreement there; it can be done elsewhere just as well. . . . Lord Melbourne cannot refrain from earnestly recommending Your Majesty to take care about landing and embarking, and not do it in dangerous places and awkward coasts." His was the one personal touch; he best knew how easily the Queen might be influenced by a subtle and crafty mind, and also he felt for her an almost paternal love, which would guard her in the smallest as well as the greatest way. So with no more preliminaries, at the beginning of September, 1843, the Royal yacht *Victoria and Albert*, with the Queen and Prince, Lord Aberdeen acting as chaperon, slipped quietly down the Thames and round Kent to Tréport, leaving the Duke of Wellington staring after them with annoyance and incredulity, saying:

"I did not believe in her going until two days before she went. Peel persisted afterwards that he had told me of it; but I know I never heard it, and it was not a thing to have escaped me if I had."

Louis Philippe was not quite sure of it either until shortly before the visit was paid. However, he had time to make domestic arrangements, one of which, the papers announced, was to secure a large quantity of what was believed in France to be the favourite food of the English people—cheese and beer!

Peel wrote to Aberdeen: "I see that for the purpose of doing honour to his Royal visitors and their companions, he—Louis Philippe—sent a very large order to England for cheese and bottled beer. I hope you will have had calm weather that you may enjoy all these delicacies."

But the general report did not arise from this letter —which, Sir Sidney Lee says, was a jest—as it was not published until long afterwards; it was itself the effect of the announcements made in the papers, being naturally a tit-bit for the comic journals, broadsheets, and cartoonists. Gilbert A'Beckett in the *Comic Album* declared that Louis Philippe, putting fifty francs into the hands of a servant:

> "Orders him instantly to look about
> For lots of English cheese and stout.
> 'Tis done, the Monarch of the French
> Anxious Victoria's thirst to quench
> On coming from the briny water,
> Has laid in stores of bottled porter.
> Also her hunger to appease,
> A massive hill of Cheshire cheese."

The cartoon accompanying this represented an enormous cheese upon the shore, flanked by black bottles, before which the Queen gaily dances with her host, while Prince Albert, looking very uncertain upon his feet, and with his arm round the waist of one of the Princesses, is expressing his satisfaction in telling glances.

Another cartoon shows the Royal party seated round a table-cloth on the grass. Louis Philippe sits opposite Queen Victoria, a vulgar, dumpy little figure, while Prince Albert, having been very sick on the voyage, is in the distance leaning against a tree, his hat on the ground before him. Servants are running to and fro with bottles of stout and plates of bread and cheese. This is an example of the coarse and vulgar in caricature, there being at that day nothing between such and drawings in which the spirit of caricature was shown in the subject and words only, not in the drawing. An example of the latter was a representation, in perfect likeness, of these five people round a table, upon which the only food was stout and bread and cheese. In this Albert says, with a pleasant smile to the French Queen : " Lettere me perswader Your Majesty to do as we Englishmans do, drink out of de Pewtare." To which Amélie responds languishingly : " Ah, Monsieur Albert, you do always persuader me to every ting." Victoria meanwhile is holding the handle of a pewter-pot, and of her Louis Philippe asks : " Does Your Majesty prefer porter to *vin ordinaire*? " drawing the reply : " Oh, porter by all means ! Your health, Phil ! "

Louis Philippe was as careful of the method of the Queen's landing as even Lord Melbourne could have wished, and she came ashore with as much ease, though scarcely in the same way, as H. B. in an amusing cartoon foreshadowed. He pictured the French King standing at the edge of a wide stream, watching a plump duck, with the face of Queen Victoria, followed

by a drake and other ducks, with the physiognomies of
Prince Albert and her Ladies, all paddling towards
him.   On the other shore stand the cock (the Duke
of Wellington) and the old hen (Sir Robert Peel)
eagerly surveying the scene.

A'Beckett gives us his own account of the meeting;
an account supported by several contemporary caricatures.   Says A'Beckett:

> "Victoria touches foreign ground,
> Saluting all the circle round,
> The King, delighted by her charms,
> Raises her in his royal arms,
> And kisses her on both her cheeks,
> As if she had been his guest for weeks.
> Prince Albert with a languid air,
> And suffering from the *mal de mer*,
> With hat and face extremely white
> Commences doing the polite."

That Louis kissed Her Majesty with great cordiality
was a fact that gave joyful opportunity to the caricaturists, while the more sober-minded were inclined to
echo the words put in the mouth of Lord Aberdeen:

"Hold hard there, that's not English manners!"
Lord Adolphus Fitzclarence, the Captain of the
Victoria and Albert, is shown valiantly drawing his
sword, while all but one sailor look aghast.

As a matter of fact, the Royal party was taken
from the yacht to the shore in the French King's
barge, and was given a magnificent reception at the
Château d'Eu.   Five days were passed there in *fêtes
champêtres*, in concerts, and in dramatic performances,
and our Royal lady was introduced to that novel
carriage, the char-á-banc.

The Queen obeyed her beloved Melbourne in so far as no papers were signed, though she talked over with her host the matrimonial prospects of the little Spanish Queen, and gave a verbal promise that Leopold of Coburg should be withdrawn as a candidate for Isabella if Louis Philippe would not allow Montpensier to marry the Infanta until her sister was not only married but had issue. Aberdeen and Guizot also discussed the same subject, the former being far too yielding, and, according to a letter written by Albert to his brother, promising so much to Guizot that the French Minister was more or less justified in his further scheming. Lord Aberdeen was the adviser whom Victoria and Albert loved, because he agreed with their short-sighted plans, and so flattered them; yet his action at " the unfortunate meeting at Eu " brought about the storm which later agitated the two countries, and set Europe laughing with relief.

The life at the Château d'Eu was well calculated to attract Queen Victoria, for it was natural, gay, and troubled with very little ceremonial; yet though we are always told that she enjoyed natural, unaffected family life, there was probably no one in the château who could dispense with ceremony with more difficulty, as the following incident shows :

Louise of Belgium had told her mother that Queen Victoria always drank a glass of iced water at ten o'clock, so at that precise hour an attendant brought a carafe and two glasses on a tray, and offered them to the Royal visitor, who promptly refused the drink, so the tray was put on the table. Queen Amélie whispered to her son, Joinville, and he, pouring some water into a glass, offered it to Her Majesty, upon which she took the glass and drank the water. One morning two young Princes, the Comte de Paris and another, climbed a peach-tree, and offered the fruit to the Queen. She took it pleasantly from them, but there was something about her manner which made the lad turn to Lady Cowley, saying, " I fear that your Queen finds us a little too rough."

Prince Albert was evidently at this time the subject of some suspicion as to the attentions he showed to fair ladies, for over and over again he is pilloried in a too tender attitude towards one who is not the Queen. Victoria protested so much as to his devotion to herself that the temptation is to think that there was some truth in these innuendoes. Thus H. H. gave to the public a crowded picture of the great picnic in the Forest of Eu, showing Louis Philippe sitting on the grass, with his back to a tree, toasting Queen Victoria, who is on his right, Queen Amélie being on his left, and a large company gathered about. Beyond the trunk of the tree, gazing furtively round to see if his young wife is looking, is Prince Albert, with his arm round a girl's waist. Louis Philippe jovially pledges Victoria in the words : " May this be the worst day of our lives ! " To which she, her wistful eyes upon her errant husband, replies : " With all my heart, Phil."

Another drawing of the sort by another artist depicted the soldiers drawn up in line, the French King proudly marching away with Victoria, who, looking

N

back, cries with agitation : " Good gracious ! if Albert
is not stopping to talk with that military-looking
female ! " Albert himself is chucking under the chin
a *vivandière*, who offers him a glass of milk, and
saying : " I wish such a pretty *cantinière* vas in my
regiment ! "—which draws the remark from a Frenchman looking on : " His Royal Highness seems quite
smitten ! "

Another cartoon on the same subject, but much
coarser in type, makes an immense soldier tap the
Prince warningly on the shoulder as he admires in
languishing fashion a camp girl.

The people of France, being suspicious and jealous,
were not quite so pleased as was their Sovereign with
the English visit. They asked that question which has
been the subject of fun through the ages : " If she is
so gracious, what does she want ? " One report ran
that she was determined to make Louis sign a treaty
of commerce, binding the nation to buy English cotton
thread and British iron ; and a cartoon from a French
point of view showed Victoria mesmerising the King
in the presence of Prince Albert and Aberdeen—
Guizot in alarm shaking his master's shoulder to arouse
him—in order that he may sign the commercial treaty
which lies on the table, having been carried over by
Victoria in the lining of her parasol.

After five days came the inevitable farewell, " and
the Queen's spirits fell when it was over," as Sir
Sidney Lee reports. *Punch* tells us that on taking
leave of her Royal host Her Majesty looked for the
first time rather sad, and then, fearing to cast gloom

on others, added : " Je vais m'éclaircir " (I am going to brighten = Brighton).

Another picture shows her marching down to the boat on the shore, Prince Albert following, meekly laden with chocolate and presents for the children, while Louis Philippe stands on the stage above, his face hidden in his handkerchief :

> " He would not embitter one moment her stay,
>   Nor send her when going, in sadness away ;
>   He hears the guns sounding, he sees her depart,
>   And can't repress longer the grief of his heart."

Prince Albert's supposed letter of thanks to his host, written in a sort of French verse, might give good exercise to young students of that language, for however queer the French, the sound of the translation will be correct :

> " L'ancre est pesé, la vapeur est en haut ;
>   L'écorce est sur la crinière,
> Le vent du levain souffle comme il faut,
>   Et feuilles la France par derrière.
> Louis Philippe, nos marins sont une planche,
>   Et disent que vous êtes un atout,
> Ils souhaitent avant que nous croissons la Manche
>   De dire un bon par à vous,
> Nous allons prendre le gage du Père Mathieu,
>   Les casseurs sont à tête ; adieu Louis, adieu ! " [1]

The Queen left Eu with a feeling of real affection in her heart for her very attentive host, and Louis Philippe was more than pleased with the visit, for it

[1] Écorce = bark (of a tree) ; crinière = mane ; levain = yeast = east ; une planche = a board ; un atout = a trump ; un bon par = a good by ; le gage du Père Mathieu = Father Mathew was at that time preaching temperance in Hyde Park ; les casseurs sont à tête = the breakers are ahead.

was the first time that he had been admitted into the pale of the legitimate monarchs, and he hoped for great things from that admission.

From Eu the Queen and her Consort went to Brighton, where the Royal children were staying, and after a few days there, sailed on to Belgium, entering a social atmosphere absolutely the reverse of that they had breathed at Eu, for Leopold had not grown more generous with age, and his people were too phlegmatic to rejoice with anything but caution at the visit of the Queen of England. Leopold's home was noted for its gloom, the King being egotistical and too much troubled about small things ever to indulge in a laugh, while Louise was too devout and too suppressed to be joyful.

Victoria kept her good spirits there, and thought the visit a happy one. She and Leopold were a curious pair. In their letters they professed the deepest devotion to each other, the Queen saying that, excepting Albert, she loved Leopold and Louise better than anyone in the world (alas! poor Duchess of Kent). Yet there were black spots in their intercourse when Victoria-Albert commented upon Leopold's constant absence from his kingdom and also upon other things, the youthful pair considering that their position justified the tutoring of a fatherly relative; so Leopold was never allowed to forget that he was a much more insignificant person than the niece he had succoured as a baby. On his part he had no relish for his visits to England, Louise, writing on one occasion to her brother that one consolation for her

husband's illness was that *la corvée* (literally, toil
demanded by a superior of a peasant) of a journey to
England would be spared her husband, who liked
neither Windsor nor the life there.

For the jovial five days at Eu, Victoria and Albert
had to pay the price. The great European countries
were angry, and Nicholas of Russia was particularly
suspicious, thinking that an Anglo-French alliance
must mean an Anglo-Russian quarrel. Hoping to
dissipate this dissatisfaction, the most royal preparations were made at Windsor to receive the Grand
Duke Michael, who visited England in October.

That visit upset Louis Philippe, who almost shed
tears also over the projected stay of the Duc de
Bordeaux in London. This Duke was the second
son of Charles X., and was regarded as Louis's rival,
being called by his followers Henri V. Prussia
had defied France and received the young man in all
friendship, so Louis Philippe's heart trembled lest
Victoria should do the same thing, and he wrote
pointing out that if she *did* receive Bordeaux all the
good he himself had gained from her visit would be
annihilated. Victoria-Albert, however, filled with the
glamour of the new friendship exclaimed with horror
at the idea that they could show politeness to one whom
Louis Philippe feared. So they sent urgent invitations to the Nemours, pressing them to come to
Windsor, that their presence might excuse discourtesy
to the son of a king.

Thus the young man, while in England, was cut
by Royalty, though fêted by many of the nobles, in

spite of the fact that all official people were forbidden to receive him, and that even his personal friends in Scotland and in England were approached by Lord Aberdeen, at the Royal command, with the desire that they should ignore him. Albert quite plainly showed the reason for all this when he wrote : " No good can come from the reception (of the Duke by the Queen), *and the King of the French must prefer its not taking place.*"

While the Queen-Prince were thus humouring Louis Philippe, he himself was gleefully rubbing his hands and trying—in spite of his protestations—to arrange the marriage between his son Aumale and Queen Isabella, until at last he was convinced of the futility of the idea. He had indeed given evidence of his easy morality when, during his stay in England, he frankly said in conversation that he did not understand either the necessity of keeping good faith nor having merchant-minds like the English, a saying which Queen Victoria did not forget later.

But before then many things happened, and the sound of war seemed ever murmuring in the ears of both nations, the fact being that Louis and his people had different aims. He wanted to ensure to himself and his family wealth, position and stability, while the French did not care a rap for him. They very much preferred to indulge in their emotions, and one of the strongest of those emotions was hatred of the English, intensified by their suspicions concerning the recent *Entente Cordiale.* The French were, in fact, spoiling for war. There was trouble in Morocco between the two countries, and in Otaheite, of which the French Commander of the Fleet took possession, clapping the British Consul into prison.   The French refused a treaty of commerce, and also refused to let British linen and cotton goods enter their country. The Prince de Joinville, who had made great friends with Lord Adolphus Fitzclarence when at Eu, deliberately cut him dead in the streets of Paris; and in May, 1844, published a pamphlet upon the French fleet, with such pointed reference to English ships, that some people looked upon it as a threat of war.

Through it all Victoria-Albert stuck to the French King, making excuses for de Joinville on the score of youth, etc., which drew the not surprising opinion from a member of the Austrian Embassy that the Queen's friendship for France was a piece of morbid sentimentalism.   Europe looked on hopefully, believing that, after all, the alliance in the West might not prove to be dangerous; and the Czar Nicholas determined not only to come and see for himself, but to obtain some of that English friendship which was supposed to be a panacea for international troubles. Then he carried out his resolve as secretly and suddenly as he believed that the visit to Eu had been made.

Queen Victoria had arranged a pleasant family visit from the King and Queen of Saxony, and was horribly astonished and flustered by the news that the Russian bear was almost at her doors.   She had to alter arrangements and fêtes, try to find a State bedroom for the autocrat by putting some of the Saxon suite into the attics, and it was necessary for the time to let the Saxon King, who arrived in London the same day as Nicholas, stand in the background.

With the Emperor's visit I am not concerned. He saw all the people he wanted to see, except John Russell and most of the other discarded Liberal Ministers; he went to Ascot and to a number of parties, dinners, luncheons and reviews. At a review at Windsor he had the opportunity of seeing some of the troops reprimanded and dismissed. The Queen disliked firing when expecting the birth of an infant, but the orders to the troops not to fire had been somehow mismanaged, and they gave a grand salute on her arrival, for which the Duke of Wellington angrily sent them off the field. The Emperor also saw how few were the troops that could be gathered together quickly, and when the Queen apologised for this he answered, with courtly kindness:

"Madame, your troops are exceedingly good, very superior to mine, which cannot be compared to them. But such as mine are, they are always and in all circumstances at the disposition of your Majesty."

In what a thoroughly grim manner this compliment was proved true ten years later, we all know.

There was one thing which astonished him, autocrat though he was, and that was the servility shown to the Queen, not only by the Household servants, but by all who came into contact with her in her home.

The Emperor, tall, inclined to be fat, bald, with horrible eyes, which might have been good but for

THE EMPEROR NICHOLAS I. OF RUSSIA

his habit of so raising the lids as to show white above the pupils, yet with a perfect profile, who could only talk of politics or military affairs, was not the man to prove attractive to women; and yet Court ladies clustered round him with admiration and a desire for notice which must have wearied the monarch who had no respect for their kind. He who had caused Polish women to be knouted; who, capturing a convent of over fifty nuns, had, because of their religion, given them as prisoners to his Cossacks, from whom they each received fifty lashes every week, and endured such other barbarities that only three survived by escaping, what could such a man care about women, however much he might pay respect to fine feathers?

However, he accepted the adulation, and was careful before leaving Windsor to bestow a large number of presents. Two thousand pounds he thought not too much to divide among the servants at the Castle, while to the pleased housekeeper of that Royal abode he gave a diamond parure worth a thousand pounds. The Lords of the Household had the regulation snuff-boxes with the Emperor's portrait set in diamonds, the equerries and grooms boxes of somewhat less value, while rings, watches, and brooches were freely bestowed. He touched the hearts of the people by contributing £500 to the Nelson statue, the same to the Wellington statue, and assigned that sum annually to buying a cup for Ascot; there were sums for the poor, for the German Hospital; and to prove how far his bribing capacity would carry him, he actually had the effrontery to offer £500 to the Polish Ball—a ball, tickets for which were sold at a guinea, got up to relieve the thousands of Polish refugees who had fled from their country to escape his tyranny. Lord Dudley Stuart, who was helping to arrange the ball, naturally refused this offer.

If Russia had felt particularly annoyed at the visit of Queen Victoria to Eu, Louis Philippe was in despair at the visit of Nicholas to England, for he wanted England for his own bosom friend, and no rivals. The vexation was not confined to the King, every member in the Tuileries felt it; the Queen saying with a grimace of disgust to Lady Cowley, our Ambassador's wife : " So the autocrat has arrived."

Again came threats of war between England and France over the French occupation of Mogador. However, once more matters were smoothed out, and Louis came over to England in October, of which event Charles Greville grumbled : " These Royal intimacies strike me as being very unnecessary, and calculated to lead sooner or later to inconvenience and embarrassment."

His Majesty was keenly anxious to get the English hallmark of distinction, the Order of the Garter, so he came, bringing Montpensier with him, for whose marriage to the Infanta he was already scheming. Prince Albert met them at the steamer, and drove with them to Windsor, placing himself in the carriage by the side of the King, and leaving his younger guest to sit with his back to the horses, which was popularly commented on as not very civil. The Queen made amends, however, for on their arrival at the Castle she went to the very doorstep to meet her visitors, extending her arms in the most cordial way while Louis Philippe descended, and then they embraced most affectionately, she giving him two kisses on either cheek. The usual entertainments took place, the English people showing as much cordiality to Louis as they did to the Russian Emperor, and everyone, high and low, talking a tremendous amount of humbug.

Louis was most gorgeously installed as a member of the Order of the Garter under the introduction of Prince Albert and the Duke of Cambridge, and he earnestly replied in response to the condition : "You will enter into no unjust war?" "To that I will heartily pledge myself!" A pledge which, as far as England was concerned, he meant to keep, though it is quite certain that he was making a promise which his subjects at least were eager to break, for the Paris papers were full of abuse of him because of this visit.

Jasper Judge tells in his Louis Philippe book that Victoria, visiting one of the French ships, liked some cakes extremely, and a parcel of them were sent to the Royal yacht. When the messenger saw a woman on the yacht's deck dressed in a "common-looking black gown, dark bonnet, and plain red woollen shawl," he held out the packet, saying, "Take it, miss; they are cakes for the Queen. Take care of them! Now mind, do not fail to give them her." It was the Queen herself, and she laughed heartily over the mistake.

CHAPTER VIII

THE QUEEN AND THE SPANISH MARRIAGES

WITH the downfall of Peel in 1846 the complacent Aberdeen gave way to the truculent Palmerston, and Guizot, knowing the man, and knowing too that he would never endorse his predecessor's vague and pleasant promises, began to work with a will. He was determined that France should get something out of Spain, and that the Coburg Prince should get nothing. Into the details of the squabble and the intriguing I need not enter. Leopold of Coburg did not want to marry the Queen. She was rough, un-educated, plain, and troubled with eczema, but he was ready to do so if the Powers willed it. The other suitors were the girl's own uncle, Count Trapani, who, thought to be dangerous, was ruled out, and her two cousins, Francisco and Enrique. Francisco seems to have been a perfect horror, with a large, white face and short, square nose, weakly in health, an imbecile, and incapable of being the father of children. Duke Ernest of Coburg declares in his Memoirs that the man who was forced upon Isabella as a husband was no man. " It was everywhere spoken about and jested over." This was perhaps the reason why the English were so angry over the match, the poor little Queen being so obviously sacrificed to French intrigue. She would quite pleasantly have taken the younger boy Enrique, but in the end was forced to take the youth whom she loathed. Her mother, Christina, who had unfortunately become far too much of a tool to Louis Philippe, was herself filled with disgust at the idea of Francisco, and tried to get the healthy, clean young Leopold for the girl. But at the silly Eu conference Victoria and Albert had promised to withdraw the Coburg youth, and when appealed to they refused to break that promise, so French tactics won. On coming into power, Palmerston, not having been told of all that had passed between Christina and others, wrote to Spain that he hoped the Queen would choose between her three suitors, Francisco, Enrique and Leopold. Then when Guizot wrote to him, he was obliged to lose three weeks before he could answer the letter, because his Queen, who was at the time cruising about the Western coasts, was insistent that she should have all despatches sent back and forth to her. These two facts gave Guizot his chance. Crying that England was cheating, and that Palmerston refused to answer his letters, he said that he and his master were relieved from all promises, so he forced Christina to force the deadly Francisco upon Isabella under threat of a single life for years to come. At the same time he demanded the hand of the Infanta for the Duke de Montpensier, and all the indecisions, the pourparleyings, and intriguings were over. Instead of the Montpensier marriage being deferred until the Queen of Spain had children it took place directly after that of the Queen, and then the arch-plotter Guizot and the half-fearing, half-delighted Louis Philippe, had to face the music.

It was said that Isabella went to her marriage looking white and sad, while her duped and duping mother "was radiant with smiles, and looked very handsome;" but Montpensier was the sad partner at his wedding, while the Infanta was quite taken with him. The Spaniards, however, hated the French, hated the marriage, and hated the young Prince, who gained nothing from his match, for Isabella was not only ready to take a favourite, but had one forced upon her by her Government, who were determined that Spanish heirs should be born to the throne, if only to keep the French at arm's length.

As for Victoria-Albert and Louis Philippe, as a near relative rudely said, "a fit of ill-temper had broken out amongst the confederates at Eu over the mad marriage affair." The Queen blamed Louis Philippe, Albert blamed Bulwer, the English Ambassador at Madrid, and the King of the Belgians laid the whole burden on the back of Palmerston. Guizot took the virtuous attitude. "Of what do you complain?" he said to Lord Normanby in Paris, "I told you that the two marriages should not take place at the same time, I told you the truth, for that of the Queen was solemnised an hour before the other." Even the French papers derided his words as a *pasquinade* which was a disgrace to the man who uttered it.

The three great Powers watched with delight this rupture between England and France, and in England feeling ran riot to such an extent that many would have liked war, though the Duke of Wellington summed up "the pother about Spain" as "all d——d stuff."

Victoria was furiously angry, considering that her dear friend had not only been guilty of a low, dishonest political intrigue, but had forfeited his word of honour *to her personally*, while pretending the most sincere friendship. She refused to allow the picture of himself, which he had sent her, to be hung, and it was reported that she ordered all her portraits and busts of him to be put in the lumber attics. The matter was aggravated by the fact that Louis Philippe was afraid to write to her; his wife made the communication for him, doing it with a wonderful *naïveté*, talking of her eagerness to impart the news of the engagement, and how they were overwhelmed with joy, as the happiness of their dear son would be assured by it, and because another daughter would be added to the family, for whom she begged Her Majesty's friendship.

The Queen answered coldly, with a reminder of what had been said at Eu, of the zeal with which she and Prince Albert had worked to maintain the *Entente Cordiale*, and of the way in which they had refused to help one of their own family to marry the Spanish Queen.

Though there was much correspondence on this matter Louis Philippe never wrote to Victoria, trying to maintain the attitude of being unjustly dealt with.

" I am induced to think that the good little Queen was as sorry to write the letter (one to Louise of Belgium on the subject) as I was to read it. But now she sees things only through the spectacles of Lord Palmerston, and these distort the truth too often," he wrote. In another letter he accused her of being resentful. So though Victoria kept her dignity and resented bitterly the idea that she had shown resentment, it was really a pretty little quarrel, and one which was cheered on by the French and English people. The former made Coburg their gibe, and from one end to the other of France " the marrying family " was again the subject of talk, article and song. It was said that Ferdinand of Portugal had, despite the internal wars and national shortage of food, sent large sums of money to the King of the Belgians to invest for him. The whole array of Coburgs sprinkled about Europe was brought up for public inspection, and Prince Albert who, like his uncle Leopold, felt anger when subjected to cartoon or criticism, suffered constant pricks to his pride.

The English retaliated with all vigour, and *Punch*, as chief spokesman, delightedly represented the French King as the central figure in its clever cartoons. He appeared in the jester's pages as Fagin, teaching his boys how to steal the coronetted handkerchief out of his pocket; as royally presenting Victoria and the King of Prussia with half an oyster shell, he having swallowed the oyster; as defeating Leopold of Coburg in a tournament, singing, after disposing of Prince Trapani :

"' Ha, ha ! I guess that's one the less ! Now, Sir Coburg, for
  you ! '
And he tipped his lance with gold, for well his foe's weak
  point he knew ;
A rush, a thrust—a cloud of dust—and when it left the air
There lay the Coburg, dead to ' time,' and much the worse
  for wear."

Then we have him as a matador, the *Entente
Cordiale* wrapped round his arm, smilingly advancing
to stab the (John) Bull.   In another picture he stands
smug and smiling with cannon balls beneath his feet
and pictures of tragedies in Spain, Tangiers, Algiers,
Ferrara and Italy round him.   For this woodcut
Punch was banished from France.   Then are shown
the Emperors of Russia and Austria, and the King of
Prussia, "dancing the last cracovienne" upon the
Treaty of Vienna, and finally Louis Philippe tripped
up and sitting down "hard and sudden," while the
three monarchs look on.   But the bitterest of all was
one showing him as Fagin manacled in prison : "A
proud man without honour, a rich man without friends."

Louis evidently had meant it when he said that he
could not see what good faith had to do with politics,
and had not anticipated any real trouble with England.
He became more and more disturbed at his want of
success with Victoria, and by the end of the year the
papers declared that he was obsessed by the idea.
He rose in the morning determined to regain the
English alliance ; he passed the hours calculating how
best to piece together the broken friendship ; he
foamed at the rancour of Palmerston, and wept over
the unkindness of Victoria ; he summoned his Minis-

o

ters, he consulted and wheedled the English Ambassador, and, it was declared, that as a last resource he fee'd Brougham to champion him. Then, being piqued at the utter futility of it all, he would turn cold to England. Not being able to win he must hate, not being able to cajole he must calumniate. And so he ended his day by swearing lustily at John Bull.

The Spanish business might have been of international importance had Europe been in a healthier condition; as it was, it was almost a personal matter. Victoria and Albert had tried to guide foreign politics and had failed, because they and their Minister were too pleasant and yielding. Had it not been for their promises, Isabella might have had a decent life with some other bridegroom, as it was, she was miserable for years, though she became the mother of six children, who for purposes of State it was deemed advisable to regard as Francisco's.

While Louis Philippe was seeking to renew the friendship with Victoria, the French were amusing themselves with stories of Palmerston, and English people learned from one of their papers that Lord Palmerston had called a meeting of Whigs and Tories at the "Crown and Anchor" (presumably in London) to explain to them what he had done and what he meant to do with regard to the Spanish marriages, and to utter a maudlin tirade on the love he felt for the power and glory of his native land. Another French paper said he had sent invitations to several members of the Parisian Jockey Club to attend a fox-hunt that he proposed to give in Piccadilly!

Victoria wanted to blame Palmerston for what had happened, but could not, as she agreed with the result of his policy; though later she and Albert did not scruple to declare that the whole trouble was caused by him. So does prejudice colour our reason!

The Queen had accepted her new Government with fear, for her love for Whiggism had gone like smoke. She thought Lord John was weak, and *Punch's* well-known cartoon of Russell as a very little man dressed in Peel's clothes, drawing the remark from his Sovereign of "Well! it is not the best fit in the world, but we'll see how he goes on!" thoroughly described the situation. She said of her new statesmen the day after the Cabinet was fixed: "There is much less respect and much less high and pure feeling," adding, however, that she and Albert "had contrived to get a very respectable Court," alluding to those officials who had to be changed with the Government. All her fear of Palmerston returned, and she wanted to give him the Colonial Office. She was so credulous even then—just two months before the Spanish marriages—concerning French tactics, that she demanded that Palmerston should do nothing to disturb the friendly relations between herself and Louis Philippe, and demanded also that he should understand that the Foreign Office was a department of the Government, the affairs of which were to be considered in common and not to be decided by him. Sir Sidney Lee says of the struggle, in his "Life of Queen

Victoria ": "The Constitution did not provide for the regular control by the monarch of the minister's work in that or any other department of the State. The minister had it in his power to work quite independently of the Crown, and it practically lay with him to admit or reject a claim on the Crown's part to suggest even points of procedure, still more points of policy. For the Crown to challenge the fact in dealing with a strong-willed and popular minister was to invite, as the Queen and Prince were to find, a tormenting sense of impotence."

Lord John himself was in doubt about his standing with the Queen, and he dreaded the friction which he knew would be coming, and of which he, as go-between, would have to bear the brunt. Then both he and Lord Palmerston regarded not only Prince Albert, but King Leopold and Baron Stockmar, with suspicion. Here were three people brought up with foreign ideas all claiming to understand English foreign policy better than any Englishman in England, all waiting to guard French and German interests, their eyes so filled with those countries that they sometimes forgot Britain altogether, and Stockmar definitely claiming to the Queen to have an expert knowledge of the English Constitution.

Victoria-Albert applauded all he said on this point, and they and Stockmar together spent six years trying to break Palmerston to their will, demanding the obedience of a schoolboy from him, and hoping to reduce him to the position of a secretary carrying out their ideas. The more Palmerston did what he considered his duty to his country rather than to individuals, the harder grew the Prince, who was always perfectly certain that he was right and the experienced practical worker was wrong. There was no way out of it excepting war to the end, and war to the end it was.

Russell was very short and slight, and when he first contested Devonshire it is said that the electors were disappointed at his size, but felt satisfied when it was explained to them that he had once been larger, but was worn down by the anxieties and struggles of the Reform Bill. He was versatile, having written dramas, history, biography, and a novel; as Sydney Smith said of him, he was "ready to undertake *any*thing and *every*thing—to build St. Paul's—cut for the stone—or command the Channel Fleet." He was "the most cheery little man that ever was," "earnest about trifles, with natural kindliness concealed under serious aims"; "free from any spirit of jobbing or favouritism in making appointments, honourably and wisely disposed"; while Disraeli said of him that he was "quick in reply, fertile in resource, takes large views, and frequently compensates for a dry and hesitating manner by the expression of those noble truths that flash across the fancy and rise spontaneously to the lip of men of poetic temperament when addressing popular assemblies." At the same time he had not the tenacity of purpose which had animated Peel, nor the quick decision which made Palmerston a successful Foreign Minister—"Lord Meddle and Lord

Muddle " was a title his opponents liked to use about him.

So with Lord Stanley as Opposition Leader in the Lords, and Disraeli as Opposition Leader in the Commons, John Russell took up his work, and made so good an impression on the Queen that in 1847 she gave him Pembroke Lodge in Richmond Park, which Lord John took gratefully, as he had only a house in Chesham Place.

Concerning their supervision of despatches, Victoria-Albert contended that they were held responsible for everything that was written to foreign Powers, and therefore should have the decision as to what was said. This was nonsense, as all Europe knew just how the English Constitution allocated the power. Yet as soon as the other rulers realised that the Queen wished to grasp full power, they instantly tried to make capital out of it by applying to her personally by letter, and by showing animus against her Minister. When Palmerston thought the occasion warranted it he evaded the Royal commands by sending drafts to the Queen at the same time, or even after, the despatch itself had gone. Sometimes he forgot to send the draft at all, and when the Prince altered his letter too drastically he on more than one occasion re-inserted the deleted paragraph. He knew that he was dealing only nominally with the Queen, in reality with the Prince, and still more with Baron Stockmar, whose advice in big matters was always solicited. *Diogenes* hit off the situation when it published a picture of Pam standing in Downing Street watching the shadow

BENJAMIN DISRAELI.

of Albert thrown upon the blind, and saying : " There he is again ! I'll not enter if his influence is to negative mine."

A further point of difference lay in the Prince's adhesion to Monarchy in any form, autocratic, tyrannic, or otherwise, while Pam cared little for Monarchy, but much for the peace of Europe and the well-being of the people.

In 1848 Palmerston sent a despatch—without showing it to the Queen—to Sir Henry Bulwer at Madrid, pointing out that the Queen of Spain, who was in great difficulties with her people, would be wise to make certain changes in her Government, and approach nearer the Constitutional idea. Bulwer, who hated the French influence, caught at a method of annoying the French Ambassador, and not only sent the despatch to the Spanish Foreign Minister, but—without authority—published it in the Opposition papers. Whereupon in a rage Isabella gave Bulwer forty-eight hours in which to leave Madrid. There was a great row, and one comic paper published the following letter, which Lord Palmerston, in his desire to be Dictator of the World, might be likely to send :—

"LORD PALMERSTON TO SIR HENRY BULWER.
"SIR,
        "You will be pleased to read this despatch immediately to the Minister of Foreign Affairs. I see that the Queen has been in the habit of driving out in her carriage in the afternoon. This I cannot permit. As the Minister of the foreign policy of Great Britain I must protest against this undue assumption of power; and I beg likewise to add, that I have observed with disgust

that General Narvaez wears a green coat buttoned up. This cannot be permitted—I wear black. By the bye, it rained at Madrid, I see, last month. Were you consulted beforehand on it as British Ambassador? "

It took two years to adjust this trouble, and it is certain that had Isabella and her Ministers taken Palmerston's advice the Queen would not have been shown in a cartoon twenty years later walking out of Spain, carpet-bag in hand, and a small crown falling off her untidy hair.

In France the King had lost the confidence of his subjects; because of his duplicity over the Spanish marriages, said Victoria-Albert, though that really was but one proof among many of his intriguing character. His aristocracy thought themselves too good for him, yet they were licentious and corrupt, so much so that the Duc de Praslin, who most brutally murdered his wife, and to escape punishment was allowed to poison himself, was popularly regarded as a type of the whole. Louis Philippe had to invite as guests a lower stratum of society, men who dug him in the ribs and tapped him on the head—literally, and walked about his rooms with their mouths and hands full of pastry.

In February, 1848, these familiarities came to their height, when a mob headed by soldiers marched to the Tuileries, and to save the King's life, gave him the chance of signing his abdication. When this crowd faced him and offered the already written deed for his signature, it is pleasant to know that though he had lost his head, and feebly asked advice of everyone round him, Queen Amélie was one of the two people present who urged him to be a man, saying, "My dear, you must not abdicate, it is better to die a King." She, so gentle, so religious, was the only one of the whole family with spirit. I must do the King the justice to say that his great objection to doing anything decisive was that it would mean the shedding of blood. Directly after signing he and his Queen left the Tuileries on foot, escorted by the National Guard, who put them into a carriage to go where they would. From a little cottage at Honfleur they escaped by the aid of Mr. Featherstonhaugh, the Consul at Havre, just an hour before *gensd'armes* came to arrest them. Louis Philippe, his whiskers shaved off, his wig gone, a casquette on his head, and wearing immense goggles, was Mr. Smith, uncle to the Consul, who remarked that, having got him to the shore, "My dear uncle talked so loud and so much I had the greatest difficulty to make him keep silence." Someone else said that the Queen prayed so persistently on the ship that Louis told her to keep quiet or she would be found out.

On landing at Newhaven Louis Philippe cried "Thank God, I am on British ground!" Possessing nothing but the clothes they wore and a little money, they waited until they received a letter from Victoria, and then went straight through to Claremont, which Leopold had lent them. With all his intriguing there was not a single castle in Spain which would take the exiled King.

It seems too bad to joke about these fugitives, but

the national punster made a neat jest on the escape—

"Poor Louis Philippe from the Tuileries ran
And tore off his wig like a desperate man;
His children came rushing pell-mell into town,
And found that papa had no hairs to his crown."

The disguised Duc de Nemours arrived on our shores with two children, and no one knew where the Duchess and the other two were; Princess Clementine came by the same boat, but did not recognise her brother. Guizot was so disguised that his " dear friend and evil genius," Madame de Liéven, did not know him, though he travelled all the way from Amiens with her—she passing as the wife of an English artist; the Montpensiers came, Prince Metternich, the well-punished suppressor of free speech and the Press, and many others. Guizot, once starred, be-ribboned, golden-fleeced, surrounded by princes and ambassadors, took a house in Pelham Terrace, Brompton, at twenty pounds a year. And at this time a man who knew little of spontaneous gratitude was in hiding in King Street, St. James's, wondering always where his next meal would come from, and nursing his often-expressed conviction that it was his destiny to rule over France. This was Louis Napoleon, who paid a hurried visit to the new authorities at Paris, and felt flattered by being asked to go away again as his presence might lead to more trouble. However, before long he went for good, until in his turn he blessed the British shores which received him as an exile.

What was at the beginning of 1848 going on in the

Western part of Europe may be told in Prince Albert's own expressive words in a letter to Stockmar: "European war is at our doors, France is ablaze in every quarter, Louis Philippe is wandering about in disguise, so is the Queen; Nemours and Clementine have found their way to Dover; of Augustus, Victoire, Alexander Wurtemburg, and the others, all we know is, that the Duchess of Montpensier is at Tréport under another name, Guizot is a prisoner, the Republic declared, the army ordered to the frontier, the incorporation of Belgium and the Rhenish provinces are proclaimed. Here they refuse to pay the income tax, and attack the Ministry. Victoria will be confined in a few days; our poor good grandmamma is taken from this world.[1] I am not cast down, still I have need of friends and of counsel in these times. Come, as you love *me*, as you love *Victoria*, as you love *uncle Leopold*, as you love your German Fatherland."

But Stockmar was too ill, or thought he was, to travel, and with the birth of the Princess Louise, the tranquil good sense of Victoria, who was at such times both physically and mentally a perfect mother, the Prince's troubled mind calmed.

The tragedy of the nations was far more complete than Albert indicated; Spain and Portugal were full of factions and military unrest; the Italians were ripe for revolt, and Palmerston sent Lord Minto to warn the Government to save itself by making concessions. The Prussian King went into the streets to promise the mob anything they wanted, and was chased back into his

[1] The Dowager Duchess of Gotha.

palace, afterwards flying to Potsdam; the Crown Prince was forced to run for his life, the King of Austria had to leave his capital; Pope Pius availed himself of the hospitality of Sardinia; the Duke and Duchess of Coburg sought refuge in England, and last and perhaps least, King Leopold was wearily hoping to lay down the burden of his ill-fitting crown. He was ill, poor man, and weary of things, but like a good, dutiful minor King, he came to consult the greater monarch, his young niece, and was sent home with sage advice and royal injunctions to stick to his task, returning to his capital "with the greatest sadness imprinted on his face." One other King was at peace with his country, and that was Ernest of Hanover, who declared that at the first sign of rebellion he would abdicate. That his subjects did not rebel is a proof that in spite of his autocracy they felt safe with him.

As for England, there were riots everywhere, and Fanny Kemble, in her airy style, speaks of London thus :—

"We are quite lively now in London, with riots of our own—a more exciting process than merely reading of our neighbour's across the Channel. Last night a mob, in its playful progress through this street, broke the peaceful windows of this house. There have been great meetings in Trafalgar Square these two last evenings, in which the people threw stones about and made a noise, but that was all they did by all accounts."

One evening a mob, headed by a youth wearing epaulettes, marched to Buckingham Palace, breaking lamps and shouting " Vive la République ! " in a very English accent, but as they approached the Queen's house the guard turned out, and the very sight of the soldiers quelled their noise. When the leader was arrested he begged for mercy, and " let the tears doun fa' ! "

The Chartists were in the midst of their agitation, and Louis Napoleon was back from his Parisian trip in time to act as Special Constable in Trafalgar Square on the 10th of April, when the great procession was to take place. Half London shivered in its shoes and the other half laughed at the idea of real mischief. As a matter of fact, though English folk were willing to agitate, they did not feel themselves sufficiently aggrieved either to die or to kill for their troubles. So that the people who were wise enough to gauge public temper laughed with justice. Many ladies went for walks and drives as usual, yet London was practically in a state of siege, for there were a quarter of a million " specials " enrolled, one for every Chartist expected. The Duke of Wellington had command of the military, and though not a soldier or a gun could be seen, armies were ready to be turned into the streets at a bugle call. Alas ! Royalty, perhaps unnerved by European events, gave way to panic, for though the new baby was only twenty days old, the Queen, Prince, and their family fled to Osborne two days before the great march was to take place. Greville, Clerk of Her Majesty's Privy Council, keenly desired that the Queen would remain in town ; Sir James Graham was strongly against her going away, saying that it looked like cowardice in her personally, and indicated a sense of danger which ought not to be shown; Peel agreed with this, and said he would speak with the Prince. However, Lord John Russell, who was not often listened to unless he said that which he was desired to say, may have thought differently, and advised Her Majesty to go, for away they all went to a house of which a part had collapsed, and most of which was in the hands of workmen, the Prince thinking Windsor too near London to be safe. The poor old Duchess of Kent who was in a very scared state of mind, was not taken with them, so she had to be content with the—to her doubtful—security of Frogmore.

The Chartists were met by the Chief Constable at Kennington and warned that the procession was illegal, upon which, in great relief, the men gathered there, from fifteen to twenty thousand, some say only ten thousand, dispersed, though their petition was taken in cabs to the House.

The Royal flight was a great error. Such measures had been taken for public, as well as Royal, safety that no danger was expected excepting to shop windows along the route; and it led to a recurrence of unfavourable opinion about the Prince, which was fanned by such verses as :—

> "That Albert's a very great ' leader '
> Of troops, must be plain to a dolt,
> But this you'll allow, my dear reader,
> He's deucedly given to ' bolt.' "

He was called the Flying Dutchman, and was said to have gone suddenly to Osborne to defend it against

Ledru Rollin (the chief of the French revolutionaries) and fifty thousand *sans culottes;* but as they did not come he returned to London to defend it against the Chartists, only to find, to his disappointment, that the movement had already been suppressed.

There is little doubt that Palmerston's policy at this time was worthy both of himself and of England. He did not truckle to the despotic Kings, great or small, which, as the Queen was a strong believer in the sanctity of monarchy, and thought it "*infamous* to sacrifice the little rulers," seemed very wrong to her, so that she described his advice given abroad as " bitter as gall and doing great harm." He could see what was hidden from her eyes, that in some countries, to avert destruction, only a loosening of the tight bonds of government was needed, the giving of more freedom, the recognition of humanity in the poor; and in these cases he counselled concessions, a course which prejudiced and less observant people like the Queen declared was simply encouraging revolution.

It is the misfortune of those in power, of those who possess, that their very position blinds them to facts patent to others. They take as their motto : "What I have I keep," and so sometimes lose all, when if they would but concede a little they might keep almost all and gain in credit.

The attention of the Queen and the Prince was truly concentrated, not on Palmerston's real work abroad, but on his relation to themselves and to those Royalties in whom they were interested. They felt that he thought he knew better than they did—which was true, and they saw that he intended to go his own way in spite of them, which was annoying. The conflicts became constant, and in almost every one the Queen-Prince was worsted, and so the whole strength of their dislike was turned upon the man who had kept the fame of England healthy when Europe was in convulsions, who had made this country an asylum for all kinds of Royal fugitives, friendly or inimical with each other, and who in turn was consulted by the Chief Minister in each of the invalid kingdoms. As Nicholas said: "What now remains in Europe? England and Russia!"

Making allowance for their limitations, it is quite possible to sympathise with the Royal pair, for it was not a dignified position for them. Greville, for instance, said somewhat approvingly of the Minister: "Palmerston's defects prove rather useful in his intercourse with the Court. To their wishes or remonstrances he expresses the greatest deference, and then goes on his own course without paying the least attention to what they have been saying to him." Surely one of the most irritating forms of opposition it is possible to endure! Lord John was treated by him in the same way, but he knew Palmerston's value and understood his aims better than the Queen, and he also knew how far Pam had a right to do as he did, and so felt no real resentment. In one despatch Russell took exception to various things, and pointed them out to Palmerston, who listened but said nothing. Later, in talking this over with the Queen, she replied: "No, did you say all that?" "Yes," he said. "Well then, it produced no effect, for the despatch is gone. Lord Palmerston sent it to me. I know it is gone."

Pam was accused of forgetting to answer letters, as in the case of the letters over the Spanish marriages, the blame of which delay he had to bear, though it lay with Victoria-Albert, but he never really forgot. If he himself delayed it was generally a matter of policy. On the contrary, he was quick and businesslike, and demanded the same qualities from his subordinates. Thus he decreed in the Foreign Office that his clerks should come themselves when he rang the bell, instead of being solemnly summoned by an intermediary. The dignity of the clerks was outraged, they said they were being turned into menials, and did their best at resistance. Odo Russell, however, made the sensible remark that whatever method took him most quickly to his chief was the method for him, and he was regarded as a traitor by the habit-encrusted and blind clerks, whose names were never included in the book of fame, while Russell eventually filled the proud post of an Ambassador.

On one occasion Victoria told Palmerston that she was ashamed of the policy he was pursuing in Italy, for she hated the idea that the Italian provinces should be taken from Austria's weak grasp. She told Russell that he simply *must* get rid of Palmerston, she could endure such conduct no longer. Russell sympathised, but did nothing. Later, after innumerable complaints and painful friction, Victoria again told him she was seriously anxious; in fact, felt quite ill with anxiety,

P

and that some plan *must* be found to get rid of her Foreign Minister. And she had the bright idea of suggesting that Clarendon, Secretary for Ireland, and Palmerston should change places. As the Secretary-ship of Ireland was then regarded as a sinecure so far as work was concerned, she could hardly have offered Palmerston a more deadly insult. Lord John, with every respect, replied that his colleague was a very able man, entirely master of his office and affairs, never interfering in other questions, though resenting any interference with his own office. He, however, promised to do what he could for the Queen, and so for a bit the matter again rested.

Pam was accused of cutting open some letters addressed to the Queen at the Foreign Office before sending them on to her. This made her véry angry, though, of course, business letters about foreign matters should not have been sent to her personally at the Foreign Office, and being sent there the responsible Minister was right in opening them. But everything Palmerston did was wrong.

The Queen-Prince loudly accused him to their relatives of showing friendship to France at this time through personal motives, just as they had said his enmity to Louis Philippe had been personal. They could not see that the French Republic, which was not likely to fight England, was valuable as an ally, and that Palmerston was very skilfully training it as such, whereas the French under Louis Philippe were always anxious to spring at England's throat. This want of comprehension was scarcely worthy of Albert, but it was characteristic of Victoria—it showed the same defect in character which made her love country dances and round games; if her cards were on the table she could not believe that the cards in the hands of her partner or her opponents might form combinations with her own at which she could not guess.

Thus while the Foreign Minister was working at an elaborate policy which should bring peace, and settle matters, generally with concessions to the revolting side, his dual Monarch was demanding not only to be kept primed with every move in the game, but to interfere with every move. Unless the Monarch had a head for understanding in every point what was being attempted, this would be destruction to the game almost as soon as it was begun; and only a simple-minded or shallow Minister could put up with it. Had Palmerston been always on the side of Kings and the confederacy which later became Germany there would have been no difficulty; he would have told his plans, they would have been approved, and everything would have gone lightly in the mutual relationship—how things would have gone internationally would have been another matter.

This Royal demand for the power of interference was not made upon the Prime Minister nor upon the other officers of State, who carried out their policies in conjunction with the Cabinet and the House; but the Prince had been so imbued by Stockmar and his training with the idea that the foreign policy should be dictated by the Crown, that, in spite of all rebuffs, he went on torturing himself over it, and the Minister

P 2

continued to be put to all kinds of subterfuges in resisting his demand.

There was a dispute over sending an Ambassador to France during the second Republic, the Queen's affection for Louis Philippe making her desire to affront the French nation by sending a Minister only, an act which would have jeopardised all Pam's European work. So, without further argument, he coolly sent Normanby back as Ambassador! From the Queen's point of view he *was* impossible.

He did more than that, though, for when Queen Maria of Portugal found that her misrule was likely to cost her her throne, and wrote to Victoria for help, Palmerston insisted that the cause of Donna Maria's troubles was her reliance upon her Coburg adviser Dietz, and that she should dismiss him. Victoria's indignation at the idea that a native of Coburg could be an ill-adviser may be imagined! But Pam dictated a letter to the Portuguese Queen which he insisted upon his own Queen copying with her own hand, and sending to Donna Maria; just as he demanded a personally written letter from her according to his dictation to be sent in answer to a private one on international affairs from the King of Prussia. It is not to be wondered at that Victoria-Albert hated the man who so lowered their pride.

Then there came a quarrel with Greece. Its King Otho, *un enfant gâté de l'absolutisme*, had no regard for persons, and as his Government followed his lead, the foreign residents, English and other subjects in Greece, had no safeguard against oppression, and

LORD PALMERSTON.

From a Painting by John Partridge in the National Portrait Gallery.

were for years robbed and cheated. Many remonstrances had been made, and at last Pam decided to follow words with action. When an Englishman had some land taken from him and added to King Otho's garden, and a Jew, native of Gibraltar, had his house pillaged by Greeks, both being refused any compensation, Palmerston demanded it. Three years were spent to no purpose in attempted negotiations by the British Consul at Athens, for Greece did not believe that England would truly interfere. Then Palmerston ordered the Fleet to the Adriatic, and Greece, like the little old woman with her pig, began to call upon Russia and upon France, and those two countries began to make a conference, and the Queen and Prince began to pity, not their poor subjects who had been and were being ground down under a legitimatised robbery, but the autocratic King Otho, and the Prince began to call upon France to have a conference in London as to the exact amount of compensation which strict justice demanded. Then while the Queen and Prince, Russia, and France were discussing matters, the affair ended, for Pam had carried out his settled policy, had wrung the required compensation from Otho, and had taught Greece a lesson about England. In fact, he had "forgotten" to obey orders, —and the little woman did not get home with her pig.

The French Ambassador was recalled from London dramatically on the Queen's birthday, the Russian and Greek Ambassadors did not appear as usual at the Foreign Office dinner that day, and the Duke of

Wellington, when asked what he thought of the situation, replied: "Oh, oh, it's all right; it's all nonsense."

Russian agents in conjunction with Madame Liéven were at work, hoping England would respond by recalling their Ambassador from Paris, and that a real quarrel would be caused between France and England, which was not, however, in Palmerston's programme, and he, by various conciliations, smoothed France down; but before the matter was settled the Queen's agitation and the Prince's anger had forced a crisis at home. Lord Stanley in the House of Lords moved a resolution which was practically a vote of censure on the offending Minister, and it was carried by a majority of thirty-seven. A week later Mr. Roebuck introduced into the Commons a motion approving of the foreign policy of England, which was calculated "in times of unexampled danger to preserve peace between England and the various nations of the world."

This was debated for four nights, and then "from the dusk of one day to the dawn of the next" Palmerston replied without note, pause or hesitation, as Gladstone said. Sir Theodore Martin—under the Queen's influence—belittles Palmerston's speech, but Peel, in concluding the debate, said that it was "a most able and a most temperate speech, which made us proud of the man who delivered it." At its conclusion every party in the House cheered Pam enthusiastically, and the majority for him was forty-six, thus reversing the decision of the Peers.

How far the Queen and Prince were responsible for
this it is not easy to say, but the former, in writing
to her uncle Leopold, remarked, most significantly:
" What do you say to the conclusion of our debate?
It leaves things just as they were. The House of
Commons is becoming very unmanageable and trouble-
some. . . ."

Palmerston himself said: " The attack on our
foreign policy has been rightly understood by everybody, as the shot fired by a foreign conspiracy aided
and abetted by a domestic intrigue; and the parties
have so entirely failed in the purpose, that instead of
expelling and overthrowing me with disgrace, as
they intended and hoped to do, they have rendered
me, for the present, the most popular Minister that
for a very long course of time has held my
office."

Sir Theodore Martin naturally deals with the affair
entirely from the Queen's point of view, and, like her,
he judges the Greek matter as an incident, whether
A and B should each receive a certain sum in compensation, or whether they were not extortionate in
their demands. The principle behind the action, the
real great question of British honour, its strength to
protect its own people, and to stand unafraid and
unashamed before the whole of Europe seemed in
no way to have been grasped by them. Yet both would
have called themselves Imperialists!

One sees, however, where the Queen-Prince stood.
They were eminently honest, straightfoward people,
who believed in the Christian principle of " Judge as

you would be judged," and they thought it natural to treat foreign countries as individuals, accord to them all the forbearance, courtesy and patient hearing that they would accord to their nearest and dearest, indeed more, for one is apt to get angry with provocation close at hand. It was an ideal which, with the help of their beloved Lord Aberdeen, they carried out later with the Czar of all the Russias. They talked nicely to him, made little concessions, not doubting he would return them in kind, and Nicholas—like Guizot at Eu —remembered a certain talk he had had with Aberdeen at Windsor, and vague promises which had been made, and he said to himself, " England is in my hand, they will let me do as I like. Wellington is dead, Palmerston is nowhere. Then I may do my will with Turkey." And so came death to tens of thousands.

On reading about this prolonged struggle between the Queen-Prince and their Minister in the pages of Martin and in the Queen's letters my sympathies were at first with the Queen, but a deeper study proved without doubt that the power and the understanding lay on the side of Palmerston, and that his actions raised the reputation of England to a higher point than it had ever stood before.

That the royal feeling against Palmerston was definitely personal as well as political, is proved by the Queen's own letters; but Pam showed in no way any feeling against the Queen in his correspondence. In 1845, when Peel's evasiveness and Russell's consciousness that no one but Palmerston could be Foreign Minister, prevented Lord John from forming a Ministry, it was said that the Queen had triumphed all along the line, and the issue was completely satisfactory to her. On the other hand, the feeling of the Whig Cabinet and of Palmerston himself was shown when Palmerston, remarking to Lord Broughton that the Queen's real feeling towards them on foreign, and particularly Austrian politics, was very unfriendly, Broughton replied : " That cannot be helped, we must do our duty irrespective of all personal preference." " To be sure ! " replied Palmerston, " it does not signify a single pin."

Later the Duke of Buckingham, a great Tory, paid a high tribute to Palmerston when he wrote : " His experience, his tact, his judgment, his inexhaustible good humour and rare political sagacity, have maintained his party in power when blunders of every kind have most severely tried the patience of the nation."

CHAPTER IX

THE QUEEN'S HOMES

THE Prince gradually absorbed into his own hands all the political work of the Sovereign, though the Queen on occasions copied out despatches, and still took a lively interest in things that were passing, but motherhood offered her so much that was new that she had time for little more than the outer forms of royalty. The Prince was also active in other ways; he altered the gardens of Buckingham Palace and Windsor, was interested in small building operations on the two estates, raising an aviary, dove house, dog kennels, etc., and when at last in 1842 the devoted Lehzen had been induced to take a long, long holiday, he turned his attention to domestic finance.

Gradually rumours had arisen as to the Queen's debts, and people began to say that she was a true chip of the old Georgian block, as exemplified in George IV. and his brothers. We are so used to the nice suave paragraphs in biographies as to how judiciously little Victoria spent or gave a shilling, that it is forgotten that the starving person may gorge when opportunity offers. The little Princess had been kept so short of money that she did not know how to use it when she had wealth, she spent what she desired, ordered what she wished, and never inquired into cost. Thus on her marriage she had not—and somewhat naturally —sacrificed her desires concerning clothes for the good of her people; she had ordered many things in Paris, and it was reported that to one foreign firm alone she had paid fifteen thousand pounds for linen, including handkerchiefs at ten guineas apiece; and later she was not less extravagant.

So the Honourable Charles Murray, as Master of the Household, found himself in 1840 face to face with a difficult task, that of limiting Royal expenditure, without troubling his Royal mistress, and he tried a futile sort of economy. He could not reduce the forty pounds a year paid to the housemaids in wages, without higher authority, so he turned his attention to smaller things, and taking a hint from the Continent—some say from Prince Albert—he announced that thenceforth the underlings of the Palace would—find their own soap! A little later tea was knocked off the list, only cocoa being dispensed to the servants, and then it was reported —though it is hardly credible—-that hearthstones, mops and brushes were to be found by the users thereof !

Apropos of this it is curious that there seems always to have been a dearth of small things in the Palace. Candles have furnished material for talk over and over again. The custom was retained until Prince

220 THE MARRIED LIFE OF QUEEN VICTORIA

Albert and Stockmar began to sweep the Palace clean, of lighting the ballroom on State occasions with eight hundred candles, the remains of which, at the end of the evening, became the perquisites of the footmen. This had the amusing effect of causing these men to forget their duties when guests were departing that they might linger in the vicinity of the ballroom, and as soon as the room was empty they would swoop in like an army and tear the candle ends from the sconces, each fighting and struggling to gain the greatest number.

In later years, when reform was an accomplished fact, Madame Titiens often told the story of how, being summoned to Windsor to sing before the Queen, she found herself condemned to dress by the light of two candles only. On asking for more, she was informed by the servant that the allowance to each room was just two candles and no more. "But," added the maid considerately, "there is no regulation which would prevent you cutting those two candles in halves and making four."

Matches, too, seem to have been at a premium, for Baroness Bunsen tells that once her husband, when staying at Windsor, rose before dawn to do some work, which pressed on his mind, and hunted everywhere for a match. However, there were none in the room, and by skilful blowing he managed to fan enough flame from the dying coal to get a piece of paper ignited. Apropos of another occasion of the sort, the Baroness says: "One must make an N.B. when one visits queens, they give you everything but matches. I was in the extreme of distress for one at Queen Adelaide's."

Though wonderful economies were gradually effected, and jobbery on a small scale was much reduced, the Queen was cheated by her loyal servants and tradesmen to the end of her days, for there seems always to have been a firm belief in Windsor that the town should live on the Castle. I have been told that every chicken which appeared on Her Majesty's table cost half-a-guinea, and other charges were not less light; while a bottle of brandy brought to some fortunate, but not too conscientious, official an income for many years.

It happened that on one long drive in Scotland Prince Albert fainted. The distracted Queen could only wait until they got to some place where brandy was to be secured to revive him, so in terror she supported her husband while the coachman galloped his horses over three or four miles of road until houses were reached. After that Victoria commanded that a bottle of brandy should be placed in her carriage every time she drove out, and as the bottle was removed before the carriage went back to the stables, and as a new bottle was put there each time it again came to the door, and was never opened by the Queen, someone had cause to congratulate himself on the fainting attack.

Another curious little incident which gave rise to domestic heartburnings is told in *The Times*' life of Her Majesty. The Prince, examining a list of Palace charges, was puzzled over a weekly expenditure of thirty-five shillings for "Red Room Wine." He investigated this charge, being naturally hindered at every step, until at last he discovered that a certain room at Windsor had been used temporarily during the reign of George III. as a guardroom, and that five shillings a day had been allowed to provide wine for the officers. The guard had been removed many years before, but the item for wine which still figured in the cellarage account had become the perquisite of a half-pay officer, who held the sinecure of under-butler. The Prince offered him the choice of relinquishing the wine money or of really becoming a butler, much to his horror.

Then came a gradual weeding out of servants, including a reduction in the number of the Yeomen of the Guard. The news of the dismissals appeared in the *Court Journal*, and inquiries soon elicited the fact that while twenty-five thousand pounds were to be saved to the Queen in wages, all the servants were to be pensioned from the public purse. Sarcastic articles appeared under the title of "Royal Cheese-parings," and there was a general sentiment that had Prince Albert loved money less the English would have loved him more.

The Queen knew well how to ensure a better income to her beloved than Parliament had voted him, by conferring upon him valuable sinecures, and there were always the Duchies of Cornwall and Lancaster to add riches to their wealth. The Prince was already a Field Marshal, and Colonel of the 11th Hussars; when Lord Munster, eldest son of William IV.,

committed suicide—it was said because of his unhappiness with his wife—Prince Albert became Governor
of Windsor Castle and Warden of the Round Tower,
which offices carried considerable emoluments with
them.   An unpopular appointment was the lucrative
one of Lord Warden of the Stannaries,[1] which
required an expert knowledge of tin mines and the
mining world.   There were, of course, not wanting
some who asserted that the Prince was eminently fitted
for the post, as he had shown himself so well able
to look after the " tin," but a contemporary paper was
severe in its comments on his first Court.   " Here
was a beardless young gentleman, hardly able to speak
consecutive sentences in English, totally unacquainted
with English jurisprudence, to say nothing of the com-
plexity of our laws, solemnly sitting for six hours,
as judge, hearing long legal arguments of abstruse
character.   What a farce ! "

As for the Duchies, that of Cornwall became the
property of the Prince of Wales at his birth, and was
governed by a Commission which gave the Queen what
she wished for the babe's support, and accumulated the
remainder, after the charges had been withdrawn, the
income from it rising gradually to £66,000, a prosperity in which the labourer upon its many estates
did not participate.   The men whose work made much

[1] Stannary Courts held jurisdiction in Cornwall and Devon
over the tin mines, the miners being exempt from all other
jurisdiction excepting in cases affecting land, life, and limb.
Twenty-four Stannators were returned from Cornwall, presided
over by a Vice-Warden.   The Crown appointed a Lord Warden,
who assembled " Parliaments " from time to time, to revise old
or enact new laws.

of the land's success received in 1846 seven shillings a week for six twelve-hour days; young men had from half-a-crown to six shillings a week, much of the wages being paid on the truck system, wheat, butter and cheese being charged market price. These people only tasted meat when some animal was slaughtered "to prevent its dying," such as a sheep with the staggers, "breeding-ewe mutton" or a cow with the "quarter evil," and then the farmer would value it at twopence-halfpenny the pound and force it on his labourers. Though we are told that Victoria pitied the tenants who, on making improvements had their rents raised, there is no evidence that she used her influence in commanding the Commissioners to inquire into the condition of the labourers, though the terrible lives they lived were reported in the London papers.

On the contrary, so successful was the Commission in raising revenues from Cornwall that a like Council was formed to farm the Duchy of Lancaster, with the result that from £27,000 it in a few years yielded an income of £60,000 for its Royal owner.

In three or four years, by the careful manipulation of money, the Queen and Prince were able to spend out of private income £200,000 in setting up a private estate, where they could enjoy "the simple life" to their hearts' content. At first their holiday place had been Claremont, where, weather permitting, the whole family could live in the open air, and many domestic stories are told of babies lying on a rug on the grass, of little people taking first lessons in riding, and of Her Majesty's love of dressing-up being gratified by the eldest boy and girl being presented to her clothed as "natives of that picturesque country of the Tyrol, where, as Höfer proved, peasants become heroes."

They also tried the Pavilion at Brighton, but Victoria was so mobbed every time she went out of doors that she never afterwards liked the place. She however scarcely gave it a fair chance, and the people, who, hoping for the return of the old Regency times, had been too exuberant in their joy, found themselves put permanently out of favour.

So Osborne House, with about eight hundred acres, in the Isle of Wight, was bought, and the foundation stone of a new residence laid in 1845. The building took until 1851, and when most of the rooms were up, the arch of one of the largest—all the rooms were arched—collapsed, carrying with it the joists, killing one man and injuring others. However, from 1846 the Royal Family went there constantly to live—with some reservations—the peaceful life of the middle classes.

Mr. James Baker, in his "Literary and Biographical Sketches," gives some interesting incidents and anecdotes of the Royal doings there, and has in conversation told me of others, such as the following,:

When on duty in the grounds about ten o'clock one night a young policeman saw a man passing swiftly into the shadow of some trees; so going quietly after him he clapped his hand on his shoulder, demanding to know what he was doing there. Receiving no answer, he said, "You must come with me and give an account of yourself!" and dragged his prisoner straight into

Q

the kitchen, to be received there with a scream and then dead silence, all the servants rising to their feet. Bewildered, the policeman looked at his companion, and then let his hand drop slowly from the coat-collar, petrified with confusion, for it was the Prince Consort! Albert shook himself a little, went to the door and disappeared to resume his walk, having, characteristically, uttered no word. The servants gathered, with both laughter and sympathy, round the poor policeman, who, knowing no comfort, spent the night in the deepest depression; when he was sent for in the morning, it was to receive, not dismissal, as he feared, but commendation for his prompt attention to duty.

At Osborne the Prince gained a feeling of freedom, he could walk where he would without being troubled with crowds of people, and the longed-for sensation of privacy descended upon him. Sometimes he must have heartily wished that he had married in a different station, or rather that his dear Victoria was just a very rich private lady, who could go where she desired without comment. The Queen would not have liked it, though, with her usual mental submission, she thought she would.

Once when the two were walking together a heavy thunderstorm came on, and they took shelter under the porch of the village post-office, the owner of which begged them to enter. On their refusal the woman insisted upon lending them an umbrella, so the Royal pair marched gaily away under the shelter of a green whalebone gamp. The next morning a scarlet-clad footman brought it back with a letter, containing a five-pound note. The cottage lady—for was she not a lady in all her instincts and delicacy of mind?—took her umbrella back, then saying it was impossible that she could receive payment for such an ordinary act of politeness, returned the note. The Queen, however, sent it her a second time, with words which prevailed upon the good dame to accept it.

Queen Victoria shared her husband's feeling of serenity and said of the escape from the regulations of a State house : " It sounds so pleasant to have a place of one's own, quiet and retired, and free from all Woods and Forests and other charming Departments, which really are the plague of one's life."

Osborne, of which Sir Charles Lyell said that it was a very pleasant residence, "like a small German Principality Palace," also had its summer-house in the form of a Swiss cottage, where the children were free to make culinary and building messes, and to play the host to their parents; and as it was near enough to Windsor to allow frequent visits, it still further drew the Queen and Court from London.

It was at Osborne in September, 1849, that George Anson, a man who was honest and straightforward, though sometimes blunt and outspoken, incapable of intrigue, and, though strongly prejudiced against the Germans, entirely devoted to his master's interests, fell unconscious while talking to his wife and never regained his senses. He had won the friendship and confidence of the Prince, who said of him, " He was my only intimate friend. We went through everything together since I came here. He was almost like a brother to me." Then the Prince and Victoria shut themselves away from their attendants to shed floods of tears over their loss.

Why did men weep at that time? There are constant allusions in the "Letters" to Melbourne looking at his Queen-pupil with tears in his eyes; Peel seems to have done it occasionally; and the Prince asserted that Palmerston once promised reformation "with tears in his eyes"! It is curious to think there should be a fashion in crying as in other things, for neither men nor women find much use for tears nowadays; they are, with many other Victorian peculiarities, relegated to the children. However, the German love for a sentimental scene made tears very popular during the 'forties, and the Queen and Prince shed them easily. They both indulged in a kind of loving regard for Death, and never failed to pay him homage in the shape of flowers and monuments or mausoleums, according to the nearness or rank of the friend taken by the Destroyer. They made plans for their own burial-place long years before either of them needed it, and the Queen shed such a wealth of tears over each member of the family who died that one wonders she was not entirely dissolved sometimes. Yet she was a good Christian and Churchwoman, who believed enthusiastically in the glory of heaven and the happiness to which the good dead attained. Had she been glad for them, it would have been more understandable, but grief of this kind was a luxury to her, and she revelled in the observance of anniversaries

of all kinds, gay as well as mournful, until the Prince
himself found them a burden.

A year earlier than this a terrible accident happened between Osborne and Portsmouth. The Royal
family were crossing in the yacht *Fairy* when it ran
down a boat which had put off from the frigate
Grampus, carrying five women and two watermen to
the shore. How much the Queen knew of the real
facts it is difficult to tell. Lady Lyttelton says that a
sudden and violent squall arose and upset the boat,
that the Prince was the first to see the people struggling
in the water, and shouted to Lord Adolphus, who was
in command, to stop the yacht, which his lordship
roundly refused to do, saying that the *Fairy* was
hardly safe herself. But he had a boat let down to
help the people. However, Lady Lyttelton was not
sure of her facts, for she says *four men* at least were
drowned. It is also impossible for those in a large
boat to know what has happened at the bow when they
see people struggling in the water alongside. The
unfortunate fact was that the *Fairy*, going at high
speed, ran the little boat down, that of seven people
only three were rescued, and that the commander of
the Royal yacht thought his post as guardian of royalty
of such extreme importance that he refused to stop to
save the lives of ordinary people. Sir Sidney Lee
mentions the matter casually in a footnote, simply announcing the fact that the *Fairy* had run down the boat
and that three women were drowned.

The Queen believed at the time that the accident
had nothing to do with her yacht, and wrote of it in

her Diary: "We could not stop. It was a dreadful moment, too horrible to describe. . . . It is a consolation to think we were of some use, and also that, even if the yacht had remained, they could not have done more. Still, we all kept on feeling we might, though I think we could not. . . . It is a terrible thing, and haunts me continually."

Lady Lyttelton practically destroys Lord Adolphus's excuse that it was not safe to stop by saying that "there really was some trifling bolt or screw wrong, and therefore it was particularly necessary to manage everything right."

I wonder what a King—who is scarcely likely to be so thoroughly wrapped up in cotton-wool as a Queen—would do in the same circumstances, whether he would be obliged to let his ship's commander disgrace his reputation for courage and just dealing in the same way.

If Osborne gave joy to the Queen and the Prince, Scotland filled their hearts with rapture. They liked it on their first visit in 1842, and still better when they went to Blair Athol in 1844. Even before they ever went North the Queen's romantic turn of mind brought the Highland soldiers into prominence, their bare knees much shocking the susceptibilities of the English people! H. H. reduced the matter to one for laughter by publishing a picture of the regiment standing around the porch of the Palace while the Queen, with pleasant smiles, presents colours to each man in the form of a pair of tartan breeks, saying that they are a mark of admiration for their man-œuvres.

Victoria loved the country, the people, the mountains, the lakes, and the trees, nowhere in all the world did anything comparable to them exist; England and the English were really scarcely fit to be neighbours to such a wonderful country. On returning to this unbelievably inferior land the Queen would weary her ladies and her visitors by the constant pæan of praise which she sung of the sister country, until many of them wished that the good God had forgotten to invent the Highlands. The very cairngorms found there were—sentimentally—more precious to her than diamonds, and at Balmoral she treasured a monster stone weighing two hundred and seventy-eight ounces, being about nine inches across, which had been found years before at Braemar. Scotch pearls, too, she particularly prized, especially if they were taken from the River Dee. These were of delicate greens, blues, and pinks, suffused with a kind of metallic lustre. They were, however, of no great intrinsic value.

In the autumn of 1844 the Queen and Prince, taking the Princess Royal, went to Blair Athol, where all the restrictions which their high position imposed were cast aside, and Her Majesty might be seen walking about the grounds early in the morning. Her piper had orders to play the pibroch under her window at seven o'clock, and at the same time a bunch of fresh heather and some icy water from the spring at Glen Tilt were taken up to her.

Sometimes, however, she was out of doors by seven, and on one occasion called at The Lodge, where the Glenlyons were temporarily residing, only to find that everyone was still in bed. Going back she lost her way, and asking it of some reapers they pointed to a path over the palings, which she duly climbed.

The papers published complimentary paragraphs as to the way in which Victoria lessened the work of her servants on this visit, and cited as evidence her order to the Highlanders on duty in the grounds not to present arms each time they saw one of the royal family, but to follow a rule of presenting them twice a day to herself, once to Prince Albert, and once to the Princess Royal.

The first Sunday the little church was a peaceful, half-empty place; the second it was more than filled, for strangers from the whole countryside came early, so that when Her Majesty entered there was a scrambling and scraping, the people standing up and even standing *on* their chairs to get a glimpse of their young Monarch. Then when service was over the unmannerly ones made a rush for the doors, and the Queen would have been mobbed if the Highlanders had not been there to impose a stiff living line between her and her too-curious subjects. The same thing is said to have happened at Dundee when the royal couple were returning home, for the policemen and special constables were so busy "gaping at the show" that they had no thought for their work, and let the people press so violently and rudely on the Queen that she was in some danger of being pressed entirely over the Quay side, a danger only averted by the soldiers of the 60th Rifles presenting bayonets to the crowd.

It was of this that a cartoon entitled *A Warm Recep-*

tion in the North was published, in which a frightened
Prince was being embraced by Scotch women, and men
of all sorts were leering at the alarmed Queen. Indeed,
the early Scotch visits gave much work to the caricaturists.

" Political Hit No. 28," named " First Sip of the
Mountain Dew," showed the Prince in an elevated and
happy frame of mind unsteadily holding a glass, while
a Scotch Laird pledges him. Peel is talking to a
woman at a cottage door, evidently pointing out that
the whiskey is from a private still, for the woman
answers, " Na duty! has it no done its duty to the
bonnie Prince yonder? Gin Her Majesty takes some
it would be as dutiful to her, so take yere dram, and
fash no more aboot it, ye tax sliding loon!" The
Queen, waiting at a distance, is murmuring : " Bless
me, how tipsy Albert looks"; while her spouse is
saying, " Come! We'll have another shot. I shall
bring 'em down in couples now."

As the Prince spent most of his time shooting and
stalking deer, it was an apposite allusion. These were
both absorbing occupations, though never so absorbing
to him that he was ready to forgo his dinner for their
sake. The day's arrangements had always to be made
so as to allow of his returning home at two o'clock,
for at this hour an intense hunger assailed him, and
he longed for the meal at which he was in the habit of
eating wisely perhaps, well certainly.

Probably that he might make his estate more attractive to the Prince, the Duke of Athol shut up Glen
Tilt, about twenty square miles of property, forbidding

anyone to cross it for fear of getting in the wind and alarming the deer. This was a tremendous loss to the country people, who assailed the Duke with prayers and petitions, none of which made any impression upon him. The editor of *The Man in the Moon* let his fancy run away with him when he printed a supposed letter from the Queen, remonstrating with the Duke's arbitrary act, for she was not likely to disagree with a plan which would add to her husband's pleasure. In fact, in her diary she tells how on one occasion " most provokingly two men who were walking on the road —which they had no business to have done—suddenly came in sight, and then the herd all ran back again, and the sport was spoiled."

One day the Prince shot no fewer than nineteen deer, and what he did with them " the chiel amang ye takin' notes " tells :

> " Then from the scene that viewed his warlike toils
> The blood-stained victor hastens with his spoils,
> And laid them humbly at Victoria's feet—
> To such a Queen most intellectual treat.
> So on the grass plot—to a shambles changed—
> The gory things were scrupulously ranged,
> Before the windows of the Royal guest
> Famed for the woman-softness of her breast."

At that time Scotland had the reputation of suffering from a fault which has happily been long forgotten. It was indicated in a saying of Douglas Jerrold's, to whom an artist named Leitch, one of the Queen's drawing-masters, on being introduced to him, explained somewhat superfluously that he was not John Leech.

"No, no, I know," said the wit; "you are the Leitch with an itch in his name."

On this matter the cartoonists were merciless. In one picture the Royal company are represented at dinner, all looking most uncomfortable, the Queen crying: "Oh, Sir James (Clark), do give me a back-scratcher, or I shall certainly go mad." Prince Albert, writhing, says: "Ah, ah, vat is dis I vas get? I scratch mineself all ovare into noding at all; I wish, Lady B., you would come; you can scratch me so nice."

Another picture shows them going on board for home, among the many presents they are carrying being Glenlivet and herrings in casks, and a huge jar of sulphur, the antidote for the trouble. A third drawing gives their home-coming, John Bull welcoming them, Peel in the background rubbing his shoulder against the doorpost, the Queen expatiating on the good time they have had; and John Bull replying: "Glad am I to see you back again, although these are not the times for junketing. But I hope, Victoria, you have not brought anything *in hand* which, to judge from Sir Bobby's appearance, is better left behind."

It was not until 1847 that the third visit was made to Scotland, the route being by sea along the west coast with five warships in attendance. The Duke of Argyll, in his "Life of Queen Victoria," tells how on their way the Queen and Prince stopped at Inverary. As the old Duke had died recently and his son had broken up the Inverary establishment, the royally-imposed visit would have been a matter of considerable difficulty had not the Duchess of Sutherland taken over a whole army of servants and given the deserted Castle the air of habitation, sending messages to all the country gentlemen, who arrived in Highland dress, and stood guard about the luncheon table. Fortunately, the visit only lasted two or three hours, and then the yacht, with its attendant vessels, went on its way.

The destination this time was Ardverikie, and the last bit of the journey was made in carriages, which could not be driven over the Padtoch Water boat-bridge near Loch Laggan, so a carpet was laid down for the Queen's dainty feet, and Macpherson of Cluny, with three of his sons, followed by one hundred and sixty Highlanders, escorted her over. Cluny carried the shield borne by Prince Charles at Culloden, while the green flag of the Macphersons, which had been out in 1715 and 1745, waved behind him. But the impressive welcome was spoiled by the heavy rain, and the wild beauty of the Highlanders was tempered by the fact that they waved not only glittering blades, but cotton umbrellas. As the Queen also carried an umbrella with her own Royal hands, some wag commemorated the event in the following lines :

"Macpherson of Cluny and Tulloch, I feel for them ;
   They've drawn out their men like Castilian guerillas ;
To welcome their Prince and Queen such a sight ne'er was
      seen—
   Highlanders ranked under cotton umbrellas.
      Highlanders, Highlanders, well have ye fought of yore,
         Led by the sound of your bagpipers' bellows !
      Now for your tartans green, find ye a proper screen,
         Under your chiefs—and your cotton umbrellas !

But ye had example set, under the heavy wet;
  Didn't the Queen, as the newspapers tell us,
Ay, and the Prince and train, land in the pouring rain,
  Under the shelter of ' goodly umbrellas.'
    Wet Caledonia ! who wouldn't drown for thee?
    Are not your sons loyal, brave-hearted fellows?
  Keeping their powder dry, while with a smothered cry,
  Comes a damp welcome from under umbrellas. ''

Ardverikie, the Lodge of the Marquis of Abercorn, was little more than a shooting box, and as a fairly large party accompanied the Queen, Prince Leiningen, the Duke and Duchess of Norfolk, Earl Grey, two Equerries and a Maid of Honour, some tents were taken, and an inn had to be pressed into service. Poor Earl Grey was an even worse sailor than Prince Albert, and he prayed hard to be excused, but as there was no other member of the Government at liberty, he had to submit to his fate. About the Prince's well-known tendency to sea-sickness the *Observer* had a foolish paragraph which was intended as serious news : " It has been stated that His Royal Highness suffered in this disagreeable respect (sea-sickness) to a far greater extent than Her Majesty, the fact being, that for only one day, when the weather was very bad, was either of these Royal personages sick. On this occasion there was *complete sympathy*, each having endured an equal amount of discomfort, but such as could be easily borne when it afforded the opportunity of witnessing so much loyalty and devotion from *all classes* of Her Majesty's subjects."

One would commiserate the Queen-Prince upon being the subject of such an absurd paragraph, were it not that it seems to have been royally inspired; the style is distinctly that of the Queen, and she was always so anxious to defend her Prince that she sometimes did it to an indiscreet extent, raising a laugh where she intended to gain admiration for him. She evidently agreed with the critic who asked:

> "What palace slave could adulate so well
> The Lord's Anointed, pitching in a swell."

During their stay at Ardverikie one innovation was made; in place of special messengers arriving each day with despatches for Her Majesty, she took advantage of the ordinary post, and thereupon a great pother arose, for it was stated that the seals of several letters were found broken on arrival, other letters never reached their destination, some official documents were intercepted, and several letters to her attendants were so saturated with rain as to be illegible. The papers announced that a close investigation was being instituted, but the *Caledonian Mercury*, anxious to save the credit of its country, affirmed that the Post Office authorities knew nothing of the matter and that the whole story was false.

In 1841 there had been a lively row over the opening of letters in the Post Office, and Tom Duncombe, "the grand jobman of miscellaneous grievances," had accused Sir James Graham, the Postmaster-General, of opening the letters of Mazzini during the Garibaldian wars. Graham justified his action by custom and statistics, and Melbourne, talking over this, said he had signed warrants for opening O'Connell's letters

and had urged Normanby to open those of the King
of Hanover, but that he was afraid to do it. But
why anyone should have wished to open the letters
addressed to the Queen and members of her household in Scotland it is not easy to judge.

It is notable that later Prince Albert, when writing
to the Prince of Prussia, desired that his letter should
go by common post, as he did not object to the contents
of the packet being known wherever it might be
opened.

At Ardverikie it was more lonely than at Blair
Athol, and the ways of the country were more primitive, so the cartoonists were again busy either reporting or inventing amusements for Prince Albert, the
curious thing being that they were constantly poking
fun at him as an admirer of Scotch girls. One quite
amusing scene—and there were others of the same
sort—is more or less based on the Prince's wonder
at seeing the bare-legged lassies. In it he and the
Queen are stopping at the entrance to a building,
where a " braw hielander " has just poured out a glass
of liquid—perhaps whiskey—for Her Majesty, and
respectfully stands, cap in one hand and bottle in
the other, but watching the Prince with meaning grin,
who with glass to his eye is bending down to see the
pretty, bare-legged waitress disappear up some steps.
Again, under the title of " Deer Sport in the Highlands," the Prince, in the centre of the picture, is
chucking a country girl under the chin, while she
laughs into his eyes, and his Scotch attendants stand
round in high glee, saying : " Eh, sirs, but His

Highness is ower keen at that sport." Of course, it needs very little fire to make a smoke, but really one wonders whether Albert did not sometimes allow himself at least to admire pretty women. There were, as I have indicated, whispers to that effect early in the reign, one being of a Countess Resterlitz, who was stopped at Calais when on her way to urge some past friendship upon the Prince; and another of a certain Countess penetrating even into Buckingham Palace as one of the Prince's old friends. Victoria regarded her as insane, and after that orders were given that Prince Albert should always be followed by some trusty person. Of course, these two Countesses may have been one and the same.

Perhaps the Prince was as bored as the Queen with this Scotch visit, and tried to lighten it by noticing the village folk around; Victoria certainly wearied of Ardverikie. The weather was bad, and the scenery of the very boldest type, causing her to feel that the sublime could be improved if it were combined with a gentler beauty. However, her doctors vetoed her removal elsewhere on the score of the advantage to her health, so she stayed the intended time, and then started for home in the wettest weather that even Scotland could offer.

It was while the yacht was off Campbeltown on its way home that the Queen acceded to a request made by a distiller, generally known as Long John, of Ben Nevis, to present the Prince of Wales with a cask of whiskey, which was to be kept at Buckingham Palace until he was of age.

They steamed to Fleetwood Harbour, where they lay the night, going thence to Euston by train early the next morning. Of this an enterprising journalist in the *Manchester Examiner* wrote as follows : " The great, the eventful morning has passed. The Queen has landed here. Fleetwood has been honoured beyond any other port in the North of England, and great is its rejoicing thereat. The wharf of the Preston and Wye Railway Company is the first spot on Lancashire soil on which Queen Victoria has set her foot, and for many a livelong day the inhabitants of that rapidly rising town will talk over the honour which was conferred upon them by our beloved Queen and recall the event of this memorable day. And yet those events were but of brief duration—fascinating and dazzling, like an indistinct but happy dream, which, without leaving any marked impression of individual circumstance, diffuses over the whole man a sensation of happiness."

The Times, that grave and dignified journal, had set all other papers an example of this sort when in 1842 the Queen went North. It had a political purpose to serve in so doing, for it had been inimical to Her Majesty for so long that now, when a Protectionist Government was in, it tried to cover up its trail with the grossest of adulation. It published accounts and articles upon the journey to and fro which, to people not spoiled by circumstance, seemed very derogatory to the Queen's real dignity. It chronicled the journey of the greyhounds and terriers; it told how at Harwich a crowd gathered to see the Royal boat pass :

R

" Foremost we distinguished a group of youthful children, who, having imbibed loyalty with their mother's milk, stretched out their little arms towards their beloved Sovereign and lisped a blessing upon her Royal head." Upon which an aristocratic bard, the Honourable —— (why did he not give his name?), wrote :

> "Oh, what a subject for disloyal squibs,
> Those infant courtiers slobbering in their bibs,
> And lisping mindless chatterings that day,
> As the flash pageant wended on its way ;
> And well indeed, at that most childish sight
> Might babies crow and splutter with delight ! "

The Times also told how " a simple fisherman, with a venerable bald head, held up a fine fish with both hands, as the only homage he had to offer the Queen; this act was kindly acknowledged by Prince Albert," on which the bitter critic commented :

> "Albert acknowledged (but we are not told how
> Whether with half-a-guinea or a bow.
> The last most likely, as he's seldom rash,
> Except in buying parrots, with his cash)."

The account of how the Prince saved many lives after landing is really comic. The Royal carriages were preceded and followed by those of many inhabitants, and at one point some horses in front took fright and wheeled round so that the coachman lost control of them. Upon which the intrepid Prince, " with great quickness and presence of mind, instantly called out to Her Majesty's postilions to stop; at the same moment four or five archers sprang forward and seized the horses' heads. By His Royal Highness's prompt orders, and the horses being stopped, many lives were saved ".:

> "Calmly bold, of valour such the force is,
> He rose, and bade the postboy stop the horses."

Great emphasis was laid upon a Sunday morning service held in the dining-room of the palace at Dalkeith, into which room was introduced "devotional chairs of oak with crimson velvet cushions," and at which the preacher took as his text: "O Jerusalem that bringest good tidings, lift up thy voice with strength; lift it up, be not afraid; say unto the cities of Judah, behold your God!" This text raised much comment among the quibblers, just as did a later sermon by a preacher at Liverpool, in which Albert was likened to Christ:

> "If it were needful, that to soothe her pride—
> Our little Monarch should be deified,
> He might at least—such blunders really vex—
> Have paid some small attention to the sex.
> Goddess, not God, had been the proper name,
> Why to a male transfer the royal Dame?
> He could not mean, a treason had been in't,
> By this mistake to delicately hint
> Our precious Queen was wont, as whisper some,
> To wear the ' inexpressibles ' at home! "

Such over-praise reacts, not upon the person uttering it, but upon the unfortunate person about whom it is uttered, and sheds discredit, not glory.

In the following September the Queen and Prince went to Balmoral, near Braemar, where they leased a little castle for six weeks. Of this place, Greville, who went down as Clerk of the Council in 1849, says that the place was pretty, but the house very small. "They live there without any state whatever; they live not merely like private gentlefolk, but like very small gentlefolk, small house, small rooms, small establishment. There are no soldiers, and the whole guard of the Sovereign and the whole Royal Family is a single policeman who walks about the grounds to keep out impertinent intruders and improper characters. . . . They live with greatest simplicity and ease. The Prince shoots every morning, returns to luncheon, and then they walk and drive. The Queen is running in and out of the house all day long, and often goes about alone, walks into the cottages, and sits down and chats with the old women. I never before was in society with the Prince, or had any conversation with him. On Thursday morning John Russell and I were sitting together after breakfast when he came in and sat down with us, and we conversed for about three quarters of an hour. I was greatly struck with him. I saw at once (what I had always heard) that he was very intelligent and highly educated, and, moreover, that he had a thoughtful mind, and thinks of subjects worth thinking about. He seemed very much at his ease, very gay, pleasant, and without the least stiffness or air of dignity."

It was in Scotland that Sir Charles Lyell made much the same remark about the Prince, and there can be little doubt that his nature expanded and became simplified, and the hauteur in which he so often shrouded himself was banished when he was quite away from all pretensions of royal state.

H.R.H. PRINCE ALBERT IN THE INSIGNIA OF THE ORDER OF THE GARTER.
From a Print in Mr. A. M. Broadley's Collection.

In 1852 Balmoral was purchased by the Prince, the old building pulled down, and an elaborate Castle built of granite after his own design. Though the new house was quite suitable for a royal residence, there was still every attempt made to secure the old privacy. The etiquette on the public roads was not to see the Queen if you met her; you might slip out of sight or be admiring the view, but you might not raise your hat or bow. Not to know this, and to offend by offering a courtesy, was to receive anything but a courteous smile in return.

It was also a grave offence to repeat any of the Castle doings, an offence which was, however, constantly committed. The following I found in the advertising columns of *The Times*, so that surreptitious enterprise even went so far as publishing a paper.

" The *Balmoral Gazette and Highland Herald* published every morning during residence of Crown in Scotland, 2s. 6d. weekly. From local advantages and ready access to the surest sources of information, the contributors to this journal will be ready to furnish the earliest and most interesting intelligence of the Royal movements so far as they can interest the loyal public."

How much the rule was evaded was also shown in *The Puppet Show*, which gave a cartoon, entitled " Royal Privacy in the Highlands" of the breakfast-table at Balmoral, round which the Queen, the Prince, and some children sit, while representatives of the *Daily News*, *Morning Herald*, *Morning Post*, *The*

Times, and others are hiding behind curtains, under tables, and in corners, all with notebooks in their hands. The picture is accompanied by a short article on the penny-a-liners who dogged Her Majesty from mountain to river, on the Mayors who waited at every port she passed eager to rush into her presence, and on the various other dull incidents likely to make weariness in her life.

There are hundreds of stories about the Royal Family at Balmoral, but they have been chronicled so often that they need not be included here. I would rather turn to the incident of the indiscreet clergyman, who, desiring to curry favour with Royalty, disgraced the Prince by the most servile flattery, at Liverpool, when His Royal Highness went there in 1846 to lay the first stone of the Sailors' Home and to open the Albert Dock. This visit was followed by a sermon preached by Canon McNeile at St. Jude's, from the words, *" Every eye shall see Him; or, Prince Albert's visit to Liverpool used in the illustration of the second coming of Christ."* The first paragraph, which displayed a fine mixture of the business instinct and exaggeration of sentiment, was as follows :

" We have just witnessed a stirring scene; and, to all who will take the trouble of reflecting seriously, a very instructive one. A promise was held out to our great town that our eyes should behold the Prince; and what were the consequences? Preparations of every description, eager, animated, costly; scaffoldings and stands erected; balconies strengthened; the ordinary occupations of life suspended; countless multitudes congregated; trades, professions, associations with their appropriate emblems; civic authorities bearing the badges of state; generals and admirals exhibiting the insignia of war; consecrated ambassadors of the Gospel of Peace; *the bridegroom from his chamber*; *the bride out of her closet*; old men and maidens, young men and children—all *on tiptoe, with outstretched necks* and eager eyes, to see THE PRINCE IN HIS BEAUTY; the Prince, the assessor, and, on this occasion, the manifestor of Royalty. It was a scene well calculated to illustrate and impress the *great revealed truth*, that the kingly office upon earth is at once *an ordinance and an image of the authority and majesty of God.*"

Thus did the preacher burnish up that poor tarnished thing—the right Divine, and asked his congregation to see in the pale and comely face of the good young Prince the shadow of the majesty of God. When we think of Henry VIII., Charles II., and the Georges, do we still believe in the right divine?— still think that there is a halo round the head of the sovereign which raises him or her into an intermediary position between God and man?—and, if so, does the same halo serve for all sovereigns, good or bad?

Mr. McNeile went further, for he said:

"When I saw the universal movement; when I heard on every side the bustle of expectation; when I overheard on the right hand and on the left the bursting apostrophe, 'He is coming!' 'He is here!' *I felt deeply what it seems to have been the Apostle's great*

object to impress on the Christian Church with reference to the SECOND COMING OF CHRIST. Behold He
cometh, go ye out to meet Him! Every eye shall see
Him!"

Christ and Prince Albert! The Son of God
coming in His glory to redeem mankind, and the
starred and gartered husband of the Queen—a sinful,
erring man! On the one hand, the great and awful
day; on the other, a locomotive from London bringing Prince Albert and his attendants; and the clergyman felt the same uplifting of the soul, the same fear
and rapture, over the latter as he anticipated feeling
at the second coming of Christ!

Is it wonderful that when clergymen can stand
unabashed in their pulpits and deliver themselves of
such frivolities they cannot number among their congregation the great mass of thoughtful people? I
wish I knew what the Queen and the Prince thought
of this sermon; for there at once would be a real
illumination upon their characters. At least, they did
not give the reverend Canon what he wanted, a
Bishopric!

The Reverend Hugh McNeile thought so highly
of his inspired address that he advertised it everywhere as a pamphlet, and it raised universal indignation in Church circles, being condemned as blasphemy.
Said the *Church of England Journal*: "Every eye
shall see Him! See whom? Does he mean Prince
Albert or the LORD OF HEAVEN AND EARTH? Prince
Albert and his equerries, or Christ and His angels?"
The fame of the much-prolonged advertisement

spread to our Colonies, and a Montreal paper reduced it to scorn by saying that it reminded them of the effective paragraphic style of patent medicine puffs.

Mr. Hugh McNeile was surely one of the chief of sinners, whereas we may judge that those who wrote the inscription : " To the Glory of God, in Honour of the Queen ! " for the foundation-stone of Victoria Hall in 1842 were only stupid.

CHAPTER X

THE QUEEN AND THE PRESSMAN

IN addition to the constant sense of annoyance caused by the Queen-Prince's relations with Palmerston, and the uneasiness which the alternating friendship and friction between them and France brought about, there was a third trouble in the first decade of their lives together which gave them many a pang. This was the publicity given to their affairs by a man named Jasper Tomsett Judge, who in 1839 settled at Windsor, becoming Windsor correspondent of the *Morning Herald* and other papers.

Being a strong Tory, his articles criticising the doings of the Whigs, "who filled nearly every nook and corner of the royal palace," gave offence to Queen Victoria, and in 1841, when she was in terror at the idea of losing Melbourne, either she or the Government tried to bribe Judge by the offer of a good appointment to turn Whig, and by the offer of a sum of money to leave Windsor. Such an act was not like Melbourne, who troubled little about the papers, it was too crude; but it came through George Anson and Edward Stanley, so perhaps Melbourne was over-persuaded by the Queen.

250

Judge replied with the candour remarkable in extreme party men : that the Whigs were beneath contempt, had surrounded the Queen and the Prince Consort with needy minions to act as spies or advisers, and he would have nothing to do with such a set.

At the end of a week the same gentleman called upon him again, and renewed the offers in more tempting form. Again Judge refused, and from that time declared that he was persecuted by the creatures of Lord Melbourne in the Palace.

However, at the General Election the Tory was successful over "the Court Candidate," and Judge asserted that the successful man was never forgiven by the Court. Then reason for his removal having disappeared, the pressman had a period of peace, was allowed to frequent the Castle, and get news for publication from the secretary to the Master of the Household. When he could not get information, he attributed it to the malice of the Whigs.

As a matter of fact, Judge played a fair game in the news he sent to the *Herald*, the *Dispatch*, and other papers, giving ordinary information in a respectful way. The public was informed that the Queen had been pleased to walk, and the Prince had been pleased to shoot, that their Royal Highnesses the Prince of Wales and the Princess Royal had driven in their new pony-carriage; that the Duchess of Kent and her lady had come to dine, and that Sir Robert Peel had been granted an audience—all the trifling little programme which it is supposed the world wishes to see. There was no interest in it, though it was sometimes made to meander down the greater part of a column. Perhaps idle people read it, and it pleased the Queen to know that her movements were of such importance to her subjects; it also helped to give Judge an income.

Occasionally, and especially towards the end, Judge would let himself go anonymously in little articles and criticisms, and some extravagant diatribe would appear, such as the following upon an Investiture of the Bath. This article was unsigned, but only Judge could have written it in *Britannia*, and it was at a time when the trouble was nearing a crisis :

"Civil Knights, Fiddlesticks! for we really have scarcely common patience to dwell upon the sickening details of these wretched attempts to maintain in a civilised age the ostentatious ceremonial of feudal barbarism. This stupid ostentation of the crimson velvet cushion, and the Gold Rod of Office, must appear particularly disgusting to the enlightened mind, and the whole description of the spectacle renders the Court very silly in the eyes of the public. . . . All this idle pomp and vain show produce nowadays a very different effect from what they did a quarter of a century ago; they cease to dazzle and to blind the public vision with their brilliancy, but they set people thinking on these and other circumstances associated with the existence of monarchical institutions."

This was a very different thing from the following which appeared in his Court Circular column, and which was calculated to please the public love of royalty :

"The Prince of Wales and the Princess Royal and Princess Alice have been frequently taken out in the Parks and grounds adjacent to the Castle. The Princess Royal displays great intelligence, prettily bowing to any persons she meets on her excursions, and appearing to take pleasure in the recognition and acknowledgments of the town people."

Every now and then some remarkable royal events were chronicled in the dailies as well as in the comic papers, such as that given one day under the heading of *Latest Intelligence* : "The Queen and Prince Albert walked on Tuesday afternoon in the pleasure grounds of Osborne House"; or these from the *Court Circular* : "Her Majesty was most graciously pleased during her stay at Windsor to enjoy most excellent health and spirits"; "Her Majesty attended by Viscountess Jocelyn went riding in the park on two ponies"; "The Princess Royal and the Prince of Wales walked and rode on their ponies." Why did they ever go to see a circus?

This sort of thing tempted the flippant to jest, and under the heading "Court Circular" there was to be read one morning in a comic journal : "The Marmosets, pretty little dears, are in good health. The severe frost has not in any way injured the turtle-doves in the new dovecote. The tailless cats have been slightly affected owing to their having been indulged with a *tête-à-tête* on the Castle walls; the dormice are sleeping well, though they have not yet found their tails," etc.

Lady Lyttelton says that Prince Albert was the first

person to insist upon having an official *Court Circular* published, which he supervised, and the above slips must have somewhat enlivened the deadly descriptions of daily nothings which were sent to the papers.

When the Prince began to grapple with the problem of the economic misrule in the Castle, information of what was happening or of the dismissal of servants got into the papers—as I have shown, and a man named Henry Saunders, Inspector of the Palace, was suspected of furnishing it. Judge, who had gone gleefully into the fray, and who, I imagine, had got the information he published from Saunders, wrote of the matter :

" This Whig busybody (Anson) brought a most foul charge against a Conservative gentleman holding a highly confidential appointment in the Queen's household. The charge was fully investigated by the Board of Green Cloth and found to be wholly groundless. Still this man and his friends, the Whigs at Court, were permitted to play their fantastic tricks, and absolutely to ride rough-shod over the few honest Conservatives left in the Royal palace."

Saunders was, however, pensioned off with £500 a year.

Judge further speaks of this " busybody " as having " absolutely the effrontery to announce that he had been selected by the Queen to put Her Majesty's affairs in order, and had the consummate impudence to go round to the Royal tradesmen and obtain an account of moneys owing by the department of the Lord Chamberlain—a department with which he had no

more to do than with the department of the First
Lord of the Treasury."

Peel was scarcely more beloved by Judge than was
Melbourne, so Judge began to write a little book,
describing the wicked way in which the Melbournites
at Court treated the meek and good Conservatives,
and the policy which Sir Robert Peel ought to follow
in protecting them.   This book, which was as badly
treated as the Conservatives were supposed to be,
was entitled :

"THE WHIGS ABOUT THE THRONE

and

THE PERSECUTION OF THE CONSERVATIVES.

PART I.—The Past.
PART II.—The Present.

"What are such wretches?   What but vapours foul
From Fens and Bogs, by royal beams exhaled,
That radiance intercepting which should cheer
The land at large ! Hence subjects' hearts grow cold,
And frozen loyalty forgets to flow."

The fame of Judge and his forthcoming pamphlet
reached the politicians in London, and he was induced
to show his work to the Conservative member, Ralph
Neville, and under promises of reward was further
induced by Lord Delawarr to suspend publication.
As he was to get £200 for the book, it was a hard
favour to grant, but, relying on their words, he consented.   He was evidently not a business man, or he
would have set a price upon his consent.

When Judge found out that George Anson and
others at Court knew all about the matter, and that

no fulfilment of the vague promises was intended, he wrote to Neville on the subject, and was abruptly informed that if he chose to leave Windsor he should receive a hundred pounds, otherwise he would get nothing.

Up to this point Judge had been an obnoxious busy-body, reporting Palace happenings somewhat unnecessarily; though some such person must inevitably come to the fore when revolutions occur, as both sides will somehow find a mouthpiece. But the matter of the little book was ended unfairly, promises were made to the man which those who made them could not keep, and the opportunity of drawing his sting was not taken by those who stood behind the promises. It was neither an honourable nor a wise procedure. Judge felt that he had done, and had intended to do, service to the Tory Government; Neville acknowledged that the party was indebted to him, and Lord Delawarr seems to have given his opinion that in the matter of the publication advantage had been taken of him, but admitted that he had authority *not* to give any compensation to the writer.

The Queen and the Prince unfortunately made this matter a personal one to themselves, as the end of the affair will show, and the only course they would sanction was the enforced clearance of Judge out of Windsor. Judge protested, making his charge against both political parties now:

"I have not only been persecuted and vilified, and attempted to be ruined by the *Whigs*, but abused and insulted by the very party I so faithfully served.

I have been offered £100 to slink away from Windsor."

Of course, he again refused the money and the move, and then, as the Prince would tolerate nothing less than the banishment of Judge, a Court official went to one of the most likely tradesmen in the town and asked him to be the agent in buying up all Judge's debts.   But the Castle was not in favour with the town at that time, and a prompt refusal was returned to this suggestion.

The insignificant journalist who, if diplomacy had been used, might have been made innocuous, won this battle, though with some loss, and was for years a very annoying enemy to royalty.   It was a pity that Queen Victoria, when her dignity was offended, was too easily made angry, and was so extreme sometimes in her anger as to lose all sense of justice.

This was true also of the Prince, who had a curious strain of hardness in his character, a hardness which he would show to his dearest as well as to delinquents. His mild amiability went hand-in-hand with a critical severity, and his warm, self-sacrificing love would suddenly change to painful coldness.   Stockmar had so tutored him that his feeling of superiority was not an impression, it was the backbone of his character, and those of whom he judged ill he also judged as fit for nothing.   No hint of this ever appears in the Queen's books, yet it was the inner secret of his power over her.   She may have adored his goodness as much as her enthusiastic pen betrays, but she feared it too; she believed in and bowed down before the superiority

s

which he was certain was his. There is a picture of the Queen and Prince taken some time before he died, she seated and looking up at him with eyes of dog-like devotion, he gazing down at her, grave, a little sad, otherwise stolid and inexpressive. It was a true picture of their characters. As Duke Ernest of Coburg says of Albert in his Memoirs : " He often stood on the brink of . . . allowing himself opinions and views which are wont to arise from contempt of mankind in the abstract," and that "he despised untruth and phrase-making and grew rough and positive in judgment." He was the usual two-in-one, only circumstance had not so welded the two together as to make a complete and beautiful whole. He was loving, kind, and charitable, but also hard, critical, and condemnatory.

It is not to be wondered at that such a man could not deal with one like Judge, a revolutionary Tory, hot in political principle, unscrupulous in practice, yet with a pride which prevented him from ever acknowledging defeat. To the Prince he was a worm, one of whom he personally would have felt justified in saying with the Irishman in the play, " There are some creatures you cannot crush, they lie so flat in the dirt."

But Judge was not singular in his feelings towards the inhabitants of the Castle. All Windsor was in a state of grumble, and, when one considers some of the conditions of a Royal town, there seems to be as much penalty as profit about it. The Prince was being cordially disliked by the Royal borough for many reasons, for in his changes in the park and round the

Castle he had not spared Windsor. Footpaths were diverted, and a road across the park was marked for disappearance. To secure greater privacy houses and buildings near the Castle had been pulled down, and the land either absorbed or left idle, by which course the town lost rates to the value of from six hundred to eight hundred pounds a year.[1]

There was a Castle and Town quarrel about the drainage, which, though of a primitive character in the town, simply did not exist in the Castle, nor in the infantry and cavalry barracks near it. All the refuse from the Castle emptied itself into the first open ditch in the Long Walk, and that from the barracks was equally well arranged in other ditches conveniently close to the buildings. So the "Woods and Forests" drew up a scheme for putting these buildings on a safe sanitary system, estimating the cost at £17,000, of which the town, for the improvement in its drainage, was asked to pay £10,000. Expert engineers, however, came to the conclusion that the town would benefit to the amount of £4,750, and at a hot-tempered gathering of townsmen Windsor agreed to pay exactly £5,000.

It should be realised that though the country as a whole supports Royalty, it does not pay Royalty's rates, and Royalty does not pay them either. It is the shopkeeper in the street, the householder and cottager at the Palace gate, from whose meagre purses are drawn the poor rate and all the local rates, both for themselves and for the huge buildings in which live Royalty and all its servitors.

[1] Vide reports in London and provincial papers.

The want and distress of that dreadful time were responsible for many things good and bad, and among them were the waves of hatred of the Prince which occasionally shook the people. It was in the famine years, and the cartoons accentuated the differences between rich and poor; Peel asleep in bed with a long line of ghosts of starved people filing past him; John Bull in miserable rags brought before the Queen, who wishes to relieve him with a slice from her huge loaf, while her children cry that she must not give away their bread, are examples. The *Puppet Show* gave one in which the great pensioned were casting their wealth into a cradle representing England; the Duke of Wellington £27,000; the King of Hanover £21,000; Brougham £10,000; Queen Adelaide £100,000; Prince Albert £50,000; and the Queen £350,000. The mere mention of such sums made people gasp, and when they realised that public obligations demanded of themselves were not imposed upon Royalty, such as rates and taxes, local bitterness grew deeper. In the poor parish of Pimlico there were execrations over the fact that Buckingham Palace was free. I write of this because it must be recognised that Judge was doing in his way what hundreds of philanthropists, journalists, and others were also doing, they were blindly seeking some readjustment by which the rich gave more to the common fund, and by which the poor could at least live. The Royal pair being the most prominent people, were used as types, and exactly the same inquisitions went on in other counties about rich landowners. But Judge was different from his fellow-workmen in that he had a personal grudge against the Queen-Prince, though he never gave that feeling verbal expression.   But there are more ways of showing a spite than by announcing it, and Judge's way was to keep a sharp eye upon the doings of the underlings of the Palace, and a smart pen ready with which to report them.

Among the buildings repaired by Prince Albert was George III.'s Flemish Farm. He laid down a method for cultivating the land, bought stock to be specially treated, and made the farm a success.   Little paragraphs constantly appeared to the effect that " Prince Albert won the second prize of £5 for a pen of pigs," " Prince Albert took first prize for the best two-year-old bull from the Berkshire Agricultural Association" (to which he gave £5 in subscription); he sold his prize cattle for £70 and £60 respectively; he took a prize of £20 for his ox and £3 for the best swede. Peel once in a speech praised the Prince for turning his attention to the promotion of agriculture, and asked a cheer for him as a British farmer, seeing the prices his stock fetched.   I have always wondered how a man in such a position could condescend to compete with business farmers for prizes; for every advantage wealth could give was on his side, and he was bound to win; to have proved that superior produce could be raised would have been honour enough.   I fear the local farmers scarcely liked such a competitor, but it needed Jasper Judge to show how the matter could be turned to advantage.   He pointed out to the Windsor Vestry that though the Prince was making money from the farm, he was paying no rates. The rates, at eightpence in the pound, would amount to fifteen pounds a year, and for this sum the Vestry sent in a demand. The Prince refused to pay on the grounds that he had no beneficial occupation, and that the property belonged to the Queen. At the discussion of vestrymen there seemed to be plenty of evidence to show that the sale of the produce of the farm brought in good profit, for not only were cattle and pigs being sold well, but turnips and mangel-wurzels. So a further application was made, and not replied to for several months, during which the Royal Farmer was consulting the legal authorities as to his responsibility. The lawyers agreed with him, and Anson eventually wrote denying *in toto* the Prince's legal obligation. The parochial authorities bowed to the law, and replied that under the circumstances they regretted the claim they had made, but they hoped, as the maintenance of the poor pressed so heavily on the parish, "that the Prince would take the state of the parish into his most gracious consideration."

It was probably as much caution as unwillingness to lose money that caused Albert to refuse to pay rates on a farm which was used for commerce, whatever may have been the idea in starting it, for the demand being withdrawn, the Prince wrote that he felt himself at liberty to take the course which was most satisfactory to himself, and to pay as a voluntary contribution a sum equal to that named, and that this payment should be made as from the year 1841.

This "act of grace" was unfortunately followed by

an incident arising from it which gave further handle
to the critics, though it may be that the Prince was
not directly responsible; for one in his position must
leave much to subordinates. A man named Richard
Webling, a worker on the Flemish farm, was pensioned
at the age of seventy-two with five shillings a week.
In 1846, some months after the affair of the rates, old
Webling, then seventy-four, went for his money as
usual, and was told that he need not come again, for
the parish, having compelled His Royal Highness to
pay poor rates, must for the future support him. The
next week Webling went to the Guardians, and was
given three shillings, with a promise of three loaves
weekly. His wife had broken her leg three years
before, and, having never regained the proper use of
it, was unable to work, and the old couple had to pay
half-a-crown a week to keep a roof over them. For
all their other wants there was left sixpence and three
loaves; they had managed hardly enough with half-a-
crown, now they could not exist. In such a case it is
not surprising that the worn-out workman went to the
one man in the town who had gained a reputation for
championing the distressed, and it was equally to be
expected that Judge would take up the case hotly.
He drew up a memorial for Webling, exactly stating
the facts, and sent it to the Prince's Secretary. After
waiting some days in vain for an answer, Judge detailed the affair in the London papers, raising an unpleasant amount of criticism; and at the end of three
weeks the pension was restored. Presumably Prince
Albert did not realise that while he was indulging in

the luxury of considering the matter, starvation wasted no time, and there was necessity to act quickly. However, the publicity given to the affair was another reason for hating Judge.

There were other things, little to a Prince but tragic to a peasant, proving with horrible precision that the amusement of the rich is more precious than the lives of the workers; and Judge pounced upon them all, blazoned them to the world, and wrung justice from the hands of time-servers.

One arose from the Prince's reverence for the Game Laws. He spent much time shooting, employed many keepers, and impressed them with a sense of the extreme importance of their work. These men were always on the watch for poachers, and used much ingenuity in devising traps, verbal or otherwise, by which culprits could be made to betray themselves. One of Prince Albert's gamekeepers trapped a man of between sixty and seventy, named Dean, trying to sell four pheasants and six pheasants' eggs. As it was not pleasant to bring the Prince's name forward as a prosecutor in a small affair like this, two County magistrates heard the accusation in the Town Clerk's private office—not in the usual Court room—and sentenced Dean—about whose offence there was no doubt—to pay in fine and costs £10 11s., or in default four months in Reading Gaol. Judge learned of the irregularity beforehand, and insisted on being present during the hearing of the case; and then, fired with compassion and disgust, reported the affair in *The Times*, the *Morning Chronicle*, the *Morning Adver-*

tiser, and the *Morning Post*.   Upon this a little whirl-
wind of comment arose, for in truth, in spite of the
way in which Queen Victoria took delight in reflecting
that everyone thought so much of her "dearest
master," Albert had by no means made himself
popular, and folk like to feel justified in a prejudice.
Mr. Collett, M.P. for Athlone, brought the matter
before the House of Commons, and the same gentleman paid the fine and got Dean released.   Judge's own
comment upon this runs :

" The publicity which I thus gave to these oppres-
sive proceedings, on the part of a man in the service
of the Prince (His Royal Highness not escaping
some severe animadversions for having such a person
in his employ) gave great annoyance, I regret to hear,
in the highest quarters."

But he should have realised that the magistrates
were more blameworthy for their severity than the
gamekeeper, whose most important work in those days
was recognised to be, not the care of game, but the
detection of poachers.   At that time gamekeepers had
become the curse of the countryside.   Most magistrates were sportsmen, had an exaggerated idea of the
sanctity of game, and would take a gamekeeper's word
against that of all others.   A gamekeeper could easily
swear away an enemy's liberty, and commit acts of
brutality and oppression without punishment.   Many
of them were callow youths, wanting in judgment and
knowledge, and one such brought scandal again upon
the Prince's name.   A youth of nineteen found a
woman, named Maria Wells, picking up dead sticks

on a corner of Albert's land. He first shouted and then set his dog—a young bloodhound—upon her. The woman, who was expecting the birth of a child, had no chance at flight, and the dog knocked her down, biting her in the hip and back.

Someone—it may have been Judge—persuaded Maria Wells to charge the young gamekeeper, and at the trial one reporter was present—Judge, of course! The magistrates wished him to withdraw, but he refused; then a delicate attempt was made to "negotiate" with him, and to find out what he would take to keep the matter out of the papers. "Not for five hundred pounds!" was his curt answer. So he was present while the youth was fined two pounds and ten shillings costs!

Put the two cases side by side! For four dead pheasants and six eggs, ten pounds; for a woman's health, sanity, and the life of her unborn child, two pounds! She and her child were worth just a pheasant and an egg in the minds of these "most just judges." It was no wonder that Judge dwelt on the larger aspect of the case, and troubled little about the details, and so caused a correspondent from Windsor to write to *The Times* and accuse him of misrepresenting facts. For instance, he had not stated in his reports that the magistrate had urged that the young man did not set the dog, which also was only a young dog, on the woman from any motive of revenge, but because she was trespassing on property he was paid to protect. But what a damnatory accusation was such a plea! It admitted at once the whole evil of the system; that revenge was regarded as a natural motive for such official assaults by gamekeepers, and that the poor were of so little value that they might not even gather the Castle's refuse! Then, again, this virtuous correspondent grumbled because Judge did not report that the woman *did not lie in bed* from her fright and injuries *for more than a week*. Now what a perfectly awful picture of the social standard of that day does this give us. A little time earlier Prince Albert when skating fell through some thin ice close to the shore and got partially wetted. It was reported in every paper with exclamatory horror, and the Queen was lauded as a heroine because she had the common sense to hold out a stick to him and help him to land, instead of running screaming away. But when a woman—a human being just as real as the Royal couple—was torn by one of the Prince's hounds, wilfully set upon her by one of the Prince's servants, a Windsor man indignantly complained that serious criticism of the matter was unjust because the injured woman did not lie in bed more than a week, and further contended that the gamekeeper was the person to be pitied, as in consequence of his mistake (!) he lost his situation.

Mr. Collett again came to the rescue, had full inquiries made, substantiated the charges, and gave Maria Wells five pounds to help her over her confinement. There is no record that Prince Albert compensated in any way this subject of the Crown for his man's brutality.

The recurrence of little matters of this sort in and

around Windsor kept alive in the district a bitter spirit of dislike for the Prince, which was accentuated by Albert's reserve and parsimony. He could not or would not atone in any personal way for the faults of his servants, either by sympathy or by money. Yet he could theorise about the working classes and work out ideas of reform, for when famine in the British Isles was at its height, the Prince could take the chair at a meeting of an Association for the Improvement of the Working Classes, make a most judicious speech, assume the patronage of the Society, and contribute to the funds needed to supply baths and wash-houses for the poor!

Game preserving has been responsible for more class hatred in England than all the agitators that ever lived and lectured, and Berkshire was dully angry with the Prince's innovations in the sporting world. He forbade the destruction of either foxes or rabbits in Windsor Park, on the assumption that the rabbits were the natural food of the foxes, and that therefore his partridges and pheasants would not suffer; but the farmers knew that both animals were deadly pests to the crops and fowls around the park. Yet when the spirit moved him, the Prince shot rabbits in great numbers, which he sold to a contractor at Egham. *Punch*, comparing him with Prince Hal in his wild-oat days, was satiric upon the Prince's constant amusement of shooting:

"He rose up to breakfast and shoot—and he came home to lunch. His life apparently had no better aim than the bearing of his fowling-piece and rifle. He could bring down a stag indeed at a long range, and knock over partridges and pheasants right and left. But he was only great in a *battue*."

A further matter which produced both indignation and laughter in Windsor was a plan for removing the town to a greater distance from the Castle, as " the only effective means for improving the Royal residence and its vicinity."

The pulling down of houses, the diversion of paths, the raising of fences, by which any near view of the Castle from the park was prevented, the unending attempts of the Prince to secure an abnormal privacy, had built up a belief that he would only be happy in an absolute solitude. Thus a firm of architects, Messrs. Kyle and Kerle, of Carlton Chambers, Regent Street, drew up a pamphlet addressed to Her Majesty's Commissioner of Works, entitled " The Outline of a proposed Plan for Building New Towns at Windsor and Eton : in order completely to improve the Castle and Parks." The necessity for this was given in the following sentence : " Windsor Castle and Parks, penetrated and intersected by thoroughfares from the town, bear, in their *general* appearance *alone*, the *royal character*; in their minute features not even possessing the advantages of some neighbouring residences."

The hill was to be cleared of buildings to its very base, the parks extended, only one public road to run across at such a distance that it could offer no inconvenience to sacred Royalty. Further, all that portion of the town east of the Long Walk and the Hundred Steps and between the New Staines Road and the river would become private to Her Majesty.

Messrs. Kyle and Kerle seemed to think blandly that the Crown would lend—would purchase—would make up the deficiency—and that the national feeling in the town and elsewhere would do the rest. What confiding innocents!

One sentence is worth quoting for its mixed metaphors: "One argument, above all, cannot be resisted in conclusion—the great and unrivalled monument which the erection of both towns would be to Her Majesty, when Eton, *taking Windsor by the hand, inscribed on their joint structure the Record of a people's love.*" There would be certainly something original about putting an inscription on a joint knuckle or fist.

This precious scheme was sent round to the newspapers and all people in authority; it was commented on here and there, and promises of subscriptions were secured, seemingly to the extent of £250,000. But that was the end of it, excepting for a soreness in the minds of timid Windsorites, who could never be sure that the first promptings of such an idea had not come from Royalty.

When there was an effort made to buy Shakespeare's birthplace for the public, it met with no response at first, and the following letter was sent to the editor of one of the weeklies:

"SIR,

　　　Suffer me through the medium of your journal to ask the public to

Look upon this Picture	And on This.
For the proposed removal of houses at Windsor, more out of the whiff and wind of royalty, and for otherwise improving the Windsor estate,	For purchasing the house in which was born the greatest poet England or the World ever had,
£250,000.	ooo (or nothing).

H. D. GRIFFITHS."

But Judge committed more serious offences than that of championing the oppressed. He wrote little books with such suggestive titles as: "Court Jobbery"; "Sketches of Her Majesty's Household"; "Royal Correspondence, being Letters between the Queen and Louis Philippe (1848)"; "A Voice from Windsor"; "A Handbook to the New Royal Stables and Riding House at Windsor Castle"; "An Act of the People's Parliament"; "The Court and the Press"; and the last one, "The Royal Etchings," published by William Strange, Junior, was, as it were, the end of the affair of Jasper Tomsett Judge and the Royal castle.

The second of these books gave a list of salaries paid to servants, and told many interesting secrets. Thus while the Dean of the Chapel Royal received £200 a year, the Surveyor of Pictures £150, and the Principal Painter-in-Ordinary (for a time Sir Thomas Lawrence) was given £50; two of the kitchen men, the clerk and the chief cook, had £700 each, the master cook had £350, with permission to take apprentices at a premium of from £150 to £200; one confectioner had £300, and two others £250 each. England's Admirals and Generals did not receive so much as the Queen's cook, and many well-educated gentlemen were poorer than the royal chimney-sweeper, who was given £150 a year. In the early 'forties, too, out of the £1,200 a year allotted to the Queen as pension money, six lucky individuals who had at some time taught Princess Victoria Italian or music or singing or French, etc., received £100 a year each. Baroness Lehzen took £400, but probably from the Privy Purse.

It is easy to imagine how very angry the Queen would be over such an *exposé* of her domestic arrangements, especially as the Press wrote widely of it, spreading the information far and near.

Another of Judge's publications, "An Act of the People's Parliament," had a sub-title which quite sufficiently explained its contents. It ran, " For the reduction of Her Majesty's Civil List, and for promoting the welfare and prosperity of the People of the United Kingdom of Great Britain and Ireland, by the reduction of Her Majesty's allowance of £385,000 to £200,000 per annum in conformity with the recommendations of the Liverpool Financial Reform Association."

These little books produced deep rancour at Court, and the " Sketches " were probably responsible for what followed. To the Prince, with his German training, it was a dreadful idea that a man of this sort could not be summarily imprisoned, or at least prevented from publishing such books, and he was eager to get rid of Jasper by hook or by crook. Men have been imprisoned in Germany during the last few years for saying and doing things which were trivial compared with those boldly said by Judge. I must, however, that affairs may be understood, make a digression concerning one of the amusements of the Queen and the Prince.

After their marriage, Prince Albert initiated the Queen into the mystery and delights of etching, and they often together followed this pleasant diversion. Miss Skerritt, the Queen's wardrobe woman, whom Lady Eastlake for some reason designated as the "original" of the Court, being required to do the "biting" of the drawings. The Queen-Prince drew their dogs, their children, the landscapes, the houses, and it goes without saying that anyone who could secure a specimen of their work valued it highly. The etchings by the Prince I do not know, but I saw several of those by the Queen in Mr. Broadley's portfolios, one of which is reproduced here. The two little figures are well drawn, though there is an echo of the Queen's personality in the way that the subject is handled —no suggestion, no idealism, no real artistry, just what was there to be seen by the physical eye.

These etchings were discussed, as all royal accomplishments are discussed; people liked to know that their Queen and her husband were clever enough to produce such things. Judge several times made them the subject of admiring notes in the *Morning Herald*.

T

the *Weekly Dispatch, Britannia,* and other journals, and several of the etchings were reproduced in the papers, no annoyance being shown at the friendly mention of them.

On September 7th, 1848, an announcement appeared in *The Times,* and in other London and provincial papers, that a collection of about one hundred etchings by Her Majesty and Prince Albert had been made. "We understand that this perfectly unique collection will shortly be exhibited to the public, and thus enable the whole nation to form an opinion of Her Majesty's and the Prince Consort's great merits in a branch of the fine arts in which it is so difficult to excel. That both the Queen and the Prince rank very high in this department of art, their united and separate productions most amply testify."

This announcement is to be attributed to Judge. He may have had some doubts about the Queen's approbation of his scheme of holding an exhibition, but as no notice of *The Times* paragraph was taken by the Court, he thought it was safe; so he made out a catalogue, had it printed by William Strange, of Paternoster Row, and sent a copy to Her Majesty and one to Prince Albert.

Judge should have asked permission to form the exhibition first, but in spite of his conservatism he was a strong democrat, the etchings were his property, and he did not realise that a right in the actual drawings remained with the artists. The catalogues were, however, sent before steps were taken to form the exhibition, and both Judge and Strange seemed to think

ONE OF QUEEN VICTORIA'S ETCHINGS

From Mr. A. M. Bradley's Collection.

that if any Royal dislike to the plan existed, they would be duly informed.

The Queen and the Prince did object strongly, but they did not say so in any ordinary way; and we have here in some sense a new version of the Lady Flora Hastings affair. For a week after receiving the catalogues no sign was made, probably advice was being taken and plans laid; then the impulsiveness which had characterised the early lamentable mistake, strengthened by the Prince's hardness, impetuously swept away any thought of justice, and ended in devastating two families, banishing Strange from England, and breaking the man whom the ;Queen-Prince regarded as their enemy.

The Royal pair were no judges of character, and they did not stop to think that a man who had always shown himself above bribery would never consent to insignificant peculation, they also did not realise that the injustice shown to Judge in the matter of the pamphlet, and the injudicious attempts at bribery and banishment, were the cause of his rancour against them. They just saw their chance of smashing an annoying subject and they took it.

On a Tuesday, exactly seven days after the catalogue had been sent to the Queen, her solicitor called at Strange's office, and there learnt from his son that Strange had gone to Yorkshire to take benefit from the baths, as he was in ill-health. The son undertook to write to his father, and the solicitor, a Mr. White, arranged to wait for the reply. Young Strange communicated with Judge, who told him to

T 2

make no secret of the fact that he was the author of the catalogue.

White consulted with those who represented his employers, and the very next day, without any further word to the Stranges, or any communication with Judge, took all the steps for a case in Chancery. By the Friday the information of the Attorney-General acting for Her Majesty, and the Bill of the real complainant, Prince Albert, were drawn up, engrossed and put upon the file of the Court, as well as affidavits in support of the information and the Bill, these last being sworn to by Prince Albert, George Anson, and White the solicitor. Injunctions and affidavits were obtained to restrain the publisher from publishing the catalogue or holding the exhibition; instruction was given to counsel, and an absolutely unnecessary case set in motion. After White's visit—he made no other—to Strange's office, the first thing the defendants knew of the matter was that they were, without option, involved in a long and expensive lawsuit, one which, by the position of the prosecutors, was already prejudged.

Prince Albert rested his case on the fact that the etchings were made for private use, that when they were printed it was upon a private press, that the plates were kept locked up by Her Majesty in order to prevent them becoming public, though some copies were occasionally left about the Queen's private apartments, and sometimes given to friends, and that, therefore, no such collection could possibly have been made excepting by a person who had stolen them him-

self or through some other person. His extremely
long affidavit says that he first heard of the collection
on the day the catalogue was received, and that such
an exhibition was in the highest degree offensive to the
Queen and himself.

If Prince Albert, on receipt of the catalogue, had
instructed George Anson to write to Strange and forbid
the exhibition, that would have been the end of the
matter, but he took this extraordinary course of setting
in motion the most unwieldy form of English law that
he might get even with a man who was obnoxious to
him, without giving him a chance of defence, this alarming affidavit being sworn to nine days only after the
catalogue had been received.

Then the weary case began, affidavits and informa-
tions were added to and amended, until there were
no fewer than twenty-four of them, copies of all of
which the three defendants—they had included
Judge's son that the revenge might be complete—
had to secure at great cost.

J. A. F. Judge, the son, had translated the letters
between Victoria and Louis Philippe, so the lawyer
made an affidavit to the effect that he believed he
was also a writer, and on this supposition alone he
included the young man's name. As a matter of fact,
young Judge had been for ten years in Boulogne, first
at school and then as an apprentice to a chemist, from
which he had returned only a few months earlier.
The case against him was eventually quietly withdrawn, there being not the shadow of evidence against
him, but that was not done until he had been made

responsible for costs to the extent of nearly two hundred pounds.

Sentiment was against Judge. The papers spoke of a young and lovely Queen being constantly annoyed by a cantankerous pressman, and asserted that no fate was too bad for him. On the other hand, the evidence was for Judge, but all the evidence was not always published, and from the first Judge was popularly regarded as too despicable for it to matter what became of him. The Prince had branded him a thief, and a thief he was.

Judge based his defence upon three facts : that the etchings were not printed at a private press, but at various times between 1840 and 1847 at a public printing press in the heart of the town of Windsor; that the copper plates were not always kept locked up by Her Majesty; and that these etchings were not taken surreptitiously from the Queen's private apartments, for they had never been within some hundred yards of the Royal residence.

The Prince, however, asserted that : " We had a private printing press, from which we occasionally printed impressions of the etchings, and the plates were and are kept locked up by Her Majesty in order to prevent the same becoming public."

This implied that the plates were never out of the Royal possession. Subsequently Albert remembered that some of the plates were once sent to a printer named Brown, but that the plates and all the impressions were returned, and that that was the only time any of the plates were out of the Royal Palace.

Had the Prince really forgotten, or did he not know what was done in the Palace? Various witnesses were drawn from the printing offices of Mr. Brown, proving that for seven years etchings were sent to the press there to be taken off. Judge affirmed that Miss Skerritt, Sir George Hayter, the Police-Sergeant-Footman, and half-a-dozen other footmen, knew this, but none of them was called as witness. Two printers, named respectively Whittington and Middleton, gave evidence, that the latter being a copper-plate pressman, did from time to time take off impressions of plates from Windsor Castle. Mr. Brown gave him a correct amount of print paper, all of which was returned engraved, but it was shown that it was the custom for the first copy or so to be taken off on common paper, as they were worthless, and also that Middleton habitually took off copies for himself on card or common paper. By this means Middleton secured about a hundred and thirty of these etchings, some being first prints which had been thrown away and trampled under foot. He made no secret of possessing them, showed them to many people, and asked Judge if he would not buy them. That gentleman offered him fifty shillings, which was refused. Later young Judge came home, and hearing casually about these pictures, thought he would like to see them. So he and his father went to Middleton's house, and saw the not over-clean collection pasted in a little album. For this Judge bitterly and with justice complained that the young man was put into the Court of Chancery, accused of robbing the Queen's Palace, made a defendant in two suits, had two injunctions as well as a Bill filed against him by the Prince Consort, and so, at the age of twenty-two, had come home to start life in England with a blackened character.

Some time after the visit to Middleton, Judge, probably hoping to gain something by the transaction, gave Middleton five pounds for a large number of the etchings. Then arose the idea of the exhibition, and Judge asserted that, " Everything that we contemplated doing and hoped to accomplish was based wholly upon obtaining the permission of the Queen; " that " no catalogues were sold, or intended to be sold, without the Queen's leave."

There was plenty of evidence to show that Middleton had the prints as he stated, and there was no doubt that Judge had bought them from him. Whether he had also been given any by the servants at the Palace at the time when he went there daily as the accredited news reporter is not shown, but the case produced no evidence that he had stolen them, though there was plenty to prove that he had caused much annoyance to the Queen by giving publicity to Windsor matters.

Then the case against Judge changed into a demand that he should give up the pictures. This, in accordance with his character, he refused. He had bought them fairly and they were his; he would undertake not to publish them, but considered that he had his rights as well as Prince Albert.

Strange's costs came to upwards of £700, an execution being put upon his premises for £200, for he had first resisted the injunction, and then appealed;

thus his costs mounted up, so having lost his business, and, as he said, fearing further persecution, he went abroad.

At a certain stage of the proceedings Judge pleaded *in forma pauperis*, which reduced his costs to something like £180.

The case ended, there was no punishment to be allotted other than imprisonment if the fine and costs were not paid, and Mr. and Mrs. Judge were left to face the problem of how to find the money. Mrs. Judge had common sense and an independence of mind which allowed her to say openly the things she thought. She had already taken action on behalf of her son, her sense of justice deciding that those who had brought so grave a charge so wantonly against the young man were the real debtors in his case. So she wrote a straightforward letter to the Queen. It had been constantly asserted during the trial that in this case Her Majesty wished to be regarded as a private lady, and not as the Sovereign of the Realm, but when it came to paying this was forgotten, by all but Mrs. Judge. For a Sovereign is exempt from law costs, and the other side has to pay both for his King—or Queen —and himself. Mrs. Judge pointed out that had Her Majesty been a private lady she would have been obliged, on withdrawing a charge against a person she knew to be innocent, to pay the costs, but that as in spite of her desire to act as a private lady she was really the Queen, this lad, admittedly innocent of all false charges, was called upon to pay. She continued:

"It is your Majesty's high privilege, even under such circumstances, to be exempt from the payment of costs. I venture, very firmly, to expostulate with your Majesty's advisers, upon placing your Majesty in such a position. It is not a position your Majesty ought to be induced to assume. That 'the Sovereign is the Fountain of Honour' is fully admitted. I trust I may venture to hope, in the cases both of my husband and of my son, I may find that your Majesty is the Fountain of Justice."

To this the lawyer sent a curt answer to the effect that Colonel Phipps had transmitted to him a letter "appearing to be written by you."

Mrs. Judge at once wrote both to White and to Colonel Phipps, saying that the letter was certainly written by her, and that she hoped it would be laid before the Queen.

Ultimately the son's costs were paid by the order of Prince Albert.

At the end of January, 1849, I find Judge saying : "If Her Majesty and Prince Albert send me to prison for costs, and my wife and children to a workhouse for food, we must endeavour to bear our afflictions with patient endurance."

For want of his costs he did go to prison, and remained there until the autumn, when, through the insistence of his wife, the sum of £180 was paid by the Queen and Prince Albert. The letter from Mr. Anson to Mrs. Judge is somewhat curious, as it indicates the real reason for the trial of Judge :

For many years it has been the unremitting efforts of your husband " to inflict every possible injury upon Her Majesty, the Prince, their family and the Court; by a system of *espionage* into, misrepresentation and vilifying of, all the acts of their private life; you will be the best judge whether he deserves such a boon at their hands. Nevertheless, it is repugnant to the feelings of Her Majesty and His Royal Highness that innocent people like yourself and children should suffer in a cause with which their names are in any way connected, and I am commanded to forward to you a cheque for £180, with which you may pay your husband's costs, and extricate him from prison; and may he in future support his family by a more honourable industry."

Punch called this killing a wasp by dropping oil upon it, but it is a pity that the drop of oil had not fallen several years earlier.

Judge wrote a full account of all that had happened concerning the etchings, which was published as a small book. The Windsor booksellers received hints not to offer this for sale, and most strenuous efforts were made by agents of the Castle to buy up every copy, as well as copies of all Judge's other little books, which were thus put out of circulation. Naturally some copies of these were missed, and are to be found here and there, but I imagine that no public library in the Kingdom could produce among its volumes a book bearing upon it the name of Jasper Judge. I have seen two in a private library, and two anonymous productions are in the British Museum, though from the way they are catalogued it seems that the authorities do not know the name of the author.

The mystery of the private press was never publicly cleared up. That the Queen possessed one could not be doubted, but it seems to have been little used during several years.

It was an ignoble quarrel upon small matters. Judge was a cantankerous grumbler, a man who saw evil in things done by the high and rich which he probably would not have given a second thought to if done in a like proportion by humbler people. He was a man who must have a grievance. On the other hand, the Queen and Prince treated him in a childlike, unwise way at first, raising a fierce pride and resentment, being too blinded by their own high position to believe that a poor journalist might not be guided by reverence for them. And so they were hurt, and he was hurt, and the country had the spectacle of their ruler going to law on a frivolous pretext to crush a fly. As in the Queen's Diaries, recently published, the Lady Flora Hastings affair is ignored, so in the long " Life " of the Prince Consort the whole Judge affair is also ignored. Kings can do no wrong.

CHAPTER XI

THE QUEEN AND THE PROFESSIONS

To the rich much shall be given, but yet more is likely to be bestowed upon the powerful; thus to Queen Victoria, especially in the early part of her reign, came an accumulation of presents which might well have frightened anyone with less chance of dispersing them into places of safety. From a jewel to a tiger, from a parasol to a char-á-banc, they ranged, and the Queen was often at a loss to know what to do with them, or how most graciously to thank the donors for gifts which she would rather have been without.

Space forbids the mention of all, but some had a touch of unconscious humour about them. Thus from the Imaun of Muscat came Arabian ponies with an entreaty that the Great Queen would not disturb his little slave trade, which was very necessary to the prosperity of his finances. " Surely she, being possessed of such great wealth and extent of dominions would not grudge an inferior ruler his trifling profits on the only produce of his dominions which he could turn to advantage ! "

With the same intent of bribery came from the

Court of Shoa in South Abyssinia a museum of articles, a jet black mule with wonderful trappings, a crown worn by a former Queen of Shoa, shields ornamented with gold, silver and precious stones, spears, gauntlets, cloaks, and robes made of the skins of wild animals, solid silver armlets, badges, and baskets.

The Emperor of China, among other things, sent Victoria a gold bedstead; and some detestable person at Portsmouth made her a table from the coffin which, as the *Royal George*, went down

"With twice four hundred men."

Victoria, with a lamentable lack of imagination, was quite excited and pleased over this last, ordering the packages to be opened in the presence of herself and the Prince as soon as they arrived.

From Russia came furs, diamonds, carriages, and the ugly Malachite vase still to be seen at Windsor; from the Channel Isles cows, fruit and vegetables; from other parts of the world tigers, jaguars, marmosets, Spanish horses, Mexican pheasants; from Isleworth a pumpkin weighing one hundred and forty pounds; from Louis Philippe, as a peace offering, a great St. Bernard, which promptly bit the Queen's arm, drawing blood, when she stroked it; from India came a Cashmere sheepdog of a most ferocious kind; from America flour and smoked delicacies, begging for a return in substantial orders.

A gift from Bristol testified to the real business capacity of a bird-fancier, who sent a parrot to the Queen. Poll was too shy on her arrival at Court to speak, but when Victoria, "struck with the beautiful plumage and fine symmetry of the newly arrived guest, entered, with great condescension, into conversation with her," Poll's shyness wore off, and she suddenly screamed: "If you don't send twenty pounds I'll go back."

The Queen sent the twenty pounds: "an inducement to all teachers to impart profitable instruction to their pupils."

The Koh-i-noor was presented in 1850 by the Directors of the East India Company, as it "had ever been a symbol of conquest," and it had been taken from the conquered Lahore state; while a crabbed old miser named Neild, for the sake of notoriety, left Victoria a fortune of £250,000 in 1852, which she refused to accept until she knew that there were no relatives who should have had it.

It may seem curious that fierce brutes of all kinds should be sent as gifts to a young Queen, but the fact was that Victoria had acquired such a reputation for liking animals that everyone believed that no beast, however ferocious, would be unwelcome.

In 1839 she gained renown by going frequently to Drury Lane, where Van Amburgh exhibited performing lions, and Lord Broughton tells in his "Recollections" how, after the show, she went close to the tiger, and the brute made a spring at her that nearly overturned his cage, but Her Majesty did not move a muscle nor did she show the slightest sign of fear.

In 1841 Van Amburgh was so favoured by the Queen that he was a greater financial success than

Macready; and she was so pleased with the spectacle of the cowed lions, brutal though it was, that she commanded Landseer to paint a portrait of Van Amburgh and his beasts upon yards of canvas to add to the Royal collection. Whenever Astley or Wombwell was within reach, the Royal children were taken to see them, and several times Wombwell was commanded to Windsor to exhibit his animals in the Royal quadrangle. Another animal wonder was a learned horse which came to Windsor to show its cleverness, and an exceptionally great dog was commanded to appear before the Court, to be fondled and photographed.

Some laughed at the taste in amusements shown by the Royal pair, and some grieved, for the theatres began to be neglected. The Prince could not keep awake through the late performance, and when he did go out he preferred music, so for years they went very occasionally to the German or Italian Opera or the French play, but scarcely ever to the English drama. English singers and English actors gradually fell out of the ranks, and some of the theatres were shut or turned into wild-beast shows. Appeals such as the following were made to Victoria through the columns of the papers, but with little effect :

"Wherever the 'most illustrious lady' of the land goes her Court will go; and wherever the Court goes the world will follow. So that a kind example in one quarter is all that is necessary to give an impetus to our native talent. Surely the admiring hosts that flock to see a Rachael, a Bouffet, or a Grisi, might take some

pride in fostering the talents of their countrymen. . . .
It is a melancholy fact that the walls of our national
theatres are deserted."

Punch was by turns bitter and humorous, telling in
its fictitious "Court Circular" that Her Majesty and
His Royal Highness had honoured this or that theatre,
when "Better Late than Never" or "The Illustrious
Stranger," "She's Come at Last," "An Agreeable
Surprise," "Are You Sure 'tis She?" and other plays
with such suggestive titles had been acted.

Quips upon the loss of popularity which one William
Shakespeare had sustained were constantly appearing,
such as "I beg your pardon, sir, but could you
inform me of any theatre where Shakespeare is performed?"

"I'm afraid you may think the distance inconvenient, but New York is the nearest place I can
remember."

And when an attempt was made to stage a Shake-
spearean play, the Queen was reminded of his existence in such announcements as: "To an illustrious
Lady.—Persons desirous of becoming acquainted with
Mr. William Shakespeare may frequently have the
pleasure of seeing that gentleman at Sadlers' Wells."

When it was decided that Shakespeare's house at
Stratford was to go to the hammer, great efforts were
made by literary men in London to get up a subscription to buy it for the country. The Queen and
Prince were approached, but it was not until the list
of subscribers included many influential names that
the latter consented to recognise the scheme by

U

becoming its Patron and giving £250 towards the purchase.

Yet, awakened by public comment, there came a time when the Queen was eager to prove that she enjoyed Shakespeare's plays, and had weekly performances of them at Windsor.

Occasionally, too, the Prince showed interest in some particular English play, as when in 1845 a private performance was given of Jonson's " Every Man in his Humour." The caste included Henry Mayhew, John Forster, Mark Lemon, Charles Dickens, Douglas Jerrold, John Leech, Dudley Costelloe, Percival Leigh, Frank Stone, and Miss Fortescue, an assemblage of writers and artists then rapidly becoming famous. The Prince was anxious to see this, and as it was being repeated for the benefit of a sanatorium he and a brilliant assembly were present.

As years passed the Queen-Prince grew much more favourable to English drama, and in January, 1853, I find Mrs. Cowden Clarke writing to her father-in-law : " Your royal Douglas is to appear in Royal Presence this week; I hear that next Friday his new comedy is to be played for the first time in the Rubens Room at .Windsor. This is a delightful and most due honour, is it not?" The play, *St. Cupid: or Dorothy's Fortune*, which was thus produced at .Windsor, began its run at the Princess's on the following night.

The Prince's love for music was very sincere, and it was not perhaps unnatural that German musicians were preferred before all others, though the favourites were Mario, Grisi, Tamburini, Lablache, Jenny Lind, etc., and it is not to be wondered at that this made people say that he loved a German organ-grinder better than an English singer.

Mendelssohn being in England, was commanded to the Palace in June, 1844, and as the story of the way in which he played for the Queen and she sang to him is well known, it need not be repeated here.

Popular opinion humorously affirmed that all the sailors on the Royal yachts had to pass a musical examination before being appointed, and that all the orders were given by means of song! While one English singer declared that "he wondered how the Queen was able to endure the noise of her baby, she had so little liking for English singing. "Pooh, pooh!" replied Tom Cooke, "she will put up with it on account of its being of German extraction."

It is perhaps fortunate that by this time both theatre and concert hall are independent of royal patronage, a matter for which improved social conditions generally are responsible.

That Queen Victoria kept a sharp eye on newspaper reports is evidenced by the fact that when a reporter at the Drury Lane dinner omitted to mention that Prince Albert's health had been drunk, she wrote to Sir Robert Peel for an explanation, and Sir Robert at once dutifully set about finding out the truth of the matter. The Duke of Cambridge had been Chairman, and he—poor man—had "thought he could not give the health of the Queen in a more satisfactory way than by coupling with the name of Her Majesty that of her illustrious Consort." It was the custom at that time to place reporters as far away from the centre of interest as possible; and so, because some newspaper man did not understand the proceedings, hours of time had to be wasted by the Prime Minister in inquiring into this little matter, and in writing two long and humble letters to Her Majesty.

If there were a belief abroad that the Queen and her circle despised the English Theatre, it was no less bitterly believed of Art. In September, 1845, there was a letter upon the subject in *The Times*, in which the writer asserted : " It is no use to conceal the fact— British high art is hated at Court and dreaded by the aristocracy. They don't want it, they can't afford it; they think any art which does not cultivate their vanity or domestic affections can have no earthly use."

In a tragic way, this ignoring of any English art but that of portrait painting was bound up with the history of " Tom Thumb's " royal progresses in England.

On Tom Thumb's first arrival here he was twelve years old and twenty-five inches high. He appeared in the characters of Napoleon Buonaparte, Samson, Romulus, Cupid, a Highlander, and so forth, his exhibitions being purely a matter of size, clothes, and impudence; but Queen Victoria was enchanted. She had him to Court several times, presented him by her own hand "with a superb souvenir, of the most exquisite handicraft, made of mother-of-pearl, and mounted with gold and precious stones. On one side was the crown and V.R., and on the reverse a bouquet of flowers in enamel and rubies." She also gave him a gold pencil-case, with the initials T.T. and his coat of arms!! engraved on the emerald surmounting the case.

There was a far more wonderful little woman at Earl's Court during the past summer who could converse in half a dozen different languages, but she made little stir, and I think that is some proof that the general standard of taste has risen in England. Yet I do not know! If Queen Mary had commanded this diminutive lady to Court three different times, had presented her with valuable jewels, and had allowed the gentlemen of her suite to kiss the tiny freak, she might perhaps have been worked up into a celebrity, and have at the end of a year gone back to her native habitation including in her luggage three thousand six hundred and seventy-eight pounds' weight of gold; for such, a New York paper affirmed, Tom Thumb had secured. "What a transmutation of metals! Such a mountain of gold for such a heap of brass!"

The English Queen in this way most obligingly made Barnum the showman's fortune; and when he returned from a round of visits to the European Courts, his little puppet had acquired such an easy assurance in high society that the piquancy of his manners rendered him doubly endearing, so that fair and titled ladies competed for the privilege of kissing him. The lower stratum of society followed their example, and untold thousands were spent—in shillings—for the honour of being in the same room with an artificial freak. Meanwhile, legitimate British art was left to starve, and all the world was shocked when B. R. Haydon committed suicide, leaving behind him the most inconsiderate expressions of despair and jealousy. In 1846 he had written a letter to *The Times*, bitterly airing his grievance concerning the " Exquisite Feeling of the English people for High Art "!

" General Tom Thumb last week received 12,000 people, who paid him £600; B. R. Haydon, who has devoted forty-two years to elevate their taste, was honoured by the visits of 133½, producing £5 13s. 6d., being a reward for painting two of his finest works, 'Aristides and Nero."

Poor Haydon, he should have realised that it was not to see a mere dwarf that the English people paid so much, but to do reverence to that which Royalty delighted to honour. He further wrote in his diary of the sightseers :

" They rush by thousands to see Tom Thumb. They push—they fight—they scream—they faint —they cry Help ! and Murder ! They see my bills and caravans, but do not read them; their eyes are on them, but their sense is gone. It is an insanity— a rabies furore—a dream—of which I could not have believed Englishmen could be guilty."

And then he was found dead beneath his picture, and Mrs. Haydon realised that a dead husband—and a dead artist—was more valuable than a living one. Her Majesty granted her fifty pounds a year, Lady Peel assigned her twenty-five pounds a year out of funds at her disposal, and Sir Robert Peel sent a cheque for one hundred pounds to start a subscription, and promoted one of Haydon's sons who was in the Customs.

There was not much sense, however, in fastening the responsibility for this calamity upon the Queen, who had been brought up without ideals and with a mind intellectually untrained, and she could not alter her preferences, though she might have better realised her position. She entertained the Ojibbeway Indians with wonder and delight, while a Chinaman with two small-footed wives and a sister-in-law were welcomed at Osborne. There were other dwarfs too, three from the Highlands, two brothers and a sister, each about forty-four inches high, who were commanded to Buckingham Palace. That they were Scotch was sufficient recommendation.

Though Her Majesty wasted no thought on high art, she was not entirely indifferent, for her real taste lay in portraits, of which a tremendous number were done of herself and her family. "Oh, dear, I wish no portraits were being done of the Princess Royal," remarked Lady Lyttelton on one occasion. The dogs, parrots, horses, and other animals also occupied the time of foreign or English artists. Prince Albert was more catholic, and in his position on the Art Commission came to know many artists, among them Eastlake, for whom both he and the Queen showed great partiality.

Lady Eastlake tells in her volume of Memoirs how the Queen-Prince secured her husband's presidency of the Royal Academy, conveying through Colonel Phipps their earnest hope that the Academy would elect him, "for it was of the utmost importance that the President should not only practically illustrate the rules of Art, but also be a gentleman of erudition, refined mind, and sound theory," adding that none fulfilled these conditions but Eastlake—which was complimentary to Eastlake, but scarcely so to other candidates for the position.

On another occasion Her Majesty made the Academy elect as one of their number Richard Wyatt, a sculptor of great merit, by remarking one day to John Gibson: "I expected long ago to have seen Mr. Wyatt's name on the list of Academicians." "So did I," added the Prince Consort; and Gibson, having the Queen's remark repeated at a meeting of the Academy, caused the members to decide that Wyatt should be elected.

When Gibson drew up the design for the recess in the Prince's Chamber in the new Parliament House, that design which showed the Queen seated with Wisdom on her right and Mercy on her left, Prince Albert took three or four Ministers to see it, and praised it to them exceedingly. Then the Royal Commission, with Lord John Russell in the chair, met to consider the various models, and the chairman handed a note round the table, which everyone read in silence. It was from the Prince, expressing his own entire approbation of Gibson's model. All present most dutifully voted for the Prince's candidate, and the business was finished. It may be wondered whether any member of that Commission even dared to feel a preference for any other design.

LORD JOHN RUSSELL.

From the Painting by Sir Francis Grant, P.R.A., in the
National Portrait Gallery

There had been a dire suspicion that Albert would advocate the securing of foreign artists to decorate the House of Lords; and Eastlake told him that he could not take the Secretaryship of the Commission if English artists were not employed. When Melbourne asked Sir F. Chantrey what should be done if foreign artists were given the work, the veteran replied:

"Why, their heads ought to be broke and they driven out of the country, and, old as I am, I should like to lend a hand for that purpose."

The literary man of the period fared worse than any, though, from all evidence, Prince Albert would have preferred him to anyone else as an occasional companion; but the Queen could not bear to have about her those whose intellectual level or attainments were higher than her own; she preferred to guide conversation, or, in default of that, to play games. But in later years these little restrictions relaxed, and both she and the Prince grew more wide-minded when the golden nineteenth century forced the acknowledgment from them that English men of letters and poets could find their equal nowhere. Yet it is always with surprise that I read of a meeting between the Prince and Thomas Carlyle the rugged; while, on the other hand, it seems natural that he should seek Tennyson, the high polisher.

When Prince Albert was asked to be Chancellor of Cambridge University, Victoria's heart was filled with happiness, though the brightness of her content was dimmed by the fact that there was another candidate in Lord Powis, who had been busily defending the

Welsh bishoprics. It is not easy to say what excellences are necessary to form the Lord Chancellor of a University; it seems to have been enough that the Duke of Northumberland, who had previously occupied the post, had sufficient wealth to give away yearly £36,000 in pensions. Lord Lamington, in his volume " In the Days of the Dandies," says that the Prince " had just invented a new infantry uniform hat, which had not obtained the approbation of the Army," and he gives the following verses by Augustus Stafford :

"Prince Albert on this side, Lord Powis on that,
We will not say which is the brighter;
But we give up the youth who invented the hat,
For the man who has saved us a mitre.

Then why, oh collegiate dons, do you run
Into all this Senate-house bother?
Can it be that the lad who invented the one
Has a share in dispensing the other? "

The Members of the Senate, however, invited the Prince to become Lord Chancellor, on the grounds " That His Royal Highness Prince Albert's exalted rank and high position in the State, his admirable virtues, with his known love of literature, science, and academic studies, mark him out as the person most fitted to be elected into the office of Chancellor of the University."

Both Prince and Queen thought that as he was offered such an honour there should be no competition for it, and the Prince wrote that he would not contest it. Bishop Bloomfield, however, turned this refusal into an acceptance by calling a meeting, at which it was resolved that "this meeting has heard with feelings of deep gratitude the terms in which His Royal Highness Prince Albert has been pleased to express the pride and pleasure he would have in filling the office of Chancellor of the University." And the Bishop immediately arranged the poll, when the result showed a majority of one hundred and sixteen for the Prince in a total of seventeen hundred and ninety. It was not a large majority, and Albert was inclined to refuse the honour, but took counsel with Peel, who showed six good reasons why he should not do so.

So Royalty went to Cambridge in July, 1847, with a great crowd of German Princes, Bishops, diplomats, statesmen, and *aides-de-camp*, to be met there by still greater crowds of excited, cheering people, causing Baroness Bunsen to exclaim : "How any woman's sides can bear the beating of so strong a throb !" to which she added, "but the Queen has royal strength of nerve."

The Master of Trinity was at that time Whewell— he of whom Sydney Smith said that "science was his forte and omniscience his foible." Of him Stafford wrote :

"Through the realm of invention wherever ye travel,
  And the secrets of worlds and of nature unravel,
  You will find when you've mastered the works of infinity,
  The greatest of all is the Master of Trinity."

The house in which he lived, Trinity Lodge, was once a Royal palace, and therefore was said to belong to the Crown; so when Her Majesty descended at its door, and Dr. Whewell begged leave to welcome her to his house,

"*My* house," corrected careful Victoria.

Not that the Master was unaware of the fact, for it has been said that because he lived there he considered himself to be almost royal, and would not allow undergraduates to sit in his presence.

The Queen's choice of dress on this "auspicious occasion" was even less happy than usual, for she drove through Cambridge on the morning of the Installation wearing a claret-coloured silk gown striped with black, an amber-coloured Indian shawl embroidered with a wreath of flowers, and a bonnet of lilac-coloured silk covered with lace and ornamented with flowers. A mixture of colours so bizarre that criticism fails.

During the ceremony of the Installation the Prince listened to the fulsome address made to him sometimes with a bow and "sometimes something like a blush passed over his countenance." On reading his address to his Sovereign he made a graceful bow, and when she read her answer she uttered with peculiar emphasis the word "approbation" in commending the University's choice of a Chancellor. At the end of the ceremony the Chancellor and his Queen had to walk to their carriage, so each undergraduate of Trinity showed his loyalty by pulling off his gown and spreading it out for the Queen to tread on; in which way they managed quite nicely to supply the omission of a red drugget.

There was some trouble about the Ode for the occasion, Wordsworth being chosen as the poet by the Prince and affirming his utter inadequacy for the honour, and a second poet called upon also feeling unequal to so noble an occasion; then Wordsworth was again invited, and he succumbed to royal blandishments. How can an honest man give the unstinted praise and adulation which royalty demands? "He who has bequeathed to the world *The Thanksgiving Ode* and *The Evening Ode*, in which grandeur, sublimity, and pathos take the most solemn and touching utterance—he at least ought not to have written an *Albert Ode*, in which a ceremonious sophistication—a great University Flam—is sought, and vainly sought, to be elevated to the height of truth," said a contemporary critic.

Wordsworth's biographers affirm that he did not write it himself, but that Edward Quillinan did it at his request "after the Laureate had failed in a reluctant attempt to prepare an ode."

But was this so? In Mr. Broadley's collection I found the following letter in Wordsworth's handwriting, which is at least worth consideration. It was addressed to the composer of the music:

"*Rydal Mount*, May 5, 1847.

"MY DEAR SIR,

"I quite agree in most of your remarks—the alterations were made in the notion, mistaken as it seems, that they might better suit your music. Be pleased to understand that you may adopt or reject any alterations as they suit you or not, and whether the note you suggest for the printed ode may be requisite we will leave to after consideration. The only alteration that I wish to stand is *love* instead of *path*, because it is intended to make her *education* as a girl the means by which

302 THE MARRIED LIFE OF QUEEN VICTORIA

she acquired a fitting knowledge of the manner in which she was to tread the path of peculiar duty when grown up.

The alteration "past" and clarion's blast was to get rid of the word *trumpet* which is required near the end of the ode, but it may be repeated if you like. I will try to supply you with the sort of chorus you wish to conclude with. I felt the need of it, but I was willing to leave the matter where it was, till I was sure that you were desirous of an addition.

The heavy domestic affliction that presses on me, the very dangerous illness of my only daughter, makes it impossible for me to exert myself satisfactorily in this task.

I am, dear Sir,

Yours truly,

WM. WORDSWORTH.

"T. ATTWOOD WALMESLEY, ESQ.,
  "Univ. Coll., Cambridge.

"Do not misunderstand the word *task*; I only felt it one in reference to the great anxiety that I have alluded to; for I was not called on to furnish the Installation Ode in my capacity of Laureate, but simply as a poet to whom His Royal Highness was pleased to apply on the occasion."

I do not give the ode, as it may be found in any collected edition of the poet's works.

That the undergraduates would be satisfied with a real, genuine pæan of praise is not to be imagined, so they had an "Ode" all to themselves, which, however, they obligingly showed to a multitude of friends. Part of it ran:

> "Sons of the Cam, awake!
>   Come, stir, ye sleeping elves,
> Arise or else your Prince will take
>   A rise out of yourselves.
> Fast man—come breakfast faster,
>   Slow man—drink off your sloe:
> Proctor and doctor, gyp and master,
>   Do show some little go!
> Ye Principals majestical, move on;
> And all ye Dons, come rolling like the Don."

Of course the caricaturists were busy over the event. There was Prince Albert taking the *Pons Asinorum*, rushing in cap and gown over a wooden plank, with an encouraging force of University men behind him and an opposing one before him. Again, in Chancellor's robes, he is standing over a woman in a Roman toga, who is sitting with her head back. The end of the Albert Hat converted into a funnel is inserted in her mouth, and through it Albert drops a pill, the description of the picture being, " The Prince Chancellor administering to Alma Mater his patent pills compounded of English, French, History, Geography, and the use of the Globes."

The Rev. W. H. Brookfield tells[1] how the old duke (Wellington) came pacing across the Court in his scarlet Doctor's gown over a full dress black suit, and wearing a Doctor's hat. " You can guess what a locomotive mob of gowns surrounded and accompanied him."

At the Vice-Chancellor's dinner to his new superior, the only people who charmed the company with song were Lablache (the Queen's singing master), Albani, and Salvi; and there is a touch of irony about the fact that, when taking a late walk in Cambridge, Victoria grumbled, " Nothing seemed wanting but some singing, which everywhere but in this country we should have heard." She so well encouraged the English in the art !

The *Morning Post*, in reporting the return journey

[1] *Mrs. Brookfield and Her Circle,* by Charles and Frances Brookfield.

to London, mentioned "that the Royal party halted for a few seconds at Bishops Stortford to take in water."

So to all his other dignities Prince Albert added that of Lord Chancellor of the University of Cambridge. He could already put after his name K.G., K.P., G.C.B., G.C.M.G., D.C.L., LL.D., Ph.D., etc., Duke of Saxony, Prince of Saxe-Coburg-Gotha, Field Marshal, Colonel of the 11th or Prince's Own Hussars, Colonel of the Scots' Fusilier Guards, Elder Brother of Trinity House, Grand Ranger of Windsor Park, Lord Warden of the Stannaries, Governor and Constable of Windsor Castle, First and Principal Knight Grand Cross and Grand Master of the Order of the Bath, Chief Ranger and Keeper of Hyde Park and St. James's Park, High Steward of Plymouth, and Captain-General and Colonel of the Artillery Company. One facetious person announced that he was also to be made Bishop of Manchester as his wife was mother of the Church.

The Queen was very jealous that the command of the Army should be retained by herself, and a suggestion was made in 1842 that, after the death of the Duke of Wellington, Prince Albert should become Commander-in-Chief. Stockmar—probably warned by the case of Ferdinand of Portugal—snubbed the project, which was, however, again raised in 1846, to the great indignation of military circles. The Army had not forgotten that Prince Albert, a civilian of twenty, had been put into one of the highest military posts before he arrived in England, and it still had little confidence in him as a military leader.

The *Morning Post* denied the rumour, saying that "The Prince is not an ambitious man. He is satisfied —and he has good reason to be so—with domestic endearments . . . with the position he so deservedly holds as the liberal Mæcenas of the Fine Arts . . . with the pleasure he must derive from giving a laudable example to English county gentlemen as a master of hounds, and to English agriculturists as a successful breeder."

In 1850 the Duke of Wellington, then nearing his eighty-first birthday, himself made the suggestion, saying that "it was of the utmost importance to the stability of the Throne and Constitution that the command of the Army should remain in the hands of the Sovereign, and not fall into those of the House of Commons." His plan involved the appointment of a responsible man as Chief of the Staff, but the Prince was to be the link which chained the Army to the Royal will.

Fortunately for everyone, Prince Albert refused the honour, and in writing his decision to the Duke he wrote the memorable passage which, though often quoted, must be added here. He said that he ought to "sink his own individual existence in that of his wife —that he should aim at no power by himself and for himself—should shun all contention—assume no separate responsibility before the public, but make his position entirely a part of hers; fill up every gap which as a woman she would naturally leave in the exercise

x

of her royal functions; continually and anxiously watch every part of the public business, in order to be able to advise and assist her at any moment in any of the multifarious and difficult questions or duties brought before her, sometimes international, sometimes political or social or personal. As the natural head of her family, superintendent of her household, manager of her private affairs, sole confidential adviser in politics, and only assistant in her communications with the officers of the Government, he is besides the husband of the Queen, the tutor of the Royal children, the private secretary of the Sovereign, and her permanent Minister."

There is something very touching about the first part of this, but at the end the letter comes near to farce, and brings to mind the Lord High Everything Else in *The Mikado*, who was the First Lord of the Treasury, Secretary of State, Chancellor of the Exchequer, Lord High Admiral, Lord High Chamberlain, Solicitor-General, Groom of the Second Floor Back, and a few other things.

That the Prince should have regarded the mere fact of being a husband as a post in itself was absurd, and equally absurd was his claim to being the tutor of the Royal children, when an army of teachers was engaged for them; also, why should he have frittered his time in doing secretarial work for the Queen when there were so many people able and willing to do it? and he certainly was not her Minister, unless he meant that he advised her; but that again was a farce, for he decided everything for the Queen. What sins Stockmar had to answer for in changing a lively youth into such a careworn, stolid man !

When the Queen conferred upon him the title of Prince Consort, the question arose as to whether there were any more worlds for him to conquer, and a cartoon showed him in despondent mood, the verse beneath running :

> "Say, aren't you Field Marshal and Warden besides
> Of the Castle of Windsor and all that?
> You've a regiment—a kennel—and then you have got
> The famous—dear me—what d'ye call, hat."

Subsequent verses betray the Prince making up his mind to secure " the belt" and to vanquish the champion, Ben Caunt, by deigning to inform him of his intentions.

X 2

CHAPTER XII

THE QUEEN'S VISITS

QUEEN VICTORIA had a sentimental desire that the
Prince Consort should see with her the chief places
she had gone to with her mother in her childhood,
and from year to year arranged visits to the most
notable houses in England, visits which sometimes
brought consternation into the minds of her hosts. In
the early progresses she had driven through the
country roads; now, however, she determined to use
the railway, and it is curious to note that her first trip
by train was as late as 1842 from Windsor to Paddington. That little journey worried a good many people,
chief of whom was the Master of the Horse, who, with
the chief coachman, had been under the obligation of
carefully examining every equipage before the Queen
used it. So there was the funny spectacle of a lord
of the realm going down to Windsor station in a
ruffled frame of mind to inspect the engine and its
appointments, just as he would have inspected a horse
and carriage! The coachman went further, and insisted that if he could not drive Her Majesty he ought
at least to pretend to do so and to travel on the engine,
and he would not be content until arrangements were

made for him to go with the pilot engine which preceded the Royal train. However, the damage done by smuts to his spotless scarlet livery was so disturbing to his mind that he did not again seek the honour of being a pioneer.

In later years, if not then, it was customary to take extraordinary precautions against any accident occurring to the Queen's train, one being that men should be stationed all along the line at a distance of half-a-mile from each other; thus her journeys to and from Balmoral would cost her £5,000 a year.

After the Prince's death she took to travelling at night, which caused great regret to the railway directors, because of the increase of risk and responsibility.

One of the earliest visits made by the Queen-Prince to subjects was paid to Sir Robert Peel at Drayton, "a very nice house," said Victoria; "our visit to Drayton has made the Premier very happy, and is calculated to strengthen his position," added Albert in the cheerful spirit of the philanthropist.

They went to Chatsworth, and the Duke of Devonshire—"albeit he would willingly have dispensed with this visit"—made tremendous preparations with coaches and horses, with a ball, and garden illuminations, all trace of which last named disappeared in the night by the aid of three hundred workmen. They went to Belvoir, where the Duke of Rutland arranged a fox-hunt, at which the Prince made his much-vaunted impression upon England by his gallant riding. "One can scarcely credit the absurdity of people," wrote the

Queen, "but Albert's riding so boldly has made such a sensation that it has been written all over the country, and they make much more of it than if he had done some great act." She did not realise that the Prince had thus for the first time proved to a certain section of her subjects a capacity to enjoy an exercise regarded as both manly and British, and much more satisfactory than dabbling with paints, or playing the piano.

By the Queen's desire, Rutland had invited Wellington and Melbourne, and to please himself he had added the Palmerstons and quite a number of Whigs, a pleasure in which Victoria did not participate, as she already felt shy of her old servants and had a strong dislike for Pam.

In 1844 came the great City event of the opening of the Royal Exchange, concerning which, though a description would be dull, the remarks of the satirists were somewhat amusing. This is how *Democritus in London* described the coming of the two City magnates to beg the Queen to stand sponsor at the christening of the 'Change.

The Windsor people meet Goodman Grig running, and ask :

"Neighbour, neighbour,
What new mountain is in labour,
Is the earthquake coming down,
Is the comet's tail in town? "

To which he replies :

"The day is fast coming of doom
The Castle's astonish'd, astounded !
From the Master of Horse to the Groom
Answer I'll not for a sound head !

> For suddenly came marching in,
> Surely the couple were crazy!
> O, such a riotous chin,
> O, such a rollicking jazey!"

The chin and the jazey—probably paunch—turn out to belong to Sir Peter Prolix and Mr. Pumpkin, Knight and Alderman, come to proffer their request:

> "We post to-day to petition and pray
> The Crown, with sceptre and garter,
> Prancing in state with the cream-colour'd eight,
> (And the more blue-ribboned the smarter).
>
> With the Beef-eating chaps in their muffin caps,
> And the Guards in their helmets glist'ning,
> Will drive us poor cits fairly out of our wits
> By coming to honour the christening!"

To this the lord replies:

> "Citizens, the Lord's Anointed
> Has commanded and appointed
> Tom Thumb to try his mimic power
> On royal *ennui* for an hour.
> Crowns, with high debate and discourse
> Overdone, have taken this course.
> When the Imperial Presence from
> In state has strutted Tiny Tom,
> I, your *batterie de Cuisine*,
> Will humbly lay before the Queen."

It is Sir Peter also, while the two are waiting over wine for the Queen's answer, who utters the famous verse in anticipating the success of their mission:

> "What exclaim'd the gallant Napier,
> Proudly flourishing his rapier!
> To the army and the navy,
> When he conquered Scinde?—' Peccavi!'"

So the Royal Exchange was opened with great pomp, by a Queen dressed in white satin and silver tissue, flashing with diamonds, the Star of the Order of the Garter upon her bosom, the Garter itself set in brilliants round her left arm; and the City Fathers had all they needed of smartness, for to please them the Queen was doubly crowned, with a miniature crown of diamonds at the back of her head and a diamond tiara surmounting her forehead.

When the Queen rolled home again in her luxurious carriage she was glad it was all over, and yet still keeping her enthusiasm for a show. She was honestly and naturally gratified by the good-humoured, loyal shouts of the great crowds, and she read with avidity all the accounts in the papers, that her vanity might be stroked with a still softer touch.

"They say *no* Sovereign *was more loved* than I am (I am bold enough to say) and *that*, from our *happy, domestic home*—which gives such a good example." And she adds about her husband : "He is *so* beloved by all the really influential people and by *all* right-thinking ones."

I am afraid our Queen had no idea of what a multitude of her people she thus consigned to the outer place. To her "the influential"—those about her who were powerful and rich—would mean about a score or so of people, while who shall judge which are the right-thinking in this world of a myriad ideals?

She also could not have realised that her people believed that her home was not at that time so happy as it had been, as the following verse attests :

"In youth's springtide and beauty's pride
Behold the radiant, ROYAL BRIDE
OF MERRIE ENGLAND ! merry still,
Tho' merrier once, for love's grown chill !
On her open brow and queenly
Shines her triple crown serenely !
ERIN's jewel, SCOTIA's gem,
[1] CLAS MERDIN's regal diadem."

Among other visits was one to the Marquis of
Exeter at Burghley House, near Stamford, about
which a whole book was written, though little of it
is worth recording. At Northampton, where the usual
Mayoral address was tendered, the chronicler paid
his Sovereign the most wonderful compliment he
could think of :

"Her Majesty was pleased to make an immediate
reply, not reading from any previously prepared
document, *but framing the answer on the spot as
she uttered it.* Her Majesty's answer was to the
following effect :

"'Mr. Mayor,—We receive the address with great
pleasure from the Mayor, Magistrates and Corporation of this town. We are gratified by the reception
we have met with from this ancient borough. You
will place the address in the hands of the Lord
Chamberlain and an answer will be sent.'"

How sycophants do belittle royalty while wishing
to extol them. This belauder of the Queen's wonderful mental effort further on announced with
triumph that "no less than five flags hung from
different parts of the village inn."

[1] Clas Merdin, the sea-defended green spot—England.

The weather was wet and the Queen had to amuse herself by going through the house, ending in the kitchen, where she was brought up short before "a large painting of a carcass of beef, the true ensign-armorial of English hospitality."

There was a sequel to the visit which proved that the noble Marquis loved his purse better than his name. He had hired furniture with which to make an empty house fit to receive members of Her Majesty's suite, and kept it there so long that he was liable for rates. Refusing to pay, he was dunned, and the matter became painfully public, wonder being expressed how for a few pounds he could let it be published to the world that the furniture was hired, or have so dimmed the lustre of the Royal honour accorded him.

At this time the Duke of Buckingham was on the verge of ruin and everybody, including the Queen, knew this, yet she elected with an immense following to stay three days in his house at Stowe. He had perforce to accept the honour and, sportsman as he was, determined to perish rather than fail. So his entertainment was the most magnificent of all, with four hundred yeomen to act as guard of honour and six hundred tenantry in white smocks to line the roads.

Being "commanded" to invite the hateful free corn importers, Peel and Aberdeen, he balanced the matter by including among the guests Disraeli, who was already preparing his vindictive attack upon Peel. It was the first time Victoria had met the Young Englander, and though she disliked and grew almost to hate him, she then distinguished him and "Mary Ann," as he called his wife, by her courtesy.

The programme here also included a ball and a battue, at which latter the Prince's shooting was much admired, one hundred and forty-four hares, twenty-nine pheasants, and one snipe falling to his gun. More was said about this than it merited. The beaters were stationed so that their sticks touched, the hares rushed out in such multitudes that only one out of half-a-dozen could even be aimed at, and many of the poor beasts plunged into the canal and swam to the opposite shore. As for the pheasants, "quite a cloud assembled, and the slaughter was proportionately great." Then when a Prince shoots he is not only given the best position, but he is given first chance, those around deferentially doing their utmost to secure that his bag shall be a full one. I have seen it done in Norfolk.

The Royal visit over, the Duke of Buckingham was left to reckon the cost, and—the bailiffs sitting by his kitchen fire—he made arrangements for selling his library and pictures, "for the magnificence of the reception given to Royalty had much to do with his financial collapse." Then, deprived of home, divorced by his wife, he went abroad, owing something like a million pounds. When in 1861 he died, at an hotel, one who had known him pronounced as epitaph: "Few men will have passed away less honoured in their life or less regretted in their death," and yet the Queen, with her purity of ideal, became his guest!

The Duke of Wellington was a less compliant host when the Queen visited him at Strathfieldsaye, for he refused to allow her to name the guests he should invite, as he refused to let reporters detail in their papers his daily programme.

In 1844 the Duke of Coburg, whom Victoria scarcely knew, died, over which loss the Prince cried long and bitterly, and the Queen cried in sympathy, absenting herself from her ladies, and displaying swollen eyes when she did appear. But she screwed up her love and courage to let Albert go for a week to Coburg, "if you *knew* the sacrifice I make in telling and urging Albert to go. . . . I have *never* been separated from him even for *one night*, and the *thought of such* a separation is quite dreadful." As one of her historians said of the Prince's bereavement and his journey to Coburg : " The Queen, too, had her trial to bear." This is typical of the Queen's character at the time, so emotional and so sympathetic—and so ready to pity herself.

The Queen and Prince made a state visit to Prussia in 1845 on their way to Coburg, and though they were away for a month the regency bogey was not even mentioned. At Malines the King and Queen of the Belgians met them, at Habersthal the Crown Prince of Prussia greeted them. At Aix la Chapelle the King of Prussia stood waiting; at Cologne the road-ways over which the Royal party passed were sprinkled with eau-de-Cologne (was this advertisement or because of the city's renowned smells?), and at the Prussian Palace at Bruhl the whole Court was on the doorstep, otherwise the stairs, for the carriage was driven straight into the hall.

For the first time the Queen felt the real bitterness of the refusal of her English subjects to give rank to her husband. At the state dinner at Stolzenfels, one of the Prussian palaces, Albert was not allowed to sit near his Royal wife. There he was but the younger brother of the Duke of Coburg, and had to take his place below those of higher birth, for among the guests was the third son of an uncle of the Emperor of Austria, who would not give precedence, and to him Prussia deferred rather than to the chief guest; so Ernest of Hanover was revenged for his niece's slight to himself. It was perhaps of this dinner that a German lady remarked that the Queen of England looked cross, for her expressive face did not generally hide her feelings. The whole incident is, of course, ignored in the "Life" of the Prince, but many on-lookers have chronicled it.

Thence the Royal party went to Coburg, and, arriving at the Palace, found "the staircase full of cousins. It was an affecting but exquisite moment, which I shall never forget," said the Queen, with her usual extravagance of sentiment, for most of the cousins must have been strangers to her.

Victoria was naturally delighted to stay at Rosenau, where the two little boys had lived, studied and played, where she could see for herself the views they had looked upon, and take the walks they had taken. She most enjoyed the quiet days there, though the re-curring visits of the sixty-one relatives who were gathered at Coburg to meet her must have made Rosenau lively.

It is remarkable that in the authorised description of this visit constant reference is made to the Coburgian peasants. " I sketched a lovely housemaid that is here in her costume, and three good little peasant girls." " One or two women who were making hay came close to me, and said, as all the country people do here, ' Guten Abend.'" The Queen thought all this charming in Germany! and she might have liked it in Scotland; but if the poor hinds around Windsor had come up to the castle decorated with ribbons and flowers, the women with wreaths on their heads, as the people did at Rosenau, how would they have been made welcome? With what haughty scorn would they have been refused admittance through the gates by the servants, and how the Prince would have shrunk from such an intrusion on his privacy! While the Queen was drawing comparisons between the peasants of England and the peasants of Coburg—all to the advantage of the latter—the English peasants, if they had seen her abroad, might equally well have been drawing comparisons between the Queen at Coburg and the Queen at Windsor, and to the advantage of the former.

The one incident—a battue of deer—which should have marred the happiness of Her Majesty on this visit, is treated very philosophically in the " Life," where we are told that the Queen was " struck by the mediæval strangeness of the scene." It was held where the skirts of the great Thuringian forest came down to the valleys, about fourteen miles from Gotha; a space having been cleared in readiness on the top and down the side of one of the hills. At the end of this space a pavilion of branches and leaves, open at three sides, had been built, and decorated with heather, forest berries, and flowers, the whole being enclosed with a wall of white canvas and netting. Chasseurs, dressed in brilliant colours, stood in the enclosure, and a German band with a *répertoire* of lively music stood outside.

On their arrival, Queen Victoria, Queen Louise, and the Duchess Alexandrina of Saxe-Coburg were ushered to their seats in the pavilion; the King of the Belgians, Prince Albert, Prince Leiningen, and Duke Ferdinand of Saxe-Coburg stood there also with their guns, while the other gentlemen took up their places at the side, where a neat little table for shot and powder had been let into the ground. Now all being ready, beaters in white coats drove a large number of deer into the enclosure, the gate was shut, and the band began to play polkas, just as in the olden times a band played when a man was being broken on the wheel.

So to the sound of merry dance-music the deer were driven from side to side in an endeavour to send them as close as possible to the Prince in the pavilion. The poor frightened beasts became frenzied, and tried every method of escape, and when one succeeded the country people on the hillside shouted with delight; one stag actually cleared the enclosure—a feat which woke loud applause from them. Some malicious writer suggested that the clapping was less at the escape of the deer than at the failure of the princely marksmen to kill him, but I think it meant that even with such an example before them, a trace of the sporting instinct remained with the people. One frightened doe, having so far run between the bullets and tried every point for escape, trotted straight up to the pavilion as though hoping to find mercy there, and she was promptly shot. All the beasts being now disposed of, the dead and dying ones were dragged up to the feet of the ladies, and their throats cut, after which the bodies were disposed in rows, on either side of the pathway, so that the visitors as they went along might look upon the stiffening limbs, dull glassy eyes, and ghastly wounds, and sweep the edges of their gowns in the blood. Truly one of *Punch's* comments was well earned :

"Sing a song of Gotha—a pocket full of rye,
Eight-and-forty timid deer driven in to die ;
When the sport was open'd, all bleeding they were seen,
Wasn't that a dainty dish to set before a Queen !
The Queen sat in her easy chair, and look'd as sweet as honey ;
The Prince was shooting at the deer in weather bright and sunny ;
The bands were playing Polkas, dress'd in green and golden clothes ;
The nobles cut the poor deers' throats, and that is all *Punch* knows ! "

A letter in the *Standard* from someone at Coburg affirmed that " the deer killing was very shocking. The Queen wept. I saw large tears in her eyes, and Her Majesty tells me that she with difficulty kept the chair during what followed. . . ." She added, " For the

Prince the deer were too numerous and *must* be killed. *This* was the German method; and no doubt the reigning Duke will distribute them to his people, who will thank Prince Albert for providing them venison."

In her journal the Queen says of the event, "As for the sport itself, none of the gentlemen like this butchery."

So we have this proposition and conclusion : The Queen did not like it, the Prince did not like it, all the gentlemen disliked it; but as the deer *must* be killed, the gentlemen had to turn butchers, make a holiday of their work, and force the Queen by social rules of courtesy to sit for two hours watching the shambles !

Punch's cartoon is gruesome. Albert stands in the midst of a heap of dying and dead beasts, smiling at the Queen in the attitude of a conjurer who has just performed a successful trick, and she from her chair gazes at him with a look of fatuous admiration, while a man in the foreground is busily cutting a doe's throat. The other gentlemen with guns in their hands admiringly regard the Prince, and Lady Canning, Her Majesty's attendant, turns away from the scene, weeping.

On this day in the mountains, the killing over, the Queen admired the heavens and earth. " The day had been, and the evening was, more beautiful than any I remember, and the soft blue haze over the hills, as we left Reinhardtsbrun for Gotha, perfected the charm of the scene by the delicate veil which it threw over it."

Y

So the butchery did not spoil the Queen's pleasure in nature, and the scene she had left did nothing to impress on her mind that nature is even more beautiful in animal life than in its combination of earth and sky.

Victoria said the Prince did not like the butchery, and that is all we know of the Prince's views on the point. The *Herald* asserted that once at Balmoral Albert had a stag driven before the window of the Castle and shot it there, having called the Queen to see the feat. He may not have liked doing it, duty and custom alone may have urged him; yet his Scotch record is of a constant succession—though in a more sportsmanlike way—of deer-killing. But it is useless trying to penetrate his thoughts, though it would be interesting to see him as he really was, not as the Queen saw him, or as she wished us to see him, but shorn of his fictitious attributes, so zealously worked up after his death. A real man, thoughtful, enlightened, prejudiced, intellectual, yet conceited, warm-hearted, hard, custom-bound, weary of the little things with which his sentimental Queen choked his days, tenacious of power, yet self-sacrificing and willing to hide his light under a bushel; strong in uprightness, yet quite capable of uttering a swear-word; a dilettante, an experimenter, a practical theorist who for his health's sake should never have been thrust into politics. Great as he was, he would have been greater and lived longer had he escaped being coached, clipped, and artificially forced by his German mentor, and if the clinging ivy which lived upon his strength had been a plant of hardier growth, ready to support as well as to lean upon him.

Victoria loved her lord so well that all he did was right, and she could not understand why the general public were not fascinated by him. She thought that same public ignorant, sinful, and vindictive for never losing its suspicion of his German leanings, and was quite certain that there was no ground for such suspicions. Yet the Royal pair had in their palace between sixty and seventy foreign servants, the Queen between forty and fifty, and the Prince half that number, who were given the upper places. Their rich subjects followed their example, and at a time when thirty per cent. of English servants were out of employment there were twelve thousand foreign menials filling the best places in London alone.

Here at once was an excuse for suspecting the Prince's tendencies. The ridiculous idea that any foreigner must be better than the best English cook, dressmaker, milliner, hairdresser, singer, dancer, or pianiste is a relic of the early Victorian days, and has done much to lower England in the eyes of the world by discouraging the practice of those arts in this country. Of the Palace foreigners so much secrecy was observed that no outsider knew their number, so a story of one is a rarity.

Victoria's hairdresser, named Isidore, received £200 a year for his work, strict punctuality being required from him. Once taking a day's holiday in London, he returned to Paddington in time to see the train slide out of the station, and in excited despair called upon the station-master and all the porters for help. As there was no train for two hours, a special was suggested, and eagerly agreed to, at a price of £18, the sympathetic station-master ordering extra speed, so that the result was a pound a mile a minute.

In other ways the Prince could never divest himself of his belief in the inferiority of all classes of Englishmen. A few weeks after his marriage he said to his brother :

"When you are gone I shall have no one with whom I can speak openly of these things. *An Englishman cannot grasp or understand such matters*, and only sees in words like those I have just uttered an arrogant desire to blame on the part of the foreigner." This was not bad for a youth of twenty ! but such an attitude of mind was fatal to his popularity. Many years later he grieved over the sad fact that life in England was so dull that all his German servants had either to marry or turn rogue ! " I never heard a real *shout* in England ! . . . In Coburg with a hundred thousand inhabitants there are thirty-two gardens for the people who meet and associate in them."

I wonder if Isidore was responsible for the trying *coiffeurs* which the Queen affected, the smooth sleekness, the loops round the ears, the high plait like a little crown midway between neck and forehead, the pride of simplicity over grace !

But if Victoria's taste led her to deck out her babies in coloured velvet, lace, pearls and diamonds, Albert had the reputation of a dandy, and, like Beau Brummell, invented a stock, which was said to be

most easy and agreeable, yielding to the slightest
depression of the head in any direction, as it had
steel wire springs round the edge of the collar. Before
this he wore a swathe of silk simply, which in one
drawing the Queen is represented as knotting for him.
He also introduced the frockcoat into England, and
another caricature, based on his remark that no one
in England could make a coat, showed him in a rage
kicking several tailors, who had done everything but
fit him well for one.

One of the Queen's foreign servants, a French-
woman, attained, after leaving her employ, a horrible
notoriety in Paris by systematically torturing five
English children committed to her care, so that two
of them died. Being brought to trial and only two
years' imprisonment given, Parisian feeling ran so
high that an appeal *de minima* was lodged and she
got five years. The *Annual Register* describes this
creature as the Queen's wardrobe woman, but she was
probably only one of several engaged in the Royal
dressmaking department, for an importation of French-
women had been made for that purpose.

Needless to say, that the news that Her Majesty
was having millinery and flower-rooms fitted up in
her palaces, and had engaged two first-rate French
artists, one as milliner and dressmaker, and the other
as florist, brought consternation to the minds of the
London tradesmen. They saw that it meant the withdrawal of work from their establishments and feared
that the material itself would be bought in Paris, and
it was keenly argued that one who drew such a large

sum of money annually from the country should spend it among her people. *Punch*, as usual then, was outspoken : " It is notorious that the Queen is at the head of the Society for the Relief of the Distressed Needle-women, and she could not therefore take any proceedings by which the earnings of that wretchedly ill-paid class would be still further curtailed. Her Majesty would, we are convinced, pause before adding a milliner's workroom to the Royal establishment, when she reflects that the example of parsimony would be immediately followed by hundreds, who can only imitate greatness in its littleness, and are always delighted when fashion affords them encouragement to an act of meanness. . . . We believe the libel to have originated in the same malevolent spirit of detraction that accused Prince Albert of intending to add a slaughtering house to his personal establishment, for the purpose of chousing the butcher out of the profit to be obtained by killing the meat. We should as soon expect to see the words, ' Albert, Meatsalesman,' over the door of Buckingham Palace, or ' Victoria, Artiste in Artificial Flowers,' stuck in the windows of the ground floor, as bring ourselves to believe that the Royal pair contemplate the paltry economy of entering into competition with their own tradespeople."

That a paper which spoke thus boldly was hated at Court is not surprising, but there was need for it, as the passion for economy emanating from the Prince touched the people at every point. With the Court's continual absences from London, its long spells of middle-class life at Osborne or Balmoral, its army of foreign and Scotch servants, London especially gained little from its dual Monarch.

However, as a master Albert was punctilious and just, and much more thoughtful for his servants than was the Queen, who, it was said, did not even remember to order them a glass of wine, a dinner or favour, either at her Coronation or her wedding. In later life, however, there was no kinder mistress than Her Majesty, and men who have served her remember her still with affection.

Lady Lyttelton gives charming pictures of the Prince noisily and eagerly managing a new kite for his boys, consenting on a cold December day to go through quarterly accounts if she will allow him to do reel steps all the time to warm himself, and showing candour, truth, prudence, and manliness generally. If only the Queen could have transmitted such human impressions of him!

There is a rather amusing story of him that, when lunching next the President of the Ipswich Museum, he said to Sir Charles Lyell, who sat on the President's other side, " I will show you a geological illustration in your way; there is a glacier "—pointing to a huge block of ice—" and here is the stream proceeding from its melting, and you see where it is flowing to." The stream was just pouring over the edge of the table into the lap of the President who was in the Chair, and he had barely time to escape being wetted through.

Sometimes Albert was an unconscious humourist,

and Edward Lear tells how he stood next to him and heard him ask Hudson, the Railway King, what he thought of the Atmospheric Railway. Hudson's reply was :

"Please, your rile 'iness, I think it is a noomboog ! "

The Prince turned to Lord Farnham with : " Explain to me, what is a noomboog ? "

Sometimes he found it difficult to understand words, and during his first visit to Scotland it is recorded that someone mentioned Ben Lomond to him. This seemed familiar, and the Prince discouraged familiarity.

" What did you say ? " he asked.

" Ben Lomond," replied the Equerry.

"Oh, Benjamin Lomond," responded the Prince, laying stress on Benjamin. The story is at least *ben trovato*.

He had plenty of grit and courage, too, which was displayed in more than one serious fire, both in his youth and later. Thus in March, 1853, the very day that the family had returned to Windsor, a fire broke out in the dining-room of the Prince of Wales' Tower at ten at night. Everyone was much alarmed, for it was a serious matter, and there was every fear that the flames would spread to the rest of the Castle. The Prince first thought it wise to secure a treasure from his own rooms—as one who was there told—and called a servant to carry out a small trunk into a place of safety. The man stooped to the task, but it was beyond him, for small as was the box it was heavy like lead. Then, in his anxiety, the Prince caught at one handle, and the servant holding the other, they staggered with it into the open air. What the trunk contained no one but the Prince knew. Of the fire Albert wrote : " We had to battle with the flames from ten at night until four in the morning before we got them completely under ; nevertheless, the injury was confined to one tower of the Castle, which has been gutted by the flames through four stories. Had the fire got beyond the tower it would have been impossible to save the Castle."

Several years later the Princess Royal showed the same cool courage when, in sealing letters, her sleeve caught fire and set light to her dress. Miss Hildyard snatched up a rug and drew it tightly round her, extinguishing the flames, and the girl neither screamed, fainted, nor fussed, but said, " Don't frighten mamma ; send for papa first"—thereby betraying the custom of the family, as well as, in this case, the loving bond which existed between father and daughter.

As this chapter has become more or less anecdotal, it might as well finish by being frankly so. Among other stories, Lord Malmesbury tells in " Memoirs of an Ex-Minister " that the Queen, like every other woman, sometimes lost her keys. Once they were the keys which opened the Government boxes, that she dropped while riding in London. Lord Malmesbury met Colonel Arbuthnot walking down the centre of King's Road, his eyes fixed on the ground, while behind him was a strong body of police and park rangers drawn in a line across the road, all looking down also, which had a very absurd effect. Individuals among the amused public found it irresistibly tempting to give false intelligence about the keys, sending the seekers in all directions after people who were supposed to have picked them up.

Queen Victoria gained a reputation for extreme punctuality, which if true of her in her later life was not so concerning her early days : " As I write you will be making your evening toilette and not be ready in time for dinner," wrote the Prince when in Liverpool; and Lord Campbell tells how, at a palace party, the master of ceremonies bet him that the Queen would be twenty or more minutes late for dinner : " She always thinks she can dress in ten minutes, but she takes about double the time," he concluded. " Sure enough, it was nearly twenty-five minutes after eight before she appeared," added Lord Campbell. The Prince himself was anything but punctual, and among Twelve Hints to Railway Travellers I find : " No. 9. Should Prince Albert be coming or going, pray that H.R.H. may be punctual." In those days a Prince could command on a railway, and when Albert had been carried at the rate of sixty miles an hour on one occasion, he said to the responsible person : " You travel too fast on this line; not so fast back, please."

Very amusing is the story by Mr. Harry Furniss in " Harry Furniss at Home " of how a Solicitor-General appeared before the Queen to receive the honour of knighthood. " ' What am I to do ? ' he asked nervously of the official at the door. ' Kneel, kneel ! ' Suiting the action to the word, he immediately fell on his knees and, like the funny man at a child's party, propelled himself along the floor on his knees. The Queen was overcome with laughter, all the more that when she retreated the little man followed. And yet he rose to the highest post in his profession, and stood by Her Majesty's side as Lord Chancellor of England to read her address to the House of Lords."

It was in the House of Lords when the Queen prorogued Parliament in 1845 that the Duke of Argyll, who carried the Crown on a cushion, forgot when backing from Her Majesty that there were two steps behind him, and stumbled. The crown fell to the floor with a clatter, and lost some of its jewels. Victoria turned very grave, though she kindly begged the Duke not to be distressed, and heads were solemnly shaken over the incident. For nearly a year from that time the Queen was receiving one shock after another about Parliamentary affairs, which ended with the fall of Peel.

It was when going to open Parliament on another occasion that just as the Queen's carriage reached the Duke of York's column the harness of one of the leaders of the cream ponies broke, and the animal began to prance. An obliging policeman had the usual piece of string in his pocket, and tied up the strap, getting his foot stamped on for his trouble, the pain of which perhaps the Queen's sympathetic words salved.

From time to time the Palace inmates were horrified by the discovery of thefts from the attics and even the rooms, and two poor housemaids were on one occasion charged, then for lack of evidence discharged, as they also were from their posts. Later a cabinet-maker was accused, who was in such horror at the idea that he committed suicide. Still the thefts continued. The long pole studded with solid silver ornaments of Tippoo Sahib's tent, and a large part of the tent, silver tops of tables, silver from the picture frames, mirrors, and cornices, massive silver firedogs and candelabra, silver statuettes of great value, even chairs and furniture disappeared, and the palace keepers were in despair.

Then a silversmith in Long Acre had several things of such delicate workmanship, silver figures of Louis XIII. and of Marshal Saxe, worth £200, brought to him for melting down, that he informed the police, and they were identified as having been taken from a room next the Prince's study. A cabinet-maker who had worked for years at the Palace was found to be the thief, one who had callously ruined two people and caused the death of a third.

CHAPTER XIII

THE QUEEN AND THE CRIMEA

In the midst of the conflict with Palmerston already recorded, the Queen gave birth to her seventh child, Prince Arthur (to whom the Duke of Wellington was sponsor); and the day after his speech in the House which sealed Palmerston's triumph, Sir Robert Peel called at the Palace. Riding back in St. James's Park his horse, a vicious one, made a sudden buck, and Peel, who did not let go the reins, fell with the animal's knees on his body. He was carried home, and for a few days lived in delirium, then recovering sufficient consciousness to say "God bless you!" he died, a broken rib having pierced his lung.

The Queen, who was sufficiently recovered to go out, had been that afternoon to call on the Duke of Cambridge, and as she left his house an army officer named Pate brought the heavy head of his cane down with all his force upon her head, crushing the bonnet and severely bruising her forehead. Pate gave no reason for his act, and the jurors were so indignant that they refused to believe him insane, and sentenced him to seven years' imprisonment. Saved by her bonnet, the

Queen only suffered from the tenderness caused, though the shock made her very nervous. "I start at any person coming near the carriage, which I fear is natural."

The Queen's grief over Peel's death showed itself by incessant tears, and by dining apart from her Court for three evenings. "I have lost not merely a friend, but a father," she said, just as she said of her husband, "he felt that he had lost a second father." To the Prince Sir Robert's death was a great blow, for he looked upon him as a tower of strength in political troubles, and Peel was at that very time busily engaged in smoothing the way for the Great Exhibition. With a nature so easily depressed as the Prince's, the facts that Peel was dead, the Duke of Cambridge dying, and Queen Louise of Belgium just declared incurably ill, all combined to lower his vitality, for he was far from strong, and now there seemed no one upon whom he could lean. He suffered much from rheumatism and was constantly having attacks of nervous fever, slight in themselves, but recurring with increasing frequency. Yet he never abated his work, and in the struggle to live up to Stockmar's ideal—an ideal, alas! which he had taken as his own—he was slowly but surely sapping his strength.

The death of Louis Philippe in 1850 affected the Queen much, for nothing but her husband's good sense had prevented her from openly overflowing with affection for the Orleans family. Yet she was always so anxious not to do the wrong thing that she scarcely saw them without first consulting her Prime Minister.

Her love for them, however, made her particularly dislike Louis Napoleon, who was having a very uncomfortable time as President, remarking once when he found himself deprived of power, yet kept busy with clerical work :

"They want to make me the Prince Albert of France."

While France was in this state of flux Albert was working unceasingly at his great Exhibition scheme, approaching public bodies, manufacturers and foreign Powers, and, though most people who had a personal interest in trade and commerce took up the scheme, the public raised a great outcry.

That England should invite a multitude from other lands to see her work and productions was unthinkable. The "hated foreigner" would steal our ideas, copy our inventions, and destroy our trade. No one imagined it possible that any foreigner could teach us anything ; on the contrary, as they were mostly dirty ruffians, they would inevitably bring cholera, small-pox, plague, and every other disease into our midst. And if the diseases were not enough, the foreign rogues would carry, as of course they always did, stilettoes, knives and poison, and so deliberately accomplish that which accident left undone. Further, they would eat all the food or cause its price to rise so that famine would descend upon the land, and England would from all these causes, also from inevitable riots and insurrections, be depopulated. Over and above all this these terrible outcasts would assuredly spoil the morals of this virtuous island. So the accusations ran, and the

Prince said that every post brought him letters saying that, as a foreigner, he desired to corrupt England.

These prognostications were largely political, being got up by those who, being out of power, thought to make the Prince the scapegoat for their woes. But England was not alone in her fears. Almost every Court in Europe denounced the idea, and embroidered its disapproval with tales of conspiracy, intended assassinations, and bomb-throwing. The Diplomatic Corps in London expressed by ill-humour the sentiment of their Courts, while the King of Prussia felt the most acute irritation, absolutely forbidding the Crown Prince and Princess from coming to England. The Prince, however, eventually succeeded in securing his brother's consent, bringing with him his young son.

But perhaps the most disappointing opposition of all was that given by some members of the Government. Lord Campbell—who lived near the park—joined Lord Brougham in declaring, as lawyers, that the Crown had no right to use the park for their Exhibition. Hyde Park had been the Prince's idea, and it was not until the matter was well under way that *The Times*, inspired by the malcontents, started a wild outcry against the whole scheme, and in particular against the proposed site. Of this the Prince wrote to the Duchess of Kent: "We are to pack out of London with our nuisance to the Isle of Dogs, etc. There is to be a division in the House about it to-day. Peel was to have taken the lead in our defence, but now there is no one with influence enough to procure a hearing for justice and reason." (How like the Prince!) "If we are beaten, we shall have to give the whole thing up."

During the debate in the House, Colonel Sibthorpe, that arch-reactionary, distinguished himself by praying that hail or lightning might descend from Heaven to defeat the ill-advised project. This is as dignified as a suggestion I found in a newspaper, that birds would settle on the building in such quantities that their castings alone would break so fragile a substance as glass!

The Prince's bad opinion of the Commons was not justified, for "justice and reason" gained a majority of votes. The great public which was to be decimated by the Exhibition took the matter very lightly, and seemed in no wit frightened, having spirit enough to sing such songs as:

> "Oh, Albert, spare those trees,
>   Mind where you fix your show,
> For Mercy's sake, don't, please
>   Go spoiling Rotten Row.
>
> Where Fashion rides and drives
>   House not industrial art;
> But 'mid the busy hives,
>   Right in the City's heart!
>
> And is it thy request
>   The place that I'd point out?
> Then I should say the best
>   Were Smithfield, without doubt."

Punch had a cartoon of an angry and sulky-looking Prince turning away from a deputation of Belgravians and others, while the Queen pleads with him on behalf

Z

of Hyde Park. However, Paxton showed that the park need not suffer in beauty, for the building might be a huge conservatory, and could include even two fine elms which seemed in the way. So when the cruciform building was up, at the end of each transept stood a majestic tree. It was, in fact, an enclosed park with long glades of grass and an avenue of old trees.

At the last moment the bright young George, Duke of Cambridge, sent to remonstrate with the Prince and express his anxiety for his cousin's safety. But at such fears the Queen laughed. Probably of all people she was the most joyful on that brilliant day when hundreds of thousands of people came with delighted curiosity to see the notabilities who entered the great glass palace, for large as it was and full as it was, it could not hold a tithe of the people who were present. The radiant happiness of the Queen in seeing the success of her husband's idea was obvious to everyone, and the appearance of the Duke of Wellington brought a roar of welcome all along the line.

Charles Greville was more interested in the fulfilment of prognostications than in the ceremony, and he stayed in the park and wrote of the wonderful spectacle of countless multitudes streaming along in every direction, and congregated upon each bank of the Serpentine down to the water's edge; no soldiers and hardly any policemen were to be seen, and yet all were orderly and good-humoured. " The success of everything was complete, the joy and exultation of the Court unbounded." Then, as usual, the prophets of evil forgot to forbode, they began to praise, and at last pretended that they had been praising all along. Our own grumbling ones do the same thing now!

When the Exhibition's life of one hundred and thirty-eight days was over, there was a surplus of £150,000, and to that we owe the establishment of the Victoria and Albert Museum at South Kensington. Good as was that object, there was even a better way in which a little portion of that sum should have been used, for the success of the Prince's scheme was allowed to rest on the ruin of various people, of which I give one example out of at least half a dozen.

A man named Hicks who had saved George III.'s life from drowning in the Serpentine, was permitted as reward to keep an apple-stall in the Park. His daughter, then his grand-daughter, succeeded him, and the stall had grown into a small white cottage, to which children went for gingerbread, curds and whey, etc. The Exhibition swept away the cottage, and Ann Hicks appealed vainly to the Commissioners. She proved that she and hers had held it for a hundred and fifteen years, and had spent one hundred and thirty pounds upon it; yet the most the tender Prince and his men would do for her was to allow her five shillings a week for one year. She was reduced to such poverty that she and her little grandchild had to sleep under the sky, and then a protest in *Punch* induced kind-hearted people to send her out to Australia, where she had a son settled. As for the others who for years had gained a living in the park and had had their

stalls destroyed, a man named Lacy, a cripple named
Spicer, a blind man, and others, they were left to live
or die as they might; the dead stones of a museum
might have equalled in value a pheasant or a hare, but
they far outvalued the lives of poor people. It is
regrettable that a Prince with great aims should have
allowed the good achieved to be blotted by such
injustice. There is a real use for people like Jasper
Judge!

The great show brought, not famine and death, but
trade and prosperity to London, and there were gorgeous entertainments devised for the guests, a royal
fancy dress ball, a great City ball, which the Queen
and Prince attended, a million of enthusiastic people
remaining until three in the morning in the streets to
see the royal party go home. The gaieties were closed
by a State Ball at the Palace, of which Baroness
Bunsen's description is interesting:

"We went into one of the ballrooms, where within a
dense circle of onlookers was the Queen's quadrille
going on. . . . I caught sight of that upright, beautiful
head, crowned with diamonds, which carried itself so
steadily through all the steps of the dance. I soon saw
the whole figure, so small and yet so delicate and well
formed, that size is not noticed. We observed the
peculiar way in which she stood after the Duke of
Cambridge had made his bow: she stood alone and
alone stepped back, and mounted the throne; nobody
asked her or helped her; she went to her place in her
own right. The action was highly dramatic, but this
prevented it from being theatrical."

The Bunsens were great favourites at Court. They were from Prussia, in connection with which Victoria-Albert were already thinking of the marriage of their eldest daughter, and in whose politics they were always interested, Bunsen having the *entrée* to the Prince whenever he desired.

Mr. G. W. E. Russell tells in one of his delightful books how Victoria betrayed the same unconscious self-possession when the Empress Eugénie was visiting her in 1855. The royal party went to the opera, the Empress so robed and jewelled as to set the fashion for all Europe. Before sitting down she looked over her shoulder to see if a chair was ready for her. The Queen sat down without thinking of her seat, for she knew that her chair would be just where it was wanted.

On the whole, the Exhibition drew the people nearer to Albert than they had ever been before, and if he had been a different person he might have retained their confidence and won their affection. However, the complaint of his being a German was always cropping up under different pretexts, and in a general way, because in public his face was inexpressive, if not stern, because the British people could never win a smile from him, because he never was known to let himself go, because, as some little boys once said when they went to play with the Prince of Wales, "we cannot play, we are afraid of the Prince Consort."

Yet Albert made no attempt to Germanise England further than to insist for himself upon a hot dinner in the middle of the day, the English custom having been cold luncheon, and also to carry on and elaborate the

Christmas Tree amusement for the children, which Queen Adelaide, who loved children as much as did Queen Victoria, had brought here with her.

Where perhaps his foreign influence was most felt was in the habits of Court life, into which were imported small but rigorous laws, which, if by chance they did increase the outward respect shown to Royalty, must sometimes have diminished the reality of that respect by the inconvenience inflicted. Thus, on one occasion Lady Russell was a guest at Court soon after the birth of one of her babies, and the Queen whispered to her : " I know you are not very strong yet, so please sit down, and when the Prince comes in Lady Douro shall stand in front of you."

It was to the Prince that the Queen's ladies owed the long hours of standing which fell to their lot, and of which there were sometimes whispers among the public that some poor woman had fallen in a faint at Her Majesty's feet through exhaustion.

The Exhibition had brought to England rather a huge crowd of people than a number of notabilities, for the great had really frightened themselves with bogus fears. They preferred to come when the Queen could give them her whole attention, and she entertained a tremendous number of princes, relatives, and others from time to time. Sometimes they came to know and be known; sometimes with a hidden object, as when the young and ill-fated Portuguese princes were here with eyes upon our princesses. Victor Emanuel made a great stir, he was such a figure of a man, when, as King of Sardinia, he arrived in 1855.

THE MARCHIONESS OF DOURO.
From a Painting by J. Hayter.

The Queen said of him that he was more like a Knight of the Middle Ages than anything else; and the Duchess of Sutherland that he was the only knight of the many she had seen who looked as if he could have got the better of the dragon. He rode like a centaur, shot by moonlight, slept only two hours, going to bed at three and calling his staff up to talk and smoke with him at five: altogether a strange visitor for Windsor. The Queen bestowed the Garter upon him, and the better to show it off he donned white shorts, which, under a very short tunic, looked exactly like drawers.

But though Victoria was the most affable hostess she did not bestow upon him the gift he came for, and that was the hand of the Princess Mary of Cambridge, who, from her beauty and royal carriage, was said to be the only woman of her circle who could make the Queen jealous on general grounds. The decision in this matter having been left to the Princess, she refused the offer on the plea of difference in religion.

Among the stories of less important visitors is that of the Turkish Ambassador, who brought his wife to a Drawing Room wearing an ordinary Court dress—which was the more remarkable as the Ambassador appeared in his national Court costume. The Turkish lady, the Princess Callimaki, held her husband's arm and threaded her way serenely through the diplomatic crowd, and it is not to the credit of the Court officials that she was not presented with the forms and ceremonies usual on the introduction of the wife of a Minister. I wonder whether the Queen, with her hard-

and-fast ideas on custom concerning women, did not deplore the fact that here was a woman trying to shake off the bonds of barbarity.

One self-invited visitor to these shores caused a tremendous row; this was the Austrian General Haynau, who had helped to suppress the Hungarians by hanging brave soldiers, burning houses with the inhabitants inside, shooting those who surrendered in good faith, and mercilessly flogging many people, some of them noblemen and two of them noble ladies, the husband of one, Herr von Madersback, who was forced to stand by and watch, being so maddened that he shot himself.

This man was in disgrace, even in Vienna, for his atrocities, being nicknamed General Hyena, yet he decided to visit England, and persisted in doing so, though in Brussels he was strongly warned against it.

Among his amusements here he elected to go over Barclay's Brewery, and his first act on getting there with some friends was to write his name in the visitors' book. In two minutes it was known all over the place what kind of guest it was who had invited himself there, and as he was crossing one of the yards some workmen from a window threw down upon him a truss of straw. It was the signal for the rush of the other workmen into the yard, who flung grain and dirt upon the alarmed General, sweeping it up with brooms and shouting : " Down with the Austrian butcher ! " To quote from *The Times*, which constituted itself the General's champion and apologist : " He was covered with dirt, and perceiving some of the men about to attack him, ran into the street to Bank-side, followed by a large mob, consisting of the brewer's men, coal-heavers, and others, armed with all sorts of weapons, with which they belaboured the General. He ran in a frantic manner along Bank-side until he came to the George public house, where, forcing the doors open, he rushed in and proceeded upstairs into one of the bedrooms, to the utter astonishment of the landlady." The furious mob rushed in after him, threatening to do for the "Austrian Butcher," but a police galley was at the wharf at the time, into which he was taken and rowed towards Somerset House amidst the shouts and execrations of the mob.

Punch had, as may be imagined, much to say about this affair, and, as usual, added verse to comment, such as :—

> "The Baron was seized with blue despair,
>   And his teeth like a mill did clack, man !
> Cries he—' Vere shall I ron? ah, vere !
>   To esgabe vrom their addack, man? '
> ' You blood-stained thing ! we'll make you feel,
>   Though you may be dead to shame, man ! '
> So, though in language less genteel,
>   Cried Barclay and Perkins' draymen."

This incident was an offence against hospitality; but it was also an offence against England that a man whose name was at the moment a byword in Europe for infamy should have come to her shores. Yet the spirit which allowed ladies to fawn around Nicholas was still abroad, and there were many attempts in aristocratic circles to whitewash Haynau.

It is easy to believe that Palmerston's sympathies

346 THE MARRIED LIFE OF QUEEN VICTORIA

would not be with the General, and when he expressed
to Austria the regret of the Government he ended his
despatch with a remark condemning General Haynau's
visit to England. He sent a draft of this to the Queen,
who at once demanded the deletion of the last paragraph, and Palmerston replied that the despatch was
already gone to Vienna. Victoria was very angry, complaining to Russell : " He clearly shows that he is not
sorry for what has happened." Palmerston said in
heat he would resign rather than alter his despatch, but
eventually he recalled the letter and took out the
passage.

It was the Queen's business to ensure friendly relations with foreign countries, but there is something
pitiful in the fact that a Sovereign must be ready to
condone any chartered criminal of the rank of Haynau
and privately pretend disgust if her people are more
honest. That she should have written of " the brutal
attack and wanton outrage committed by a ferocious
mob on a distinguished foreigner of past seventy years
of age " was going much too far. One can understand
regretting as a matter of policy, but the man's age did
not prevent his acts, nor did his position give him
anything but an unenviable distinction.

The Queen and the Prince had by this time become
obsessed with Palmerston and his doings; they saw that
Russell was but a broken reed to lean upon as far as
their policy was concerned, and their only safety-valve
was in talking excitedly about the Foreign Minister to
whomsoever was with them. Lord Clarendon dined
with them one night, and " the moment he entered the

drawing-room after dinner the Queen exploded," and most bitterly discussed Palmerston and all his ways. When she had talked herself out on the subject the Prince began, and as he could not get in all he wanted to say in the evening, he asked Clarendon to go the next day, and then spent two and a half hours unrolling the tale of the royal woes, with indignant resentment.

Unfortunately, the Queen-Prince did not allow themselves the chance of being charmed by their Minister's pleasant manner, for though they wrote him long letters, and communicated through Russell, they otherwise ignored him. The last time the Prince expostulated with him personally, Pam assured him most earnestly, "with tears in his eyes," that he had never had a disrespectful thought of the Queen; and this statement is borne out in his letters. He could not help knowing that his dual Monarch disliked him; but if he knew of the petty feeling and rancour he passed it by without comment. As the French Ambassador said, "He was a daring pilot in extremity"; "and a most generous enemy," pronounced Cobden when dying.

As has been stated, for all the accusations against Palmerston, he kept England healthy and out of trouble for the five most dangerous years Europe ever passed through, when every country was sick with war fever. On the other hand, in a year or so of the rule which was so dear to the majestic heart, the Queen and her two peace Ministers, Derby and Aberdeen, failed and led us into war.

On the one hand was the man who resolutely intended to keep peace and to do the best he could for his country, on the other was a dual Monarch intent on peace at any price, who spread their sympathetic care far over Europe, especially Germany, who raised their own dignity into a fetish and, above all things, desired to be rid of their Foreign Minister.

Their love for Louis Philippe made them hate Louis Napoleon, and though they deplored French anarchy, they saw nothing in the *coup d'état* but a vile action perpetrated by a dishonest, lying adventurer; while those who studied international politics realised that it brought a chance of peace to factious Paris and steadied Europe.

At a party at Pam's house the *coup d'état* was the one subject of conversation, and one Minister after another said what he thought about it to Walewski, the French Ambassador. Among them Palmerston uttered his approval of the event in an officious way, that is, as a private person. The next day Walewski communicated Pam's words to the French Minister in Paris, who told Normanby, the English Ambassador, and Lady Normanby wrote long accounts of everything that happened in the Embassy to Colonel Phipps, Master of the Queen's Household, that her letters should be shown to the Queen. None of these communications was official, and Palmerston's words were well coloured by the time they had reached Victoria, whose anger made her ready to clutch at any straw. Her constant agitations and demands for help had already so upset John Russell's nerves that he was ready to do anything to get out of an unbearable situation; so he wrote to Palmerston saying that he had committed the Government by what he said to Walewski, and that he himself must advise the Queen to bestow the seals elsewhere, concluding his letter with : " Although I have the misfortune to differ from you in minor questions, I am deeply convinced that the policy which has been˙ pursued has maintained the interests and the honour of the country." In his next letter he offered him the Lord-Lieutenancy of Ireland, upon which Pam naturally pointed out that such an offer was in itself a refutation of the charges of imprudence and indecorum.

The ironic point in the proceedings was that Lord John had himself expressed a like opinion to Walewski at the same time as Pam, as also had Lord Lansdowne, Charles Wood, and Lord Grey. As Lord Malmesbury, Pam's successor, said : " Old diplomatists must know the difference between an *officious* and an *official* conversation. The first is a free interchange of opinions between the two Ministers and compromises neither."

The pretext of the dismissal was as flimsy as the joy of the Queen-Prince was unbounded. In a letter to his brother, Albert said :

" And now the year closes with the happy circumstance for us that the man who embittered our whole life, by continually placing before us the shameful alternative of either sanctioning his misdeeds throughout Europe and rearing up the Radical party here to a power under his leadership, or of bringing about an open conflict with the Crown, and thus plunging the only country where liberty, order, and lawfulness exist together into the general chaos—that this man has, as it were, cut his own throat. 'Give a rogue rope enough, and he will hang himself' is an old English adage with which we have sometimes tried to console ourselves, and which has proved true again here."

And yet in this fulfilment of their desires lay the greatest tragedy of their joint reign.

As for Europe, it stood at first amazed at the fall of Palmerston, then the countries all sang their own pæans of joy. Austria rushed into the arms of Russia, and they embraced with emotion; Greece all but melted on the shoulder of the two Sicilies. It was a triumph for Absolutism, a blow for the peoples. The Prussians sang in the streets doggerel to this effect:

> "Has the Devil any son,
> Sure then he is Palmerston."

Our English Minister in Madrid resigned his post, saying he could no longer be of use there, as Spain believed that concession had been made to the reactionary spirit. The Orleans family were as pleased as the English sovereigns, and all alike believed that English policy would in the future be a very lady-like, very peace-at-any-price, very simple, very blind policy, as, alas! it turned out to be.

Some time earlier the Queen had put before Lord John the principles, written out for her and Albert by Stockmar, to which she desired her Foreign Minister to conform—broadly, that she should know to what she gave her sanction, and that, having given her sanction, nothing should afterwards be altered. This sounds fair, but it did not express her meaning, for every incident in the long dispute shows that she wanted to dictate the policy, not only to sanction it, to alter letters to her liking, to refuse to send them if she did not like them, a great danger when the ruler is so distinctly a party person. This document she caused Russell to read in Parliament after Pam's dismissal, much to the latter's disgust.

The Queen-Prince were utterly amusing when the former wrote to Russell demanding that, now that they had got rid of Palmerston, they should specifically define English policy abroad, and draw up general principles which could be adapted to different states, and a regular programme defining England's relation with each country. Such a demand, which could only have emanated directly or indirectly from Stockmar's doctrinaire mind, makes one gasp with amazement. That Russell was said to "look overburdened and worried to death" is not to be wondered at, and gave excuse for a comic paper to announce:

"There was a little man, and he had a little head,
    And he said, ' My little head, let us try, try, try,
        If we can't with all my pains,
        And my little, little brains,
    Subdue the world under you and I, I, I.

The little head it ached and the little man he quaked,
    And away they went to work together, gether, gether,
        But so feeble was their will,
        And so little was their skill,
    That they got into very stormy weather, eather, eather."

The stormy weather came in four weeks, when Palmerston's amendment to the Militia Bill was carried, and Lord John resigned. Of this Pam wrote to his brother :

"I have had my tit-for-tat with John Russell, and I turned him out on Friday last. I certainly, however, did not expect to do so, nor did I intend to do anything more than to persuade the House to reject his foolish plan and to adopt a more sensible one."

The feeling of England on Pam's dismissal was deep; the people felt that the only strong man we had had been thrown aside to suit those whose sympathies were with the crowned heads of Europe, and who would sacrifice a whole people to the majesty of royalty. The Prince, naturally, was blamed, and the Queen was suspected of being entirely influenced by him, as, indeed, she was, and a deadly public feeling of anger began to grow against Albert.

Victoria always bitterly resented the fact that Albert was accused of a German bias in English politics, yet the accusation was true, for hidden behind the throne stood Stockmar, the adorer of Prussia, ready always to respond with advice and direction to the appeals of the Royal couple. He was perfectly honest, and could not help it that his leanings were all to Germany and monarchy, and his pupils could not imagine that his views did not suit England, nor that they themselves sometimes had their loyalty to England clouded by their deference to his advice and by their family affections.

As soon as Palmerston was banished from Europe,

Nicholas of Russia began to stretch his fist over Turkey; the Duke of Wellington was dead and could not reason with him; Palmerston could not threaten him; of Lord Malmesbury, a young untried man, who was put in the Foreign Office because he was quite unlikely to differ from his Queen, he had no fear; and Lord Derby, who became Prime Minister, was a negligible quantity. Only Pam in his back seat foresaw that trouble was coming, and no one would listen to him now. He would have smiled if he had known that Victoria-Albert, in the Queen's name, of course, sternly rebuked Malmesbury for allowing a Protocol (of which they had not heard) to be signed between England, Austria, Prussia, and Russia; and later scolded Aberdeen and Russell for holding a conversation with Louis Napoleon; and Charles Wood for not sending the drafts of letters until weeks after they had been written. Victoria had no realisation of how near she was getting to a desire for despotic monarchy.

Derby's Government did not last long, and then Aberdeen came in at the head of a coalition, and the Queen demanded that Palmerston should not be given the Home Office. However, Ministers, like schoolboys, have to play fair with each other, and as Pam refused to take the Foreign Office again, that was the only post he could have.

Nicholas was still happy, for Aberdeen, the Concessionist, was at the English helm—he who had conceded so much to Guizot as to make him feel justified in the Spanish marriages affair, and who later had given

A A

such vague promises to Nicholas at Windsor that he was certain that under Aberdeen's guidance we would not oppose him in Turkey.

Into the Crimean War itself I cannot enter. It was at first a Franco-Russian quarrel over the keys of the Holy Sepulchre, and at various stages Russia moved its army a little nearer Constantinople. Every time Russia moved, England started and shook herself, and then lay down again, growling " Wait and see." This began as soon as Aberdeen took office, and for over a year the occasional spasms and wait-and-see policy continued. When it was suggested to Aberdeen that a bold course would meet with general approval, his answer was quite Queen-like : " In a case of this kind I dread popular support."

> " What matter if Russia a sea-board obtain?
> Never mind till our navy she sweeps from the main,
> Which I hope she won't do, if we just cease to brag,
> And to sing Rule Britannia ; and lower our flag.
> Let us learn to be meek and submissive and tame,
> And in time perhaps Commerce may make her the same."

So while England was waiting, afraid to enter the back door as friends, the Russians had taken forcible possession of the front hall, as Palmerston said, and Aberdeen made the futile rejoinder that though Russia's first offensive action was indefensible, still, as the Emperor had made no declaration of war, we were not justified in doing anything. The " Vienna Note " was drafted, elaborated, sent to every big Power, altered, sent back to each Power, and, being trimmed exactly to suit Russia, was after some months of travel given the quietus by Turkey. Such a safe, conciliatory policy! one which forced Albert to say, when more than a year had been thus spent: "Aberdeen has, unfortunately, made. concessions which bring us nearer war." But the Emperor still did not believe that we would fight.

When Russia destroyed the Turkish fleet at Sinope, Palmerston, sick of his struggle to put pluck into his colleagues, took the excuse of the Reform Bill and resigned, upon which Aberdeen went with great alacrity down to Windsor with the resignation, and announced it in *The Times*, it being said that "certain personages were glad once more to shake off their obnoxious minister."

Then, while Palmerston was out of office, Aberdeen followed the course he had been urging upon him all along, and Palmerston withdrew his resignation.

All England was jealously waiting and watching; *Punch* gave us Nicholas as a clown trying to stuff a turkey into his capacious pockets and crying to Policemen France and England: "I don't mean any harm, gentlemen!" The more serious papers wrote of the dangers to our trade of Russian occupation of the Black Sea and the Mediterranean; and the popular suspicion of the Prince burst into a roaring flame. This suspicion having sprung into active life with Pam's dismissal, had gathered strength with the painful tension of the year of academic reasoning and inactivity, and it swept through the land, emanating from all classes. Roebuck accused Albert to the Duke of Newcastle of holding the keys to many mysteries, and papers came out with condemnations and questions, such as the following from *Diogenes*:

"Did you, Albert, cancel instructions prepared by the Ministers at home for Lord Stratford at Constantinople? despatch a Minister on your own account to the East, charging him to contradict the despatches of the Ministry? warn the Russian Ambassador of the contemplated movement of the combined fleets in the Black Sea? Is it true that you have a third key to the Queen's Despatch Box, that you open the box before the Queen sees it, and alter the despatches intended for foreign Ambassadors? that you receive important communications from Courts abroad relative to our foreign policy, which you do not show to Ministers? that you make alterations in the despatches of the Foreign Secretary before they are forwarded to the Courts for which they are intended? that you interfere at the Horse Guards to an extent which has excited general surprise and condemnation? that you exercise an influence over the patronage of the State, which is most injurious to the public service, as well as contrary to the spirit of the Constitution? that you dined off a turkey on Christmas Day, drank the health of the Czar, and led the chorus, 'For he's a jolly good fellow'?"

Thousands of people stood round the Tower one day to see the Prince taken there, and some said the Queen was to accompany him. When he did not arrive, the cry was that he was not to be imprisoned, because the Queen had declared she would share his fate.

So fierce and prolonged was this hysteria over the Prince that the most influential people in the land had to refute it, and Gladstone wrote a sensible letter in the *Morning Chronicle*. People accused the Prince of attending the Privy Council! Well, about sixty other men were also present, and no secrets were talked; he was accused of being present when Her Majesty gave audience to Ministers, and Gladstone's reply was: "We desired that our Queen should take a husband who was virtuous, prudent, and intelligent. She took one who was also accomplished, informed, able, and energetic. . . . In Prince Albert, high natural abilities have been improved by singularly careful and assiduous culture, to a rare point of excellence. . . . Is it right, is it natural, is it possible, that a wife so charged with labour and with care should debar herself of the assistance of a husband so endowed! We are certain that the voice of England will answer in the negative."

The matter was brought forward in both Houses on the last day of January, 1854, when the Queen opened Parliament. The crowds in the streets to see her pass were immense, and it was feared that she and her husband might be badly received; but though there was hissing, good humour generally prevailed.

Lord John defended the Prince in the Commons, and so good a case was made out that the wildness of abuse died down, but not until the war was quite concluded did gossip about the Prince's wickedness really die out.

How the Queen suffered through all this may be

imagined! she who fastened with avidity upon every shred of evidence that Albert was appreciated well, had to see him overwhelmed with absurd accusations. He, too, looked anxious and ill, though he said lightly: "If our courage and cheerfulness have not suffered, our stomachs and digestion have, as they commonly do when the feelings are kept long on the stretch."

As soon as Victoria-Albert and Aberdeen had made up their minds, they were keenly anxious that the quickest and best methods should be followed. But there were grave defects at the War Office, and they were not surprised when the Government was turned out in February on a motion to inquire into the conduct of the war. The Queen's emotions at this crisis were too deep for tears, for she saw *no one* fit to lead the legislative assembly: a most characteristic and yet Albertian judgment! She knew that Lord Derby was not strong enough to guide events, yet because his views pleased her she sent for him. Though he was a Tory, and thought Pam the worst man in England, besides, as he told his Sovereign, being blind, deaf, and old, he was obliged to add that the whole country cried out for him as the only man able to carry on the war with success, and that he *must* be in the Government if France was to retain any confidence in England. Yet, as Stockmar had impressed upon Albert-Victoria that Palmerston was mad, and as they were ready to believe anything against him, they were driven to desperation in their desire to avoid him.

Abroad, England was being laughed at as having neither army nor government; and Walewski wrote personally to Albert telling him that, as far as France was concerned, Palmerston and Clarendon were absolutely essential to any Ministry that might be formed.

Lord Derby failed, Lord Lansdowne was approached and refused, and then Lord John was summoned; in fact, the agitated rulers tried every side-path they could think of rather than tread the hard high road; yet they knew that Palmerston was the only man who could bind together the vacillating members of any government that could be formed, for all were afraid of the responsibility of the war. So for six days the business of the country was at a standstill, while all the world wondered.

Then the Queen-Prince made the best of a terrible situation—they sent for Palmerston, and promised to extend to him as Prime Minister the confidence they had shown his predecessors. But what a bitter draught it must have been!

So the strong man had to do his utmost to repair the mistakes of his dual Sovereign and their Ministers and help the weary war to drag its lamentable way to its ineffective ending.

Punch marked the event by publishing a cartoon of The Dirty Doorstep. Upon the door-plate is inscribed "Aberdeen, Newcastle & Co." and the step is heaped with blunders, routine, precedent, incapacity, higgledy-piggledy, delay, twaddle, and disorder. Palmerston, an active lad with a broom, says: "Well! this is the greatest mess I ever saw at anybody's door," to which Johnny, an urchin, replies, "I lived there once—but I was obliged to leave—it was such a very irregular family."

Once in power, Palmerston's energetic action, his care for the soldiers and insistence upon better regulations at the war centre, wrung from the Queen a reluctant gratitude, so that in 1856 she conferred upon him the Order of the Garter. His presence also at once altered the attitude of Russia, which for the first time showed a desire to propitiate England. Had he been at the helm at first prompt action would have shown Nicholas exactly what to expect, and every evidence goes to prove that there would have been no war.

For more than two years Victoria-Albert had had absolute power in foreign affairs. They had proved that the policy of talkee-talkee in the then state of Europe was a dead failure, yet they learnt nothing from it—they only plumed themselves upon having tried by every means to avert the struggle. Sir Theodore Martin's book is a lasting monument to Royal incapacity for truly estimating a question from all sides. It is natural, though sad, for Royal eyes are bandaged by isolation and tradition. Another King like Albert, intellectually certain that active power should be his, would for ever destroy monarchy in England, and, indeed, had Albert lived long and clung to the same privileges, that struggle would have come about long ere this.

As for Nicholas, the war killed him, for in 1855 came the sudden news : " The Emperor Nicholas died this morning of pulmonary apoplexy after an attack of influenza." He had passed through agonies at the reverses of his troops, and the previous day he had received news of the defeat at Eupatoria, which so affected him that he died a few hours later in delirium.

He had once declared in a speech that " Russia has two Generals in whom she can confide, Generals Janvier and Février." *Punch's* celebrated cartoon shows General Février laying his icy hand on the Czar's heart and causing its eternal stillness.

CHAPTER XIV

THE QUEEN AND THE END

WHILE rumours of war were in the air the Queen took a great interest in her soldiers, attending military displays, at which she wore military clothes. When the soldiers marched away the Royal Family would be on the balcony of Buckingham Palace at seven in the morning to see them pass; or from Osborne lead them on the *Fairy* out to sea, or see them off at Portsmouth, the Prince generously giving each officer a sealskin coat, and to each soldier a sheepskin. Victoria, with her usual enthusiasm, gushed over the men, "loving my *dear, brave* army as I do!" "Our beautiful Guards sail to-morrow." "I am *so fond* of my dear soldiers, *so proud* of them!"

When the poor wounded and disabled things began to come back in 1855 Her Majesty had a grand display in St. James's Park, and gave them medals with her own hands, uttering kindly words to each; and she watched—again from the balcony—the triumphant return of the broken, shabby and reduced Guards, and then drove to Hyde Park to pass them under review.

In May of that year the Victoria Cross was struck,

and the Queen, dressed in a red tunic and purple skirt, publicly in the park pinned the new order on the breasts of sixty-two heroes. Her own characteristic comment upon this in a letter to her uncle runs : " From the highest Prince of the Blood to the lowest private, all received the same distinction for the bravest conduct in the severest actions, *and the rough hand of the brave and honest private soldier came for the first time in contact with that of their Sovereign and Queen!* Noble fellows ! I own I feel as if they were *my own children;* my heart beats for them as for my *nearest and dearest.* They were so touched, so pleased; many, I hear, cried."

These are words which—in the light of the general belief in Queen Victoria's greatness—come as a shock. They are not the words of one who is absorbed in the woes and sorrows of others, or of one who possesses judgment. Had a girl uttered them one would have hoped that years would bring balance and breadth, but from a woman of thirty-six ! They show her childishly carried away by her emotions and remind me of Lord Aberdeen's penetrating remark to Nassau Senior :

" The Queen entered into the war with horror, she soon got to like it very much."

It was so. In her activities over the soldiers she enjoyed a personal Queenship which never before had been hers, and she felt that everything she did in honouring them reflected glory upon herself. She and her husband were busy, happily busy, going into camp at Aldershot, going down to Chatham, taking large parties of visiting Royalties with them, talking with the men, attending their theatricals, making speeches to them, gaily interested and always in the public eye. The soldiers were happy and honoured, and the Queen was happy in the daily excitement and the public adulation being poured upon her for the way in which she sacrificed (!) herself.

The war did something else, it cemented temporarily a friendship between Napoleon and Victoria, and gave her further exercise for enthusiasm. As has been said, Victoria-Albert for a long time refused to recognise the new French Emperor, and Louis Napoleon desired nothing so much as their recognition, giving a proof of this when, being made to understand how strong was Palmerston's feeling against the Suez Canal, he replied to Lord Clarendon : " If you say no more on the subject I will take care that my people shall let it drop."

Napoleon had been received nowhere with open arms. When the Czar wrote to him he addressed him, not with the kingly " Mon Frère," but with the lesser title of " Mon Ami," which made the sharp-tongued Frenchman reply : " How condescending ! A brother is forced upon one, a friend one can choose ! " Which, however, scarcely agreed with the spirit of the cartoon which showed him kneeling to Nicholas saying : " Am I not a man and a brother? " That he did not forgive the insult and all it implied showed itself when he joined England in its war against Russia.

Though our Government insisted upon the expediency of recognising Napoleon, Victoria-Albert would have none of him, and set their faces against his marrying the half-niece of the Queen, the daughter of Princess Féodore.

Then, hoping to conciliate England, Napoleon promised friendship to Leopold, urging him to help him with Victoria; next he invited Ernest of Coburg to Paris, and with him the Empress discussed the Queen-Prince; she talked of their beautiful domestic life, of the virtues of the Queen and her Consort, of the purity of their Court; apparently nothing could exceed her admiration of the English royalties.

Such praise—all dutifully repeated—was the shortest road to Victoria's heart; and though she looked askance upon the suggestion of a marriage between Jerome and Princess Mary, drawing the rude remark from Pam that Jerome was preferable to a German princeling, she was distinctly mollified. Then Leopold's admonitions, her councillors' strong opinion that it must be friendship or enmity, and their assertion that her attitude meant danger to her country, made her consent to recognise the Emperor as her brother.

Napoleon replied by addressing Prince Albert as " Mon Frère," and asked them both to Boulogne to see his troops. Albert alone could accept, but he carried with him a letter to the Empress from the Queen, which put a seal upon the friendship. When Albert left her, Victoria, lamenting that she had only once been so long separated from him since her marriage, laid commands upon his suite that the most minute and constant details of EVERYTHING that passed should be sent her, commands which were faithfully obeyed. The Prince, treated to the same comforting prescription of deference and flattery, thoroughly enjoyed his four days abroad. He was the great personage for once, and there were no fetching and carrying for him to do, no prompt obedience demanded to petty commands, which in itself must have constituted a holiday.

In April, 1855, Napoleon and Eugénie came to England on a visit to Victoria-Albert, and our people received them with acclaim, as eager to welcome them as was the thoroughly converted Queen. Of their arrival at Windsor she says : " I embraced the Emperor, who received two salutes on either cheek from me, having first kissed my hand. I next embraced the very gentle, graceful, and evidently very nervous Empress, and then we went upstairs, Albert leading the Empress, who, in the most engaging manner, refused to go first, but at length with great reluctance did so, the Emperor leading me, expressing his great gratification at being here and seeing me, and admiring Windsor."

Here the Emperor received his passport into society, the Blue Ribbon, and it is said that his look of triumph on this occasion was a thing not to be forgotten.

There was a State visit to the City, the London people going mad over the visitors and flocking in awful crowds into the streets. At the opera fifty, eighty, and even a hundred guineas were paid for boxes, and it was hard to secure a stall at ten guineas. All this must have been a wonderful and triumphant experience for the man who had often been penniless in

London and in the lower quarters of Continental cities.

The Royal children fell in love with the Empress, and were never out of her room; and when she left, she, they, and—someone says—the whole French suite, were dissolved into tears. The Queen gave her "sister" at parting a veritable Victorian gift, a bracelet containing some of her hair!

When, the following August, Victoria, Albert, and the two eldest children went to France, the Emperor refurnished Versailles for them, masking the fortifications with flowers. He met them at Boulogne, and going through Amiens and Abbeville they unfortunately arrived two hours late in Paris, so that French hopes had somewhat cooled in the darkness, though one courtier told the Queen that such enthusiasm had not been shown in Paris even at the great triumph of Napoleon I.—a pretty piece of French politeness, though the Queen accepted it as fact.

Among the notabilities they met Bismarck, and the Princess Royal for the first time saw the man who was to rob her life of half its brightness. One day our Royal pair took a remise at the Embassy gate, and drove privately through the streets and the Jardin des Plantes, no one recognising them. They made a sentimental journey in state to the tomb of James II., and a complimentary one to that of Napoleon I., at the latter bidding the Prince of Wales kneel. "A thunderstorm broke out at the moment, and the impressive scene moved to tears the French generals who were present."

Both Queen and Prince were treated most royally, and the former left France with all her feelings about her host entirely reversed. She wrote of Napoleon's frankness, his sincere, straightforward conduct, of his fascinating, melancholy, engaging ways, "so quiet, so simple, *naïf* even, so pleased to be informed about things which he does not know, so gentle, so full of tact, dignity, and modesty, so full of respect and kind attention towards us. . . . Then he is so fond of Albert, appreciates him so thoroughly and shows him so much confidence."

What a paragon Napoleon seems to have appeared, and yet a little earlier the Royal pair had been horrified over his perfidy.

This visit led to one very disagreeable incident for Victoria, in the shape of an insulting letter to her by a French refugee in London named Felix Pyat, who won ephemeral fame in the Parisian whirlpool of 1871. He wrote this letter for distribution among the French around him, and then sent it to *L'Homme*, a little paper started in Jersey by men exiled by Napoleon, among them being Victor Hugo. After begging Victoria to remember the fate of Charles I., this effusion ran as follows : " The Emperor kissed your hand. God save the Queen ! You have given Canrobert a bath,[1] drunk champagne, and kissed Jerome. You felt a need to escape a little from all these great men and all those beautiful things, and one morning, being languid, *abimée* with admiration and delight, no longer a Queen, but a woman, a daughter of Eve, like a plain gossip of

[1] Alluding to the bestowal of the Order of the Bath.

Windsor, you took a cab by the hour with your man and your children, and went to rest in the Jardin des Plantes with the trees and the beasts of the good God. You have tasted and enjoyed all the pleasure, the poetry, the light, the perfumes, and the strength of France. (Had you possessed another sense you could not have enjoyed more.) You could not have had too much in another sense. You have sacrificed everything, dignity as a Queen, the scruples of a woman, the pride of the aristocrat, English sentiment, rank, race, sex, all, even shame, for love of this ally! To-day when you are thoroughly refreshed and calm, returned to your home, having regained your *sang-froid*, your tea, your butter and your reason, now, Madam, what does this visit signify? What did you go to do at this man's home? Certainly you, an honest woman, that is to say as honest as a Queen can be, did not go to see the ruffian of the Haymarket."

This letter procured the banishment of all concerned —Victor Hugo included—from Jersey. It was republished in the English Press with indignation, but beyond the annoyance it caused did little harm.

The Queen could never really fathom the character of her new French ally, but he quite correctly gauged hers, and when there was disagreement over the close of the Crimean War he was clever enough to beg a consultation with her personally. So he and Eugénie went to Osborne for four days, and by reason of his persuasive tongue and Victoria's impressionability he successfully won all he wanted. Then before leaving he invited his hosts to run over to Cherbourg at their leisure and see his new arensal and fortifications.

It was rather a funny situation, Napoleon laying his hand on his heart, protesting his lasting friendship and esteem after having secured his own terms, and then saying, " Come, my dear sister, come and see the splendid arrangements I am making to add to my power of attacking and giving you a good beating."

So, with six children on board, they in the *Victoria and Albert* slipped over to Cherbourg one day, and anchored off the French coast for the night. It was said to be an *incognito* visit, but at 8.30 the next morning the fortresses saluted, and Generals came to escort the Royal party to land. Of the works Victoria said :

" It made me very unhappy to see what is done here, and how well protected the works are, for the forts and the breakwater (which is triple the size of the Plymouth one) are extremely well defended."

In the afternoon the Prince arranged a long drive into the country, and they went as far as the ruins of Briquebec, where a little incident happened which, though too insignificant for the Queen to record in the " Life," was more interesting than all the rest.[1] The curé came to offer Her Majesty a sketch done by a *pauvre brave bonhomme* who was wandering through Normandy, named Jean François Millet. On seeing it the Prince exclaimed, " That man is a born artist ! " and admired the little picture greatly, which after its

[1] *Tales of My Father*, by A. M. F.

"gracious acceptance" was given to the Princess Royal as a memento of the visit.

The Orsini outrage badly strained the friendship between Napoleon and the English Court, for Orsini had gone straight from London to throw his three bombs at the Imperial carriage, from the ruins of which Napoleon and Eugénie walked as by a miracle. France went into hysterics over *la perfide Albion*, and its colonels shook their swords in our faces in an article in *Le Moniteur*, when they wrote :

"Let the miserable assassins, the subaltern agents of such crimes, receive the chastisement due to their abominable attempts; but also let the infamous haunt (London) where machinations so infernal are planned be destroyed for ever. Give us the order, Sire!"

A demand was also made by France that England should refuse to give free asylum to French exiles, and Palmerston, agreeing with the Queen that some concession might be offered, brought in a Bill making conspiracy to murder a felony and not a misdemeanour. It was not much of a concession, and it was a just one, but the English were furious with the extravagant threats of the French; so John Russell and the Liberals turned against Palmerston, saying that he was truckling to French aggression, and defeated his measure by nineteen votes.

And so at last came the wonderful event of the Queen clinging to her old enemy, begging him not to resign. But Palmerston could not do as she wished, seeing that he had been turned out by his own colleagues, and the Queen lost for a time the man whom she now acknowledged as necessary to her sense of security.

These events made the state visit to Cherbourg in 1857 most uncomfortable for all the Royal people. Napoleon was angry over Orsini, and more angry over the temper of the English people, openly asking the Queen whether they were as prejudiced against him as ever. He made a terrific—Victoria felt almost a threatening—display as her yacht neared the harbour, for first a single gun was fired, then came the salute from gun after gun, running along each tier like a train of fire, then all the forts fired in volleys of eight at once, as fast as they could. The ring of fire came not only from the town, but from far into the country, up among little ravines, at the top of picuresque eminences, where it might have been fancied only rural villas and cottages could exist, around clumps of trees, and from the sides of cornfields : such a cannonade as had probably never before been offered for a visitor of peace.

The French cried *Vivas* for the Emperor, the Empress, the Prince Imperial, and the Queen of England, " which I dislike so much," said the Queen pathetically, seeing that the Prince was not included in the popular commendation. She endured, too, a terrible *quart d'heure* when her beloved had to make a speech, for she felt the situation to be grave, and knew that every word would be searched for latent meanings by every diplomatist and journalist in Europe. " I sat shaking, with my eyes *cloués sur la table*. However, the speech did very well."

But through the two days the Emperor did not regain his cheerfulness, and the Queen found little comfort from his remark on parting that that very day (August 6th) a hundred years earlier the English had bombarded Cherbourg.

The Queen shuddered at the idea that Napoleon was fortifying himself against England, and thought over her military commanders with doubt. The one man in whom she would have confided—the Duke of Wellington—had died in 1852. His successor as Commander-in-Chief, Lord Hardinge, had in 1855 fallen at her feet in a fit at Aldershot, and died a few weeks later. He was followed by George, Duke of Cambridge, and in him was no help. Yet he was her own choice, she believing that through him she could still keep the army under the control of the Crown.

Wellington was a greater loss than she knew, for he had always kept his independence and was a curb upon her tendency to autocracy over those near her, and she regarded him in an almost filial way. One night, when sitting near her listening to music, he fell asleep, and when Victoria rose, all rose also but the Duke. Her Majesty laughed and tapped him on the shoulder with her bouquet, which awoke him; she then made him a profound courtesy, and taking his arm in a kind, affectionate manner, drew him into the drawing-room for coffee.

It was said that the Queen was responsible for the rumour that he intended to marry Miss Burdett-Coutts, for while he was dining at the Palace one night the conversation turned upon that lady, and Victoria remarked to the Duke that he really ought to marry her, it would be such a good match in every way. This caused a general laugh, but, as a matter of fact, the Duke, who was even in his age something of a gallant, did pay much attention to that lady, astonishing the world by his intimacy with her, "with whom he passes his life, and all sorts of reports have been rife of his intention to marry her," said one of the Grevilles. *The Observer* even came out with a detailed announcement of the marriage settlements, and then—the rumour passed and was forgotten.

One of the proudest moments of this veteran's life was when he was asked to sit for a statue which was to be put up in some public place. He was a modest man in spite of the plaudits always showered upon him, but he dearly loved appreciation, and, though he hesitated, it was but to consent with something like emotion. The statue was made by M. C. Wyatt of guns taken by the Duke in war, and when it was finished it measured twenty-seven feet in height, and weighed about fifty tons. It was fixed in its place on the top of the arch at Apsley Gate among cheering crowds, with Royalty to look on, but, alas! the crowds who came to admire began to laugh, for the statue was ungraceful, badly made, and out of all proportion with its resting-place.

The old warrior was much hurt by the talk in the Clubs and the ever-recurring newspaper comments upon it, such as "an unsightly monster left until called for in Piccadilly," or a suggestion that its true resting

place was Guy's Hospital. To the gibing verses there
was no end:

> "Ride a cock horse
> The archway across,
> And see a big gentleman on a bronze horse.
> Badly he shows
> From his nose to his toes,
> But how we can better it nobody knows."

But he felt the sharpest grief when it was announced
that the Queen had decided that the statue should
be removed; upon which decision the satiric papers
declared that Her Majesty felt it to be contrary to
her state and dignity to allow the effigy of the Duke
to stand *over* the arch *under* which she drove. The
poor Duke was all the time in such an uncontrollable
state of irritation that people dared not speak to him
about it, and he wrote to Croker that people "must
be idiots to suppose it possible that a man who is
working day and night, without any object in view
but the public benefit, will not be sensible of a disgrace inflicted upon him by the Sovereign and Government whom he is serving. The ridicule will be felt
if nothing else is!"

As soon as the Queen knew the state of mind of
her faithful servant in this matter she countermanded
the preceding order, only regretting that the monument
should be so unworthy of the great personage to whose
honour it had been erected.

Wellington was such a public idol that there was
much criticism of the Queen-Prince because they did
not return to London at his death, and because the
Prince did not attend the funeral:

376 THE MARRIED LIFE OF QUEEN VICTORIA

> "He cares not, what cares he? for funeral or pall
> Who could sleep his last sleep without coffin at all!
> But if you must give him a burial in state,
> And make living pride on dead rottenness wait,
> Then do it in earnest, and not in a sham,
> And stand there chief mourner, my royal Madame;"

was an anonymous expression of feeling, to which a further verse makes the Queen reply to the reproaches of the warrior's ghost:

> "My conscience acquits me, *sans peur, sans reproche,*
> For I sent to attend you my coachman and coach
> And six spanking bays: and my Alby to-day
> From his best Durham's calving I made stay away,
> To do you more honour; and out at the show
> Looked myself from the window of Buckingham Row.
> And I hope that my people all saw in my eye
> The tear that stood glittering there as you went by."

Austria took a petty revenge for the row over Haynau by refusing to send a representative to the funeral.

So there was no Duke, and no one of his standing, to strengthen the Royal two in their intangible fear of the warlike intentions of the Emperor, nor to advise them upon the horrible Indian Mutiny. When the first news of the rebellion in the East reached them they seemed at once to foresee that it meant tragic things. They had already become unnerved about the state of the Army, weakened as it was by the war, and fretted continually that new forces could not be raised at a minute's notice. They wrote daily, sometimes twice a day, to their Prime Minister, urging speed, one suggestion following hard upon another, until Palmerston remarked in reply that measures sometimes were most likely to succeed which followed each other step by step, and ended one letter by saying that it was very fortunate for him that the Queen was not on the Opposition side of the House, the sarcastic meaning of which did not penetrate her consciousness.

They were just as anxious, after their visit to Cherbourg, to strengthen the English naval defences, for Napoleon continued to increase both army and navy, while Victoria-Albert grew more and more uneasy as to his aims. Then he declared his alliance with Victor Emanuel, and his intention to back a united Italy. This was something of a relief, though fear was turned to anger, for the Queen-Prince's sympathies were all on the side of Austria against Italy, and the anger grew loud and deep when Napoleon said he wanted Nice and Savoy as payment. As Prussia at the same time was trembling about its Rhine borderland, a French paper wittily summed up the situation by declaring :

"La Reine d'Angleterre a mal aux côtes, on lui conseille de se fortifier.

"Le Roi de Prusse a mal aux reins (Rhin).

"Le Roi de Piedmont a si souvent crié 'Vive l'Italie' qu'il a perdu sa voix (Savoie)."

If Victoria-Albert had a distinct leaning to Austria, their affection for Prussia was vivid, for they had long cherished the idea that their eldest girl should marry the young Prince, Frederick William. When this young man came to the Great Exhibition he saw the little Princess Royal, who was then not eleven years old. It was a tender age at which to make an indelible impression, but so it is recorded. In 1853 the Crown Prince, Frederick's father, definitely proposed the alliance between his son and England's daughter, and then in 1855 Fritz came over here himself to see if the flapper of fourteen came up to his expectations, and he found her pretty, clever, transparent and quick of tongue. She was then two months under fifteen years old, an age at which girls to-day are only just beginning to feel that they belong to the upper school, that they must wear their frocks a little longer than their younger sisters, and pay special attention to those details of the toilet which the younger ones so eagerly evade.

Whose fault was it that a babe of that age should be thrust into womanhood? Left uninfluenced, would the Queen have allowed it, she who would not marry until she was over twenty? Was it the Prince solely, he who had an especial love for his daughter, and who had gained a passionate love from her? Did he know so little of womanhood that he thought he was acting wisely by her? Or was it Baron Stockmar, who, with his un-English ideas, had long pressed this thing in his love for Prussia? To him the Prince wrote in September—the little Victoria's fifteenth birthday being in the following November:

" Now for the *bonne bouche!* The event you are interested in reached an active stage this morning after breakfast. The young man laid his proposal before us with the permission of his parents and of the King; and we accepted it for ourselves, but requested him to hold it in suspense as regards the

H.R.H. The Princess Royal at the time of her Marriage.
From a Painting by Winterhalter.

other party until after her confirmation . . . he speaks of himself as personally greatly attracted by Vicky. That she will have no objection to make I regard as possible."

The Queen also wrote to her uncle, "*our* wishes on the subject of a future marriage for Vicky *have* been realised in the *most gratifying* and *satisfactory* way. . . . Fritz William said he was anxious to speak of a subject which *he* knew his parents had never broached to us—which *was to belong to our* Family. . . . I need *not* tell you with *what* joy *we* accepted him for *our* part."

However, the determination to keep the child in ignorance soon broke down, and in a few days Fritz during a ride picked a piece of white heather, which he gave her, and at the same time made an allusion to his hopes and wishes as they rode down Glen Girnock.

It is not possible to see any reason why such a sacrifice should have been necessary. We are told over and over again that this was a love match, yet what does a girl, who binds herself before she is fifteen, know of love? It is true that she did not marry until two months after she had passed her seventeenth birthday, but even then, to send one's girl irrevocably out of the home-nest at that age to an alien country, to win or lose everything, is a terrible thing. Had the Princess been a woman of twenty-one instead of an immature girl, the unhappiness that attended her life at the Prussian Court might perhaps have been avoided. But it is not likely that her mother ever considered such an idea, she urged her daughter to bear with things and once was sore tempted to remonstrate, but of regret for her own share there is no evidence.

This marriage pleased no one in England but the Royal Family, for Prussia seemed a declining force, ruled over by a weak King who could not command respect. The Prussian Ministers did not like it; Bismarck was strongly against it and never ceased his enmity to the Princess until after many years when, disgraced himself, he begged her intercession, only to meet a well-merited rebuff. It was in fact, another Stockmar-formed marriage carried out by the Queen-Prince through motives of sentiment for Germany, but also because they believed Fritz to be a decent, upright, sincere young man.

That Prussia should have demanded that the Princess should go to Berlin to be married because the dignity of the young Prince would not allow him to come to England, was a pure piece of Ministerial intrigue, inspired by the hope of upsetting the match, for Prince Frederick had betrayed no thought of such a thing. Victoria-Albert were righteously indignant, and the Queen wrote that they would not hear of it, saying, "It is not every day that one marries the daughter of the Queen of England."

The ceremony, therefore, took place at the Chapel Royal on January 25th, 1858, with nearly twenty German Royalties among the guests, and the poor child did not know how to tear herself away from the father she adored. "It will kill me to leave dear papa," she exclaimed; while at the thought of the separation the Queen was also sick at heart, saying when the young people had at last driven away: "Such sickness came over me, real heartache, when I thought of our dearest child being gone, and for so long—all, all being over!"

If only she had kept her dearest child a few years longer the pain would have been less.

The people were enthusiastic enough through the festivities, though they deplored the reasons which still remained against the match, as may be gathered from the words of an old woman who stood at the end of Birdcage Walk as the bride and bridegroom drove away. The crowd was so enormous that people were pushed against the carriage, and this old dame thrust her face into its window, saying earnestly:

"Young man, you've got a good wife there; mind you make her a good husband."

"I will, you may be sure of that—I will," emphatically responded the young man.

When they first visited England after their marriage, both Prince Fritz and Princess Victoria assured folk of their great happiness and of the tender affection they bore each other, for many sinister reports were current in England as to their unhappy life together, the reports going so far as the assertion that Fritz had used personal violence and thrown his wife downstairs. But the Princess's troubles arose at first rather from her mother-in-law than from her husband, and later from the "man of blood and iron"—Bismarck.

In 1857 Victoria insisted upon doing her husband

a justice which the nation had so far refused, by giving him the title by Letters Patent of Prince Consort. It is a reproach upon the chivalry and fair-mindedness of the Englishmen of the day that they did their Queen the indignity of refusing any position to her husband. For seventeen years he was in the eyes of Europe merely the second son of the Duke of Coburg; for seventeen years, when he was out of England, personal arrangements had to be made to allow him to occupy a seat at the same table with his wife; for seventeen years he who was spending his whole life in the service of England, who was considered good enough to be the most intimate associate of the Queen, was not thought worthy of anything like equality of rank with her. The Queen always wanted some arrangement made which should save him and her from the recurring humiliations of such a situation, and at every suggestion there was someone's temper to consider; " In the present disaffected state of the House "; " Seeing the temper of the country "; " It is likely to create division in the Cabinet "; so the excuses trailed through the years.

A year earlier Victoria had put in an urgent plea that the title popularly given of Prince Consort should be ratified by Parliament. She saw her boys growing up and holding superior positions to their father, deferring to him only through affection and forbearance. " If the children resist, the Queen will have her husband pushed away from her side by her children, and they will take precedence over the man whom she is bound to obey; if they are dutiful, she will owe her peace of mind to their continued generosity."

In answer to this strong appeal to her Prime Minister, Lord Derby, with the greatest humility and deference, pointed out " the present unfortunate temper of the House of Commons," "the hostile criticisms of the Press." So the matter was left for another year, and then the Queen took it into her own hands; and *The Times* celebrated the event with a sneering attack on the Prince.

The Queen was keen upon settling her children for life, and long before it was necessary suitors came in number from all over Europe to look at the little Princesses, and the Queen was busy from 1855 gathering information as to their morals, health, and means. From sentimental reasons she would rather have liked to bestow a daughter upon the young Prince of Orange, thus making reparation in the third generation for the disappointment of the first and second. For one Prince of Orange had been refused by Princess Charlotte, and another by Queen Victoria. Eventually the young Louis of Hesse was chosen for the Princess Alice, the engagement taking place when the Princess was seventeen, which was certainly an improvement upon the age of her sister in like case.

There are many events which must be left unrecorded. The Prince of Wales's tour in Canada and America, the Royal visit to Prussia that the beloved daughter might once again please parental eyes, the visit to Coburg, all these things have been told again and again. A great grief was the death of the Duchess

of Kent early in 1861, who, having had a small operation for an abscess under the arm, died through a com-
plication of troubles a few weeks later on March 15th.

Two years before his death the Prince Consort had
agreed to work with the Queen in writing a book upon
her favourite English monarch, Charles II. Charles
II.! think of him as a hero in a Court supposed to be
renowned through the world for its purity! For such
a busy man and woman to undertake such a work it
was necessary to secure a " ghost," and a young writer
was found who was ready to gather the information and
work in the library at Windsor. He was a born book-
lover, and soon noticed that some valuable old books
had disappeared.

" Oh, they are here, there is no doubt of that, and
they must be found! " said Albert.

But they were not there, and it was only by great
pertinacity that it was discovered that many had been
borrowed by the " Poor Knights." Two of the most
valuable were found lying on a round table in the
window of one of the Knights' little parlours, being
used to raise the plants to a more advantageous height.
Years later one of the lost books was noticed by a book-
seller among a lot which he had captured, and he sent
it to Her Majesty in case she would like to buy it back
—for the sum of £150. The Queen examined the
book and wrote as a memorandum for the Librarian :
" A very nice book—but—the price! "

One morning the Queen came to the library asking
for a certain volume, and as no real catalogue had been
made, it was not easy always to discover a book. How-

ever, going to a side-table, the young writer picked up
the volume and placed it in Her Majesty's hand. This
unwonted celerity quite astonished the Queen, who
exclaimed : "Oh, how clever of you, how very clever
of you to know just where every book is." The
librarian bowingly accepted the compliment, and did
not say that he had been handling the volume the day
before.

The Queen-Prince, as they grew older, developed
in the usual way; they became keenly conservative,
especially in foreign politics, and did not recognise the
existence of patriots. To their minds, Kossuth was the
leader of rebels, to respect whom was a grievous sin
against Austria; the Italian fighters for a United Italy
were but revolutionaries who ought to be stamped out—
for they were intent upon upholding absolutism in Austria. When a Liberal Government came in, they, being
in deadly fear of Russell and Palmerston, invited to
form it one whom they thought would be a willing tool,
Lord Granville. Pam, knowing his own power, agreed
lightly to the arrangement, but Russell refused, so
Lord Granville would not act, and Victoria was obliged
to take her old enemy for a second time as Prime
Minister. During this year of 1860 the Queen-Prince
were in misery about foreign affairs; they *would* interfere, and their interference constantly recoiled upon
themselves; when things went wrong abroad, they made
—the Queen being spokesman, of course—accusations
which could not be sustained against the Ministers at
home; they were enraged with Napoleon, disappointed
everywhere. When Italy was being unjustly used, they

peremptorily demanded neutrality from Palmerston; but when Austria began to suffer, they bitterly desired action. The last straw was the scheme on the part of the Government to abolish the office of Commander-in-Chief. They protested strongly—and though events had largely destroyed the sympathy of their leading Ministers, the suggestion was for the time dropped.

With her emotional nature and exuberance of expression Victoria must have been a difficult person to live with through that year. She had never lost the habit of impressing upon those around her when things did not go right that she was the Queen, the greatest person, not only in the land, but in the house. From much that has been put into print it might be concluded that domestically at least the life of the Prince was one of unbroken bliss. That he knew himself to be loved is doubtless, but that he had at times to endure the sharp edge of his wife's tongue up to the last is also a fact. One who was much in contact with him during the last three years, often after expressed the sorrow he felt at the ultra-regal attitude—to put it in soft words—which would be shown to the patient, quiet Consort. Indeed, by that time disappointment and weariness were pressing hard on the man who had striven so unceasingly to do what he believed to be right. Duty, family affection, class sympathy had all combined to impose unremitting work. It is true that this work was largely unnecessary, even sometimes mischievous, but the Queen-Prince thought it essential, and the Queen, who was always ready to discuss foreign affairs, and to let her emotion run riot over the wickedness of her Ministers, left all the real thought and work to Albert. He was the brain of the partnership, and he was the most loyal and dutiful partner any woman ever had. No word exists which shows that he ever assumed credit for anything done, or asked recognition for the long hours of labour, which towards the end of his life he allowed to absorb each day.

He was not happy over his eldest son, upon whom he had spent much thought and time, again with the best intention, though injudicially. Yet he had had a happy life with his children. He had botanised, geologised, moth-hunted with them; had shown them how to work with their hands; had tried to induce a love of literature, and was interested in their music and drawing. His idea of literature, however, meant heavy reading, and from all that can be gathered about the children's education, it seems certain that one thing neglected was imagination. Novels and fairy tales are never mentioned—a fatal omission when dealing with some characters. If the girls liked their cooking and cleaning, and the boys their carpentering and building, as play, there was no reason why they should not do it; if they had different tastes it would have been better to have filled the world for them with the colour and beauty of fancy and human character. But the customs of the time were against children, for the elders were governed by routine rather than thought; thus when the Prince of Wales had reached his seventeenth birthday he was pronounced of age, and the

Queen—with the fatuous folly of the time—suddenly affected to regard him as a man, telling him that his training had been severe in his own interests, and now he was to consider himself as his own master. This was more sentiment than reality, for the boy, who had been brought up with no companions but his own brothers, knowing no girls but his own sisters, imbibing no thoughts or views which were not as familiar as the furniture of his bedroom, was not suddenly left to his own devices, though it might have been well if the leading strings had been more relaxed.

When he went to Cambridge he had a tutor, a governor, and an equerry to guard him, who all surrounded him when—clothed in his nobleman's cap and gown—he went as the only student to a lecture, though a specially invited audience of undergraduates was allowed to be present. The Prince, unhappily, had been so tutored in theories of purity that the theory of suggestion was exemplified, and in spite of his many guardians he had not been long at Cambridge before he got into some erotic scrape.

This was a heavy blow to the Prince Consort. The thought of his son doing that thing which of all others he had been most warned against haunted him, it chased sleep away at night and upset his digestion in the day, and an endeavour to put matters right was one of the last efforts he made before his illness. He went down to Cambridge on a horribly cold, wet November day, feeling already overburdened with lassitude and catarrh, while his depression was black as night. He was losing courage and his " pure and

H.R.H. THE PRINCE OF WALES
AT THE AGE OF SEVENTEEN.

noble will," to quote from Stockmar, was at failing point.

The Prince had many times said that he did not mind the thought of death; if only he knew that his loved ones were provided for he would be quite content to die. When he last went to Coburg, the horses of his carriage took fright and smashed into the gates at a level crossing. The coachman was injured and one horse was killed, the Prince jumping out just in time and falling. The shock threw him into the deepest melancholy, and Stockmar exclaimed:

"God have mercy on us! If anything serious should ever happen to him, he will die!"

The day that Albert was starting for home he was walking near the Castle with his brother Ernest, and at one of the most beautiful spots the Duke saw him draw his handkerchief and wipe tears away. "I shall never see it again," he said, "never again shall I be in Coburg."

When he had to keep to his room in November, 1861, he felt from the first that he should not recover, but he still went through the despatches—and was allowed by the Queen to do so. Up to the end the Queen's eyes were not penetrating enough to believe that her beloved was very ill. December 9th was the first day he was kept in bed, and on the 11th Victoria wrote to Leopold lamenting that it was very sad and trying for her, that she was well, "and I think really *very* courageous; for it is the first time that *I* ever witnessed anything of this kind though *I* suffered from the same at Ramsgate and was much worse."

The fact that Albert was suffering from fever, with despondency, weakness, and "occasional and invariable wandering," "gave her a very trying time," but it seems to have awakened no alarm, none of the insight which might have been expected.

It has been said that the Prince's critical condition was purposely kept from the Queen. *Can* such things be kept from the eyes of love, if those eyes are not clouded by the veil of self? I for one do not believe it possible. The protracted illness of a beloved person, especially of one so tuned to melancholy as the Prince, would bring unending watchfulness, insistent fear, only kept in control by hope. Every change would cause joy or horror, and a desperate determination to fight for the invalid's life.

However, to Queen Victoria death came with terrible suddenness—though days before the Prince had told his daughter Alice to write to the Princess Royal that he was dying—and she was left crushed and broken-hearted; left without support, the foundation as well as the walls gone. For Victoria had not carried out her early promise as an active Queen; she had rested everything but the outer appearance of Queenship upon the Prince. When he was dead she still clung to him, for in any decision the question she would ask was, not "Which course do I think right?" but "What would he have done?"

"It is the beginning of a new reign," she said pathetically, and she was right. Those judicial memoranda, the long letters to statesmen! There was no one now to draw them up for her or write them. It has been said that at first she asked the Prince of Wales to do his father's secretarial work, and that poor youth, frightened by what he knew it meant, dared not undertake it. Others who were connected with that period have said that Victoria never forgave her son for the anxiety his Cambridge affairs had caused and which she averred, with her usual exaggeration, had brought about Albert's illness. However it was, she never would allow the Prince to help her in governing, and so made of him just a man of idle leisure, thus carrying her theory of purity into dreadful practice by sacrificing to it her eldest son. In this matter I do not think that she consulted the memory of the Prince Consort, at least I hope not.

For a time the Queen let matters, even foreign affairs, slide, until Palmerston pointed out that her signature was necessary if state affairs were to go on. When she once more became active, it took all her time and energy to cope alone with work which had for so many years been done for her; and even then her grasp upon the reins of government was light compared with what it had been, and her statesmen suffered less friction and less interference.

The lasting work of the Prince Consort was not that upon which he had expended his energies and his life, for he did not increase the Monarchical power in England; it was the pulling of the Crown permanently out of the Georgian mud, and proving that those in high places could be virtuous and intellectual.

His character alone tended to stamp something new upon aristocracy, which is always only too inclined to believe that position, money and manners are all that is needed. The lesson has not been learned with too great an avidity, but there is now far deeper respect for mind and character than could have been traced among fashionable people in the times of Queen Victoria's immediate predecessors.

INDEX

A

A'Beckett, Gilbert, 171, 173
Abercorn, Marquis of, 237
Aberdeen, Lord, 172, 173, 176, 178, 182, 188, 216, 314, 347, 353, 355, 358, 362, 363
Adelaide, Queen, 37, 116
Albemarle, Lord, 50, 73
Albert, Prince Consort, 2; character, 3 *et seq.*, 257, 322; childhood, 21 *et seq.*; purity, 28, 108; travels, 32, 33; arrival in England, 36; marriage, 37; Field-Marshal, 39, 41; and the Tories, 46; levee, 47; dancing, 51; and Melbourne, 54; family jars, 56; description of, 59; first speech, 62; in the City, 76; and Lehzen, 78; 81, 85, 95, 97, 98; education of children, 103, 113; and income tax, 114; 118, 125; King Consort, 125; 128; and Palmerston, 126 *et seq.*, 129, 346, 348, 352; visits the House, 134; and the potato, 141; and national fasting, 142; Palace economies, 145, 219 *et seq.*, 324; as Edward III., 149; goes to Ireland, 158; and Stockmar, 163, 170; visit to France, 171 *et seq.*, 180, 186, 190, 191, 194, 195, 196, 203, 205, 207; foreign policy, 211; and the brandy, 221; Governor of Windsor Castle, 223; and the policeman, 235–6; as sportsman, 233, 268, 310, 315; and the

Scotch girls, 239; Greville's impression of, 244; sermon upon at Liverpool, 246; institutes *Court Circular,* 254; and Jasper Tomsett Judge, 256 *et seq.*; as farmer, 261; and the rates, 262; and Webling, 263; his gamekeepers, 264; the case of Dean, 264; of Maria Wells, 265; his etchings, 273; at law, 276; and the theatres, 288; and "Every Man in His Humour," 290; love of music, 290; and Sir Charles Eastlake, 295; and Gibson's design, 296; and the Chancellorship of Cambridge, 297 *et seq.*; his many titles, 304; offered post of Commander-in-Chief, 304; his estimation of his duties, 306; title of Prince Consort, 307; death of his father, 316; visits Prussia and Coburg, 317; refused precedence, 317; at battue of deer, 318; foreign servants, 323; a dandy, 324; as a master, 327; stories of, 327; unpunctual, 330; depressed by deaths of friends, 334; and Great Exhibition, 335; and the people, 341; German habits, 342; peace policy, 348; German bias, 352; public rage against, 355 *et seq.*; and Crimea, 358; absolute power in Foreign Affairs, 360; and the troops, 362; and Napoleon III., 365; in Paris, 367; goes to Cher-

THE END

Richard Clay and Sons, Limited,
Brunswick Street, Stamford Street, S.E.
AND BUNGAY, SUFFOLK.

KING EDWARD

IN

HIS TRUE COLOURS

By EDWARD LEGGE

Price 16/- net

SECOND EDITION NOW READY

At all Bookshops and Libraries

EVELEIGH NASH, 36 King Street, Covent Garden, LONDON, W.C.

A KEEPER OF ROYAL SECRETS

Being the Private and Political Life of Madame de Genlis

By JEAN HARMAND

Price 15/- net

"Félicité Stéphanie de Genlis, comtesse, adventuress, governess, copious writer of novels, plays, and homilies, needed a biographer, and M. Jean Harmand has adequately supplied the want."—*Times.*

"Extremely interesting . . . peculiarly vivid, and even fascinating . . . he has made real for us the personality of Mme. de Genlis as that of a remarkable woman, who led a remarkable life."—*Daily Telegraph.*

"The true story of Mme. de Genlis's life—a story now fully set forth for the first time. And what an interesting figure she is now that we can see her clearly! 'A Keeper of Royal Secrets' runs to over four hundred pages, but few will find it too long."—*Daily News and Leader.*

"With the help of documents in the possession of the Genlis family, and of other materials obtained from a variety of sources, M. Harmand has been able to give us the first full-length portrait of the woman who witnessed the Ancien Régime, the Revolution, the Empire, and the Restoration, and who died under the July Monarchy."—*The Nation.*

"Deeply interesting . . . she was an extraordinarily interesting woman, who lived in extraordinarily interesting times, and Jean Harmand has made the utmost of his long and deep study of both in this fascinating volume."—*Truth.*

"Highly interesting . . . M. Harmand has produced much fresh material, and has made a most interesting addition to the inner history of nations."—*Liverpool Daily Post.*

At all Bookshops and Libraries

EVELEIGH NASH, 36 King Street, Covent Garden, LONDON, W.C.

SOME AUTOBIOGRAPHIES

Published by

MR. EVELEIGH NASH

MY OWN STORY
By LOUISA OF TUSCANY, Ex-Queen of Saxony. **10/6** net.

MY MEMOIRS
By Madame STEINHEIL. **10/6** net.

MY RECOLLECTIONS
By the COUNTESS OF CARDIGAN AND LANCASTRE. **10/6** net.

MY MEMOIRS
By PRINCESS CAROLINE MURAT. **15/-** net.

LEAVES FROM A LIFE
ANONYMOUS. **10/-** net.

MY MEMORIES
By the COUNTESS OF MUNSTER. **12/6.**

RECOLLECTIONS OF A MILITARY ATTACHÉ
By Colonel the Hon. FRED WELLESLEY. **12/6.**

REMINISCENCES OF AN OLD 'UN
By FRANK N. STREATFIELD, C.M.G. **7/6** net.

HURRAH FOR THE LIFE OF A SAILOR
By Admiral Sir WILLIAM KENNEDY, K.C.B. Cheap Edition. **2/-** net.

FORTY-FIVE YEARS OF MY LIFE
By PRINCESS LOUISE OF PRUSSIA. **16/-** net.

FORTY YEARS OF PARISIAN SOCIETY
By ARTHUR MEYER, Editor of "Le Gaulois." **10/6** net.

SOME REMINISCENCES
By JOSEPH CONRAD. **5/-** net.

MANY CELEBRITIES and a few others
By WILLIAM H. RIDEING. **10/6** net.

MY AUTOBIOGRAPHY
By Madame JUDITH (of the Comédie Française). **10/6** net.

Obtainable at all Bookshops and Libraries.

EVELEIGH NASH, 36 King Street, Covent Garden,
LONDON, W.C.

Mr. EVELEIGH NASH'S LIST OF NEW BOOKS

"MY PAST"

MR. EVELEIGH NASH has acquired the world-rights of a sensational autobiography written by a relative of one of the reigning monarchs of Europe.

The memoirs, which are now in active preparation, will be published under the above title during the London season, but, owing to the terms of his agreement with the personage in question, Mr. Nash is unable to give particulars at present. The identity of the author and full details regarding the book will be announced in April.

ADVENTURES BEYOND THE ZAMBESI

Of the O'Flaherty, the Insular Miss, the Soldier-Man, and the Rebel Woman.

By MRS. FRED MATURIN

(EDITH CECIL-PORCH)

With Illustrations   Price 10*s*. 6*d*. net.

Four widely diverse, yet up-to-date people agreed to seek together the risks, excitements, discomforts and delights of sport, adventure and companionship beyond the Zambesi. One of these was Mrs. Fred Maturin (Mrs. Cecil-Porch) whose previous book "Petticoat Pilgrims on Trek" showed that she possesses a rare power of vivid and amusing narrative. Wanderers and stay-at-homes will revel in her lively description of the six months' trip of this delightful quartette in quest of big game and sport in the African wilds. Her buoyant optimism and her rich sense of humour found full play in the many adventures that befel them, and it is just this humorous, friendly and intrepid outlook of hers that lends such charm to her written record. The book is illustrated with some remarkably good photographs.

SPORTING RECOLLECTIONS OF AN OLD 'UN

By FRANK N. STREATFEILD, C.M.G.

(Author of " Reminiscences of an Old 'Un.")

Illustrated   Price *7s. 6d.* net.

A book after the heart of all good sportsmen, brimming over with cheerfulness and good fellowship. The author, who has been a universally popular figure in sporting circles for over a quarter of a century, relates many amusing anecdotes on shooting of every description, fishing, falconry and cricket, and has packed his book with incidents of interest to all who use the rod and gun.

THE ROMANCE OF THE ROTHSCHILDS

By IGNATIUS BALLA

Illustrated   Price *7s. 6d.* net.

A full and picturesque narrative of the rise of the House of Rothschild. The characteristics and early vicissitudes of the famous Five Frankfurters who laid the foundations of the House are shown, and many amusing anecdotes are related of them in Mr. Balla's book.

SOME EARLY PRESS OPINIONS

" The author takes us, in a sense, behind the scenes, gives us a hundred details of the Rothschilds' methods, and shows us, step by step, how the accumulation of these enormous sums was made possible."—*The Globe.*

" Extremely interesting."—*Daily Express.*

" Interesting all the way through."—*Standard.*

" Abounds in interesting quotations and anecdotes. —*Liverpool Daily Post.*

THE MARRIED LIFE OF QUEEN VICTORIA

By CLARE JERROLD

Author of " The Early Court of Queen Victoria," etc.

Illustrated.   Price 15*s.* net.

In this volume Mrs. Jerrold carries a stage further her interesting study of Queen Victoria's life. She endeavours to tell the real truth regarding the Queen's married life and her relations with the Prince Consort, and in doing so relies on their own recorded actions and words rather than upon the highly coloured and in many cases exaggerated pictures presented by the " lives " of Prince Albert which were authorised by the Queen.

The result is a human and fascinating story. The relations of the Queen and Prince with those around them, with their children and with their ministers —especially their hatred and fear of Palmerston— their love for Louis-Philippe, for the German confederation, and their complacency towards Russia are all dealt with and throw a strong new light upon the English Court during the years in which Prince Albert was virtually King.

THE SAILOR WHOM ENGLAND FEARED

Being the Story of Paul Jones, Scotch Naval Adventurer and Admiral in the American and Russian Fleets.

By M. MACDERMOT CRAWFORD.

Author of " The Wife of Lafayette."

Illustrated.   Price 15*s.* net.

John Paul Jones was unquestionably one of the most striking characters of the eighteenth century. Born in 1747, the son of a gardener in Kirkcudbrightshire, he was, at the age of seventeen, third mate on a slaver, at twenty a merchant captain ; at twenty-eight lieutenant in the United States Revolutionary Navy ; at twenty-nine a captain ; at thirty-two commodore, " the ocean hero of the Old World and the New," spoiled, adulated, petted by great and small. A vice-admiral in the Russian Navy at forty-three—at forty-five he was dead !

A traitor who terrorised his countrymen, known alternately as " rebel," " corsair," and " pirate," Paul Jones was none the less a man of rare distinction and ability—a brilliant seaman endowed with courage and determination ; and the record of his deeds is a story of unflagging interest.

A CANDID HISTORY OF THE JESUITS

By JOSEPH McCABE.

*Author of " The Decay of the Church of Rome,"
" Twelve Years in a Monastery," &c.*

Price 10s. 6d. net.

It is curious, in view of the endless discussion of the Jesuits, that no English writer has ever attempted a systematic history of that body. Probably no religious body ever had so romantic a history as the Jesuits, or inspired such deadly hatred. On the other hand, histories of the famous society are almost always too prejudiced, either for or against, to be reliable. Mr. McCabe, whose striking book " The Decay of the Church of Rome " attracted such widespread and well-merited attention, has attempted, in his new book, to give the facts impartially, and to enable the inquirer to form an intelligent idea of the history and character of the Jesuits from their foundation by Loyola to the present day. Every phase of their remarkable story—including the activity of political Jesuits and their singular behaviour on the foreign missions—is carefully studied, and the record of the Jesuits in England is very fully examined.

A KEEPER OF ROYAL SECRETS

Being the Private and Political Life of Madame de
Genlis.

By JEAN HARMAND

Illustrated.   Price 15*s*. net.

The career of Madame de Genlis is one of the
baffling enigmas of history.   For the greater part of
her life she played an important *role* in the social
and political life of France.

By virtue of her intimate association with Philip
Egalité, Duc d'Orleans, and her high position as the
Governor of Louis Philippe and the other Orleans
children,   the   influence   she   wielded   practically
amounted to royal power.

She cast her spell over a wide circle, winning
admiration even from her enemies, and yet her life
has been the subject of a storm of scandalous reports
and speculations.

What was her exact relationship to the Duke ?
was she the mother of the famous " Pamela " whom
Lord Edward Fitzgerald married ? what was her
share in the astounding affair of " Maria Stella " ?
what part did she play in the Revolution ?—these
are some of the mysteries surrounding her on which
M. Harmand, with the help of many unpublished
letters and documents, throws much new light.

The whole truth will probably never be known,
but M. Harmand in his elaborate biography gives
us an immensely fascinating and vivid story, and
unearths many new details regarding her curious
and romantic life.

THE TRUTH ABOUT WOMEN

By C. GASQUOINE HARTLEY
(Mrs. WALTER M. GALLICHAN)

Price 6s.

This book is the outcome of twelve years' careful study of the conditions of women in this country and abroad. Believing that the time has now arrived when women must speak out, fearlessly, the truth about their own sex, the author has endeavoured to review the situation as it appears to her after her lengthy study of the subject. Her book is divided into three parts—the biological consideration of the question—the historical consideration, and the present day aspects of the woman problem. It is a book of much plain speaking and closely reasoned argument and, whether or not one agrees with its conclusions and directness, it is a work which undoubtedly merits the attention of every responsible person, male and female.

BY-PATHS IN COLLECTING

By VIRGINIA ROBIE.

Profusely illustrated.   Price 7s. 6d. net.

Every enthusiast over rare and unique things which have passed the century-old mark will want this delightful book by Virginia Robie. It contains a wealth of sound advice upon the quest of the quaint, and much reliable information is given upon the collecting of such things as china, furniture, pewter, copper, brass, samplers, and sundials.

PRINTS AND THEIR MAKERS

Essays on Engravers and Etchers Old and Modern

Edited by FITZROY CARRINGTON

With 200 Illustrations.   Price 10s. 6d. net.

A volume exquisite in every detail of the planning and making. The chapters—contributed by notable authorities—discuss various phases of etching and engraving from the time of Raphael and Durer to the close of the nineteenth century. The plates for the illustrations (200) have all been made with unusual care from original engravings and etchings, and together form a valuable collection.

New Six=Shilling Novels.

VEILED WOMEN

By MARMADUKE PICKTHALL

Author of " Saïd the Fisherman," " Children of the Nile," etc.

A fine novel of the East telling the life story of an English girl who marries an Egyptian noble and lives the harem life. The gradual mental and physical effect of the secluded life of the harem upon a healthy western woman is shown with great effect, while the story of her ineffectual appeal to the Commander-in-Chief of the British Army of Occupation to take her back, of her escape from the harem and flight into the desert, of her return and eventual relapse into a state of resigned contentment with her lot, will appeal strongly to every woman. The wonderful world of the Cairene women, their comings and goings, their intrigues, their pleasures and pastimes, the gorgeous colouring and the subtle perfume of their surroundings, the mystery, the charm and the insidious influence of the harem life are depicted with the brilliance of characterisation and richness of detail that one has come to expect from the author of " Saïd the Fisherman."

LADY OF THE NIGHT

By BENJAMIN SWIFT

A charming story centreing round the romantic attachment of two delightful people—Ysmyn Veltry, the daughter of a wealthy French perfume manufacturer and Vivian Darsay, a great-grandson of an old Crimean veteran, Colonel Darsay—whom, years before the story opens, chance had brought together and made playmates of among the perfumed fields of roses, jasmine and all the other fragrant flowers which surrounded Veltry's world-renowned distillery at Grasse.

At the instigation of an ambitious sister-in-law, Veltry has come to London to inaugurate, on lines which shall outvie in magnificence any similar establishment, a shop in which to sell his perfumes. Ysmyn and Vivian meet again under dramatic and greatly changed conditions to find their path to happiness beset with difficulties, and it is not until the " Maison Merveille," which has quickly become the talk of fashionable London and developed into a veritable " palace of beauty culture " is, in the height of its success, overtaken by disaster, that the " Lady of the Night "—so called after jasmine, her father's favourite flower—becomes the wife of her erstwhile playmate.

THE EMPEROR'S SPY

By HECTOR FLEISCHMANN

" The Emperor's Spy," which deals with the struggle between Napoleon Bonaparte's secret police, headed by a beautiful woman spy—Elvire—and a gang of daring Royalist conspirators led by Georges Cadoudal and the Chevalier Lahaye Saint Hilare, is one of the most exciting, vivid and elaborate historical novels since Dumas's " Three Musketeers."

Famous historical characters, from Napoleon downwards, crowd its pages. Incident follows incident in quick succession, and plot is met by counter-plot, until, at last, under the shadow of the wild cliffs of Brittany the Emperor's Spy, having achieved the crowning triumph of her life, meets with a swift and tragic death at the hands of the last of the Royalists. The book is 576 pages long and there is not one page of this tremendous story which does not glow with living, human interest.

GLOOMY FANNY AND OTHER STORIES

By MORLEY ROBERTS

Author of " Thorpe's Way," " David Bran," etc.

Readers of Mr. Morley Roberts's novel " Thorpe's Way " will remember that " Gloomy Fanny," otherwise the Hon. Edwin Fanshawe, was one of the most amusing characters in that very amusing story.

I'D VENTURE ALL FOR THEE

By J. S. FLETCHER

*Author of " The Town of Crooked Ways," " The Fine
Air of Morning," etc.*

A story of the Yorkshire coast, 1745.

THE LOST MILLION

By WILLIAM LE QUEUX

*Author of " The Mystery of Nine," " Without
Trace," etc., etc.*

CARNACKI
THE GHOST-FINDER

By WILLIAM HOPE HODGSON

*Author of " The Night Land," " The Boats of Glen
Carig," etc.*

A NEW NOVEL

By LADY TROWBRIDGE

14

A HAREM ROMANCE

By E. DE LA VILLENEUVE

A very lifelike picture of the Young Turk Revolution is contained in this novel. A double love story, full of thrilling incidents, is woven into the web of public events, the two heroines, one a lovely Turkish girl, the other a beautiful Armenian, having each been prisoners in the Palace of Yildiz. The personality of Abdul Hamid is vividly realised, and the cruel oppression to which he subjected the inmates of his harem is graphically described.

Three-and-Sixpence Net Novels.

POISON

By ALICE AND CLAUDE ASKEW

Authors of " The Shulamite," " The Woman Deborah," etc.

ROADS OF DESTINY

By O. HENRY

Author of " Cabbages and Kings," " Heart of the West," etc.

Two-Shilling Net Novels.

QUEEN SHEBA'S RING
By H. RIDER HAGGARD
Author of " King Solomon's Mines," etc.

THE MYSTERY OF NINE
By WILLIAM LE QUEUX
Author of " Without Trace," etc., etc.

SETH OF THE CROSS
By ALPHONSE COURLANDER
Author of " Mightier than the Sword."

ImTheStory.com

CPSIA information can be obtained
at www.ICGtesting.com
Printed in the USA
BVOW06s0557061216

469856BV00028B/509/P